Dance and the Hollywood Latina

LATINIDAD

Transnational Cultures in the United States

This series publishes books that deepen and expand our knowledge and understanding of the various Latina/o populations in the United States in the context of their transnational relationships with cultures of the broader Americas. The focus is on the history and analysis of Latino cultural systems and practices in national and transnational spheres of influence from the nineteenth century to the present. The series is open to scholarship in political science, economics, anthropology, linguistics, history, cinema and television, literary and cultural studies, and popular culture and encourages interdisciplinary approaches, methods, and theories. The Series Advisory Board consists of faculty of the School of Transborder Studies at Arizona State University where an interdisciplinary emphasis is being placed on transborder and transnational dynamics.

Marta E. Sánchez, Series Editor, School of Transborder Studies, Arizona State University

Marivel T. Danielson, *Homecoming Queers: Desire and Difference in Chicano Latina Cultural Production*

Regina M. Marchi, *Day of the Dead in the USA: The Migration and Transformation of a Cultural Phenomenon*

Priscilla Peña Ovalle, *Dance and the Hollywood Latina: Race, Sex, and Stardom*

Dance and the Hollywood Latina

Race, Sex, and Stardom

PRISCILLA PEÑA OVALLE

RUTGERS UNIVERSITY PRESS
NEW BRUNSWICK, NEW JERSEY, AND LONDON

Library of Congress Cataloging-in-Publication Data

Ovalle, Priscilla Peña, 1976–
   Dance and the Hollywood Latina : race, sex, and stardom / Priscilla Peña Ovalle.
        p. cm. — (Latinidad—transnational cultures in the United States)
   Includes bibliographical references and index.
   ISBN 978–0–8135–4880–7 (hardcover : alk. paper) — ISBN 978–0–8135–4881–4
(pbk. : alk. paper)
   1. Hispanic Americans in motion pictures.   2. Hispanic Americans in the
motion picture industry.   3. Hispanic American motion picture actors and actresses.
4. Dance in motion pictures, television, etc.—United States.   5. Race in motion
pictures.   6. Sex in motion pictures.   I. Title.
   PN1995.9.H47O93   2010
   791.43′652968073—dc22

                                                                    2010003041

A British Cataloging-in-Publication record for this book is available from the British
Library.

Visit our Web site: http://rutgerspress.rutgers.edu

Manufactured in the United States of America

For Omar, with my deepest passion
For Cynthia Peña Sanchez and Casey Ovalle,
with my greatest love

Contents

Acknowledgments

This book is the product of many years of hard work and the tireless support of a community of friends, family, and scholars, but I must start by acknowledging the one person without whom this book would not be possible: Omar Naïm. Omar has changed the trajectory of my life yet walks beside me every step of the way. I cannot imagine a better existence than the one we have made together, and I continually look forward to our next adventure. He has loved, nurtured, and inspired me since I was a restless young woman struggling through college—well before graduate school was even a fanciful thought. This book is for him.

This book is also for my mother and my father, Cynthia Peña Sanchez and Casey Ovalle. Each of them has taught me about tireless love, strengthened me with their creativity, and inspired me with their incredible work ethic. My education and this book would not have been possible without them. I also thank my sisters, Natascia and Marcella, for helping me to become a better teacher and friend.

One of the most wonderful parts of academia is its tradition of mentorship. Every step of the way, I have been blessed with incredible mentors. First and foremost, I thank Jane Shattuc. While it was a great leap of faith that got me to college in the first place, it was Dr. Shattuc who sparked a film theory fire, told me about graduate school, and made me believe I could pursue it. She then welcomed me into her home and gave me the great gift of knowing Annie. I can never repay such generosity, but I hope to grow into the kind of teacher and mentor that she is.

As a graduate student at the University of Southern California, I had the good fortune to work with Marsha Kinder, Tara McPherson, David Román, George Sanchez, Curtis Marez, and Lynn Spigel. I can never fully thank my committee—Drs. Kinder, McPherson, and Román—for shepherding me through graduate school, for nurturing my dissertation from its unwieldy nascence, and for continuing their mentorship. I am honored to call them friends. Working with Marsha and Tara at the Labyrinth Project and the Institute for Media Literacy at the Annenberg Center for Communication, respectively, has trained me in the kind of theory and practice I look forward to emulating someday. I greatly enjoyed working and learning from these amazing women. From Drs. Román and Sánchez I learned the incredible power of professionalization—skills and strategies that have made endeavors like this book possible and that I hope to pass along to my students. I thank Drew Casper and Rick Jewell—who taught me everything from the theatrics of the classroom to the thrill of the archive—as well as Pete Chvany, Jim Lane, Rob Sabal, and Rob Todd at Emerson College, for teaching me about the wonders of production and collaboration.

Libraries and archives are magical places, and I am grateful for the many guides who have helped me navigate their treasures. I am indebted to Elizabeth Peterson at the University of Oregon. As a colleague, she has so often gone beyond the call of duty on my behalf. It is with her support that this book has matured from its gangly origins. I am fortunate to count her as a friend. The boundless expertise and generosity of Ned Comstock and Sandy Garcia-Meyers at the University of Southern California's Cinematic Arts Library and Archive have continually regenerated my passion for this project, and it is richer because of them. I also thank Barbara Hall and Jenny Romero at the Margaret Herrick Library of the Academy of Motion Picture Arts and Sciences as well as the archivists at the University of Southern California Warner Bros. Archives for preserving the dynamic bones of Cinema Studies.

I give special thanks to the many people who have guided and supported me through the manuscript development and production process. I am grateful for Daniel Bernardi's tireless encouragement and his work as my editor, mentor, and friend. I thank Alberto Sandoval-Sánchez for helping me rethink this project in new and important ways. At Rutgers, Leslie Mitchner, Marilyn Campbell, Katie Keeran, Anne Hegeman, and Ann Weinstock have gifted me with unparalleled support; I thank them for their patience and tireless efforts on my behalf. I also thank my copyeditor, Kathryn Gohl, for her exquisite eye and for teaching me so much more about the writing process. Many more thanks to the excellent support of my colleagues in the English Department at the University of Oregon—including Harry Wonham, Marilyn Reid, and the administrative staff—as well as the Oregon Humanities Center, which provided subvention funds for this project.

I thank Routledge for allowing me to incorporate parts of "Framing Jennifer Lopez: Mobilizing Race from the Wide Shot to the Close-Up," from *The Persistence of Whiteness: Race and Contemporary Hollywood Cinema*, edited by Daniel Bernardi; and Taylor & Francis for allowing me to incorporate parts of "Urban *Sensualidad*: Jennifer Lopez, *Flashdance*, and the MTV Hip-Hop Re-Generation," from *Women and Performance: A Journal of Feminist Theory* 18(3): 253–268.

Finally, I am indebted to and grateful for the many colleagues, friends, and family who have shared this experience with me. I give my warmest, greatest thanks to Jennifer Stoever-Ackerman for her tireless commitment to me and my work. She has helped me discover my voice, taught me how to be a good writing partner, and been ready to read drafts and drafts at every turn. I cannot imagine any of this without her. I have also been blessed with an amazing group of colleagues and friends at the University of Oregon. I am especially thankful for the generous feedback I received through the Center for Race, Ethnicity, and Sexuality Studies; many thanks to Kathleen Karlyn, Kate Mondloch, Sangita Gopal, Chad Allen, David Vázquez, David Li, Michael Aronson, Elizabeth Peterson, Michael Hames-García, Irmary Reyes-Santos, and Lynn Fujiwara for their exquisite feedback during this workshop. In addition, I am deeply honored that Lynn Fujiwara, Kathleen Karlyn, and Carol Stabile have taught me about grace under pressure and institutional leadership. I also thank my many excellent writing partners: Jennifer Stoever-Ackerman; William Arcé, Karen Bowdre, Marci McMahon, and Joshua Smith (also known as fABD-5); Cindy García and Melissa Blanco Borelli; Irmary Reyes-Santos and Lynn Fujiwara; Lara Bovilsky and Mark Quigley; Ernesto Martínez and Tania Triana; and Susan Quash-Mah, without whom this manuscript would have never materialized. I deeply appreciate the support of my many family members and families in San Antonio, Los Angeles, Paris, Beirut, and Eugene: Ziad Naïm, Socorro Peña, Fouad Naïm, Nidal Achkar, Justine Schmidt, Russell Lichter, the Emerson gang, Grupo Animo, the Ovalle family, the Sanchez family, the Gary family, the Gutierrez family, the Morozumi-Fujiwara family, the Aronson family, and many more.

And finally, many thanks to Mr. B for your warmth and humor. I hope you enjoy this book.

Dance and the Hollywood Latina

CHAPTER 1

Mobilizing the Latina Myth

In 2007, the dandruff shampoo Head & Shoulders ran an advertising campaign featuring a series of staged testimonials from black, white, and brown women. Each woman's extolment—delivered in a series of close-ups—praises the product according to her (hair) type: after a black woman with dark, curly hair gushes that the shampoo "actually changed my hair," a white woman declares that her straight auburn hair "feels healthy." When the Latina finally delivers her testimonial, she exclaims that her improved hair has "movement, like salsa," and the commercial cuts to its only medium shot, framing the Latina's body from head to hip as she rocks into an abbreviated salsa step.

The sight of a Latina-in-motion—euphoric to sell us something, anything— is all too familiar in the history of U.S. media and popular culture. The dancing brown female figure has been a part of motion picture history since Thomas Edison filmed the Spanish dancer Carmencita in 1894,[1] making her the first woman recorded by an Edison camera and one of the earliest dancing bodies on film (*Carmencita* 1894). Over a century later, the dancing Latina has appeared in or on everything from soda commercials to postage stamps, from feature films to billboards.[2]

Latinas-in-motion have mediated the racial and sexual ideologies of mainstream U.S. visual culture since Hollywood's formative years, and in this volume I work to understand the dancing Latina as an elemental facet of the U.S. national imaginary. By interrogating the Latina's legacy of racialized and sexualized imagery in Hollywood film, I question how and why dance has so effectively delivered the complex racial and sexual meanings that compose the myth of the Hollywood Latina. In the United States, the dancing Latina body on screen is a unique microcosm of the social conventions required for fame and nonwhite female agency in an alternately hostile and hospitable national sphere. The screen Latina is a female Other, an embodiment of the promise and fulfillment of national and sexual conquest. But her Otherness occupies a middle ground, mediating and maintaining the racial poles of difference in the service of nation formation. Because the Hollywood Latina is imagined and imaged somewhere between black and white on the continuum of cinematic racial representation, she articulates and distinguishes the purported sexualized differences of this racial binary. Dancing on screen, her brown body is caught between the liberation and limitations of both black and white female performers: she is mythologized as sexual and assertive, yet she is compatibly cast as the love interest of black and white male performers.[3]

The myth of the Hollywood Latina builds from Roland Barthes's (1972) use of the term "mythology." I am particularly interested in Barthes's assertion that myth "transforms history into nature" (1972, 129), an important process that has greatly influenced my approach to the visual history and iconicity of the Latina body documented in this project. The myth of the Hollywood Latina buries the colonial and imperial history of the Americas—long the burden of the brown female body—in the racialized and sexualized image of the Hollywood Latina. Since the Spanish Conquest and Manifest Destiny, this myth has been built upon a succession of colonial relationships organized around race, gender, and sexuality (Fregoso 1999; Lugones 2007); its visualization and perpetuation in the twentieth century, however, have relied on collapsed, codified, and reiterated depictions of dance and racialized sexuality that signify the Latina's amoral behavior and impermanence.[4] A century of cinematic conventions—from writing and casting to costuming and choreography—have reinforced the mechanics of this visual tradition. This book identifies the cinematic history that has long compelled us to recognize, understand, and ultimately believe in the myth of the Latina's innate dance abilities and the so-called fiery nature that accompanies it.

The myth of desirability and availability is the backbone of the myth of the Hollywood Latina. Every Latina star in this project—and many performers besides—began her career as a dancer, prompting me to ask why and how dance has become a requirement for Latina stardom in Hollywood film. What does this emphasis on physical mobility tell us about the intersection of performance, racialized sexuality, and visual culture? To determine the answer, I build my analysis on the following set of questions. First, what is the myth of the Hollywood Latina and how do dance, race, and sexuality operate as its intertwining code in Hollywood film? Second, how has the unique in-betweenness and racial mobility of the dancing Latina body contributed to the reiterative production of a cohesive racial identity in the United States? Finally, how does the dancing Latina paradoxically create the illusion of diversity and sexual liberation while also developing her own social and professional agency? In *Dance and the Hollywood Latina* I use the careers of five Latina stars to address these questions and determine why the historically charged and socially complex image of the dancing Latina has remained a popular figure in U.S. popular culture. Each star's tale offers multifaceted answers and illustrates the many ways in which Hollywood has reproduced a mythology around and through the brown female body. Ultimately, the dance of Latina stardom emphasizes the negotiations and strictures required for nonwhite female employment and agency in Hollywood—and, by extension, the United States.

To unpack the myth of the Hollywood Latina and its role in mitigating national tensions surrounding nonwhiteness and gender/sexual equality, I have organized this volume around five of the best-known Latina stars in Hollywood film: Dolores Del Rio, Carmen Miranda, Rita Hayworth (Rita Cansino), Rita Moreno, and Jennifer Lopez. All of these women used dance to gain agency as working performers with mainstream careers, yet many of their roles paradoxically racialized and sexualized their bodies in ways that perpetuated the U.S. myth that brown women are inherently passionate, promiscuous, and temporary nation-builders (Almaguer 1994, 61). Framed by colonization, Prohibition, and the United States–Mexico border, Mexican-born Dolores Del Rio cast the mold for this mythology through her career in the 1920s and 1930s. When Portuguese-Brazilian Carmen Miranda came to the United States in the early 1940s as the Good Neighbor policy's premier import, her arrival shifted the myth to accommodate her tropical likeness. When Spanish-American Rita Cansino became Rita Hayworth in the late 1930s, the myth bubbled beneath her makeover and eased the nation into a new era of (white) female sexuality during and after World War II. Later, the myth enhanced Puerto Rican–born Rita Moreno's iconic performance as Anita in *West Side Story* in 1961 and supported her status as an Academy Award, Emmy, and Tony winner. Most recently, Nuyorican Jennifer Lopez has mobilized the myth to exploit the multicultural and multimedia discourses that have uneasily, yet profitably, incorporated black popular culture into mainstream media of the 1990s and 2000s. Each woman's career has uniquely utilized and contributed to the myth of the Hollywood Latina for the past cinematic century.

In this chapter I set out the project's language and tactics by providing a methodology that identifies, or makes strange, aspects of the Hollywood Latina's representational value. I also offer a comparative analysis of two "commercials" to make the logic and ubiquity of the dancing Latina explicit. The 1934 Technicolor short titled *La Cucaracha* (The cockroach) and the 2006 Jell-O pudding commercial titled "Mural" use unknown Latina dancers to sell their products, highlighting the formal and cultural approaches at the core of my methodology; these case studies also showcase the historical breadth of the dancing Latina's mythological formation. By outlining the key conventions of the dancing Latina's representation through these examples—such as her physical "look," bodily actions, and their symbolic burden—I use the book's two organizing concepts of "in-betweenness" and "racial mobility" to demarcate the Latina's symbolic value according to the traditional white/black binary central to the past century of Hollywood filmmaking and to clarify how and why she has become such a potent Hollywood figure. I argue that the trajectory of the Hollywood Latina provides the racialized ambiguity crucial to the black–white racial continuum. Although her presence appears to diversify the media landscape, the traditions of her representation as a dancing and temporary love interest of white men in fact reinforce and reify the status quo of Hollywood representation and cultural citizenship within the United States. The Latina star, although mobile, is also in flux: she is a temporary figure instituted by the institutionalized racism of Hollywood conventions. The chapters that follow illustrate how the individual careers of Del Rio, Miranda, Hayworth, Moreno, and Lopez illuminate the national stage differently and at different time periods by negotiating such racialized, gendered, and sexualized expectations through their personae.

As Latinas, the women in this project represent a diverse range of backgrounds; as stars, they exemplify the narrow realm of the Hollywood Latina. In this volume I broadly use the term "Latina" to reclaim and reorient the dismissive cultural collapse that has allowed Hollywood to consistently conflate Mexico, Brazil, Puerto Rico, and other Latin American regions with each other and with Spain.[5] These slippages (Spanish for Mexican, Cuban for Brazilian, etc.) are more than innocent confusions of one so-called Latin nation for another; instead, these errors highlight the imperial power of the United States. The term "Latina" exposes how—regardless of the performer's persona or self-identification—such errors rank, racialize, and sexualize Latin American countries within the cinematic frame according to shifting U.S. social, cultural, and political interests. Despite my flexible use of the term "Latina," I have identified "Latina star" more specifically to illustrate how few brown women have achieved star status in Hollywood. In this project, I define a Latina star as someone who either regularly received top or near-top billing in A-list or otherwise financially successful Hollywood films, or achieved and maintained an iconic or legendary status in the mainstream media world. Such parameters exclude performers like Mexican-born Lupe Vélez, Dominican-born Maria Montez, and Nuyorican Rosie Pérez, women who have used dance within popular, powerful, and compelling careers but whose iconicity or Hollywood billing have fallen short of the legacies and acclaim of the women featured here.

Because Latina stardom has emerged in successive waves that coincide with U.S. imperialist tendencies in the twentieth century, these five careers function as barometers of the nation's shifting ideological beliefs in terms of race, gender, and sexuality (as well as class). Yet decoding these representations does not expose an easy equation: no one Hollywood Latina stands in for any one nation or national event. Rather, the Hollywood Latina is an alluring and amalgamated symbol of the colonial relationship between Latin America and the United States. Since the Spanish Conquest and Manifest Destiny, the history of westward expansion has suggested that—to the colonizer—land and the brown women who inhabit it were ripe for conquest. This colonial legacy is reiterated in the representational coupling of white men and nonwhite women (but not vice versa), a cinematic convention that illustrates how racialized heterosexual couplings are central to the myth-making process (Lugones 2007, 203). But whereas the Hollywood Latina is codified as desirable and available on screen, her image is impermanent since she cannot legitimately reproduce the nation when in the presence of white women (Lugones 2007, 203).

Hollywood film embodies and renders visible the racial, sexual, and gendered ideologies of the United States and these representations function as recognizable—if exaggerated—versions of the U.S. social/racial hierarchy. As Richard Dyer and Laura Mulvey have argued (and many others have reiterated), the white heterosexual male operates as the primary figure and perspective of mainstream Hollywood film, while the white female functions as a secondary figure in overwhelmingly patriarchal and heterocentric narratives (Dyer 1997; Mulvey 1989; Shohat and Stam 1994). Recently, critics have drawn attention to the intimate relationship between racial representation and the development of film technology and narrative by showing how nonwhiteness has played a pivotal role in some of Hollywood's most important films, including the technological spectacle of musicals (Courtney 2005; Dyer 1997; Maurice 2002; Shohat 1991). As a genre, the musical provides a similarly important frame for understanding the Latina body as a complex site of gendered, racialized, and sexualized negotiation on the Hollywood screen.

The colonial legacy of the Latina performer—and its paradox of racialized sexuality—is more apparent when framed against the Hollywood musical formula. According to traditional critical analysis of Hollywood musicals, the musical male performer courts his love interest through dance.[6] Dance functions as symbolic copulation: by teaching the (white) musical female to dance, the (white) musical male awakens his female partner's sexual identity. This sexual awakening is fulfilled when the musical female gains the ability to dance. Often, a musical siren intervenes to complicate the narrative, testing the musical male's fidelity to his love interest. The siren appeals to the musical male's sexual appetite and is often characterized as a dancer who requires no tutelage, such as the perfectly tempting dark-haired dancer briefly embodied by Cyd

Charisse in *Singin' in the Rain* (1952). The siren takes pleasure in seducing the musical male, but he ultimately triumphs and proves worthy of the virginal musical female and is rewarded with a legitimized social position of husband-to-be (Altman 1987; McLean 2004).

Hollywood's alignment of dance with specific interpretations of race, gender, sexuality, and class illustrates the symbolic formation of the U.S. national imagery and its ideological visualization. In musicals and in other Hollywood films, nonwhite and marginalized white women danced instinctively or compulsively, while sexually naive or innocent white women were taught to dance by male suitors as expressions of their sexual awakening and impending matrimony. This hetero-normative and patriarchal narrative structure has served as the backdrop for the Latina's characterization as a dangerous yet desirable object; she tempts white leading men and mainstream film audiences without technically breaking the white/black taboo (Hershfield 1998). Thus, the Hollywood Latina has functioned like a siren because the audience has been trained to assume that she already knows how to dance and requires no onscreen tutelage.

As an act, dance grants Latina characters a kind of agency or narrative subjectivity that challenges the traditional passivity of female representation. As a nonwhite female, her movement bucks the Hollywood tendency to frame the male body as "natural in action" while female bodies are statically "situated," a trope popular since the early film experiments of Eadweard Muybridge (Coffman 2002, 55; Williams 1989, 43). Although dance often restricts the Hollywood Latina to stereotypical roles that fit commercial expectations, this appeal to wider audiences can often result in greater box office, public recognition, and star power. As her dance produces access and agency, it paradoxically perpetuates the myth that Latinas are inherently passionate, promiscuous, and temporary.

While the Latina star's roles may be racially sexualized or seemingly reduced to characters with innate sexual prowess, her dance sequences have required great energy, emotion, and skill. Del Rio, Miranda, Hayworth, Moreno, and Lopez were each cast according to type, but they often exceeded their roles' limitations by maximizing their screen time with the use of movement and gestures that dared the audience to look away. Audiences have found Latina dance so compelling that these women became some of the most iconic—and profitable—performers in Hollywood; the seduction of Carmen Miranda's eyes, arms, and hips made her one of the United States' highest paid actresses, while the movement of Jennifer Lopez's body has made her a household brand.

Of course, I am not suggesting that a Latina is inherently sexualized or racialized when she dances. On the contrary, dance is many things, and to affix one meaning to any body's steps discredits the complexity of human movement and posits a static argument on a mobile form. The hegemonic film frame, however, trades in stereotypes and stock characterizations; this tendency explains why we expect recognizable performers to play with or against type and how star personas develop in the first place. In itself, a dancing Latina is both true and real; many Latinas do dance, and dance is an integral part of many Latino/a cultures (Aparicio 1998; Delgado and Muñoz 1997; García 2008; Macias 2008). But, in Hollywood, dance stands in for and identifies the Latina as a composite of race and sexuality—factors that mark her supposed difference in the face of Hollywood's preferred illusion of white humanism.

Dance also functions as a metaphor for Latina stardom. Despite moments of empowerment, the dancing Hollywood Latina remains a liminal performer because she diversifies but does not disrupt the black/white binary central to the U.S. racial hierarchy as portrayed by Hollywood (Shohat 1991; Shohat and Stam 1994, 189). The degrees to which the Latina can maneuver her career across the racialized continuum (or floor) depend on her looks, ability or willingness to dance, country of origin, and accent. I pose that in Hollywood film, racial representation is a sliding-scale hierarchy, one with clear parameters and even clearer zones of ambiguity; to succeed in the industry, a Latina performer needs to know where she falls on the scale and how to maximize her position. While the Hollywood Latina's narrative and professional agency remain tentative—especially when cast opposite a white actress of similar or higher star power—she still maintains some on-screen leverage.[7] Unlike many white female characters, she can often articulate her desires; unlike many black actresses, the Latina has been cast as the white protagonist's love interest without dying by film's end (Bogle 2001; Courtney 2005). Understanding how and why these things are related requires a theoretical vocabulary that illuminates the larger mechanics of this specific racial representation, especially in terms of sexuality, power, and performance. As we shall see, these constant negotiations have an oscillation—or dance—of their own.

At the Intersection of Sameness and Difference: In-Betweenness and Racial Mobility

To better explicate the Latina star's function in both film and nation formation, I have developed the terms "in-betweenness" and "racial mobility."[8] In-betweenness demarcates the ambiguously racialized space that Latinas occupy in the hierarchy of visual representation. Oscillating between the normalcy of whiteness and the exoticism of blackness, Latinas function as in-between bodies to mediate and maintain the racial status quo. Some Latina performers, however, can channel this liminality into stardom by maneuvering their in-betweenness toward the more desired racialized representation of the period (usually toward whiteness, but occasionally blackness), thus maximizing their careers in visual culture—a phenomenon I term "racial mobility." From a pragmatic perspective, in-betweenness and racial mobility maximize the Hollywood Latina's increasingly marketable image; her racially ambiguous look has become particularly attractive as the media industry has increasingly pursued multicultural markets within and beyond the United States. From a more insidious perspective, however, in-betweenness and racial mobility modify and reinstate the status quo. In the end, both are true. At the edge of power (that is, whiteness and fame), the Latina star can exercise her agency if she follows the rules; if she proves too unruly, she can be readily contained with increasingly lackluster or stereotypical roles.

The Hollywood Latina's in-betweenness is marked by a simultaneous exhibition of sameness (through accessible appearance) and difference (through dance performance). In-betweenness is greatly dependent on a prescribed look, which first determines whether she can enter the frame at all and then whether she can access the spotlight or become a breathing part of the Latin mise-en-scène. Since the 1930s, the Latina's popularity has hinged on an exotic look that could be read as "ethnic" yet remained familiar enough for white women to appropriate through hair coloring, tanning, fashion, and makeup (Berry 2000, 120). This emphasis on an exotic sameness resulted in the formulaic look of the Hollywood Latina: clear skin, a fair or caramel complexion, delicately dramatic facial features, and a trim but curvy figure. Her most distinct physical trait, however, may be her dark, often long, brown hair. Although many dark-haired white women have become stars in Hollywood, the unambiguous whiteness of blond starlets has resulted in more screen time, narrative agency, and celebrity status—especially during the classical Hollywood period and especially during World War II (Roberts 1993, 4). Dark hair, combined with fair or caramel-colored skin, has often marked a kind of ethnic difference that remains accessible to white audiences, particularly women (Berry 2000, 111; Negra 2001, 87). Although some Latinas, like Rita Moreno, have retained their naturally curly hair, most have straightened their hair to conform to a more standardized impression of the Latina look: long, brown, and straight or lightly wavy. Whether born of Latina/Latin American heritage or not, on-screen Latinas must adhere to this look, which does not stray too far from the standards of beauty set for white female performers. As we will see in the case studies of this chapter, the dark-haired women cast in La Cucaracha and "Mural" both fulfill this look, even though the star of La Cucaracha, Steffi Duna, is Hungarian-born (Negra 2001, 119).[9]

Compliance with white beauty standards does not mean acceptance, however. Because Latinas are rarely (if ever) considered white, their ambiguous racial/ethnic difference must be highlighted and contained through the action of dance. By using dance to signify a kind of racialized and sexualized difference, Hollywood merely collapses and formalizes an association that already exists between bodily movement, sex, and race in the United States. Effusive public dancing was an indication of loose sexuality to early white Protestant communities (D'Emilio and Freedman 1997). On the East Coast, this generalization developed into an early distinction between WASPs and working-class white ethnics, but as white settlers moved westward, their encounters and misinterpretations of Mexican dance practices added racist undertones to an already sexualized prejudice (D'Emilio and Freedman 1997). As the movie industry began to develop on the West Coast, it quickly codified dance, race/ethnicity, and sexuality into a unified trinity that proved increasingly popular as production companies began to showcase technological breakthroughs—such as the use of sound in *Hallelujah!* (1929) or color in *La Cucaracha*—with the cinematic spectacles of nonwhite bodies (Maurice 2002).

Despite the legacy of hysteria incited by racial ambiguity in the United States, the Latina's racial mobility and seductive nonwhite screen body are contained and regulated through the temporality of cinematic dance. Her movements and gestures are determined by the tempo of the song, the space of the soundstage, the length of her choreographed sequence, and—most importantly—the film frame itself. Locked within the tripled "voyeuristic gaze" of the "director, the camera, and the male protagonist," the Latina can be fully desired by the spectator because she is performing within a temporary space and time (Albright 1997, 99). Further, her dance functions as a hyper-performance, suggesting yet another way through which the "reality" of a film narrative's central performance is disrupted—in this case, troubling the narrative beyond her already Othered body (Dyer 2002).

The Hollywood Latina's racial mobility is dependent on her specific intersection of nonwhiteness and femaleness and her position on the sliding-scale hierarchy can be greatly influenced by the romantic lead cast opposite her. Despite the Latina's racially ambiguous look and contextualization, audiences typically know that the Latina star is not white, and she does not typically pass for white; even Rita Hayworth's contemporary fans knew of her Spanish origins (McLean 1992, 9). The Hollywood Latina's hegemonic look must be countered with a clearly racialized and sexualized characterization—especially when the Latina is cast opposite a white male lead—that marks her as distinctly nonwhite and thus a temporary companion for her white lover (Berg 2002, 71).

The Hollywood Latina's racialized sexuality is more accurately a racialized heterosexuality, demonstrating how her sexual encoding is distinctly tied to nation, race, and class in the United States (Lugones 2007). The Latina's male partner is thus an important component in the position of her in-betweenness. If he is white, she is potentially an insufficient or temporary partner in the film's narrative. If the Latina is cast opposite a Latino character (whether Latino or a white actor in brownface), the narrative or other cinematic codes suggest that she can find a better lover (Almaguer 1994, 61). Although the Latina may ultimately be assimilable if paired with a white man, she is cut off from this rosy future if paired with a nonwhite male because nonwhite men like Latinos do not possess the same opportunities for racial mobility as Latinas do on the arbitrarily hierarchical racial scale. Because nonwhite men do not have the same access to white—even white ethnic—roles that Latinas may have, their transgressions do not necessarily enhance their status; when male Latinos are able to mobilize race, it is more of a lateral move. Anthony Quinn, for example, was able to play other brown men such as Native Americans, Arabs, Greeks, and Italians but was often restricted from playing a nonraced or nonethnic white role; his early roles "oscillated between the romantic 'noble savage' *and* the dangerous racialized criminal" (Marez 2004, 149). While Latinas are often, although not always, paired with white male leads, Latinos are rarely paired with white female actresses.[10] When the narrative called for such pairings, the Latinos were cast as white actors in brownface. In this way, nonwhite male sexuality could be contained, a regulation that perpetuated the demonization of nonwhite men in the name of protecting the virtue of white women. Conversely, nonwhite women were framed as in need of rescue from their own men. Even in those instances in which interracial romance was explicitly on display, as in *West Side Story*, the film manages to reestablish the hierarchy through casting, choreography, and makeup.[11]

As these complex cinematic and extra-cinematic layers illustrate, in-betweenness and racial mobility do not shield the Hollywood Latina from racist practices within the United States or Hollywood, nor do they fully absolve her from inadvertently supporting such ideologies. While Latinas are exoticized in ways similar to black female bodies, nonblack Latina performers retain limited privileges if they adhere to the dominant cosmetic codes that are organized around whiteness as the default racial and representational identity. Once in line with the dominant U.S. standards of beauty—specifically in terms of hair and complexion—Latinas who look the part may access a wider variety of roles than black performers, including on-screen interracial romances largely out of reach for U.S. black or Afro-Latina performers (Dyer 2002, 39).[12] Even more prominent roles and careers are possible if the Latina is willing and able to combine the exoticized and racialized gesture of dance with white body codes such as lightened and straightened hair, as exemplified by Rita Hayworth and Jennifer Lopez. It is no coincidence that none of the Latina performers featured in this project identifies as or would be identified as Afro-Latina; this distinction—nonwhite, but not black—has been crucial to the Hollywood Latina's longevity, even during periods of racial unrest among black or multiracial Latino communities within the United States. In identifying the Hollywood Latina's agency, one may also hold her accountable for reifying the centrality of whiteness—but to what extent?

The Hollywood Latina thus marks a paradoxical agency. The personal and professional choices that have constituted her racial mobility have alternately become the costs and casualties of pursuing or gaining agency in Hollywood film. As a dancer, she frequently exhibits a narrative agency that challenges traditional white female passivity, but the act of dance often confines her to roles that reiterate racialized and sexualized myths. Similarly, the balance of sameness and difference required of the Hollywood Latina builds her professional and social agency while cultivating an illusion of diversity and sexual liberation in U.S. cinema. This paradox results in sacrifices that are not necessarily equal for the five women in this study, illustrating how the oscillation of a Latina's in-betweenness toward whiteness or blackness can have long-term repercussions. After Del Rio became disenchanted with her U.S. roles, she left Hollywood and became a major figure of Mexican cinema. Miranda's Hollywood roles never expanded beyond typecasting, and her career quickly declined.

To show how the Hollywood Latina helps visualize an ever-shifting ideal within the United States, I build this project's primary conversation through cinema studies and Latino/a studies, as well as performance studies. Latino/a studies provides a frame of reference for exploring the national body in terms of race and ethnicity within the United States, while cinema studies illuminates the capture, representation, and dissemination of the Latino/a body through the social institution of media. My analytical approach is anchored by cinema's attention to the rules and conventions of representation (and informed by my media production experience), but I am most interested in further unraveling the tensions that exist at the intersection of Latino/a studies and cinema studies as begun by Charles Ramírez Berg, Rosa Linda Fregoso, and Chon Noriega and recently continued by others (Berg 2002; Fregoso 1993; Noriega 2000; Mendible 2007; Beltrán 2009; Bernardi 2007). For example, the framework of Latino/a studies has enabled me to complicate Richard Dyer's influential work on stars to find that, for Latinas, stardom and the agency (however limited) that comes with it can lead to a politicized manipulation of industrial, national, and social structures (Dyer 1986, 1997). At the intersection of these two disciplines, I complicate both to focus on the concept of in-betweenness and its limited application within Latino/a studies and cinema studies.[13]

While the intersection of cinema studies and Latino/a studies establishes the perimeter of my analytical approach, this project is deeply indebted to recent scholarship in dance and performance studies. Dance provides the women considered in this project—women of color operating in a white- and male-dominant arena—with the action necessary to flex their star agency (however limited) in resistance to their doubly marginalized position. The dancing screen Latina solicits the body as well as the mind and eye of the spectator, generating a complex form of pleasure that feeds a certain racial/sexual fantasy while simultaneously producing a dynamic space for viewer and performer (Albright 1997).[14] Whereas dance and performance studies have borrowed, refined, and refuted components of visual analysis in part garnered from cinema studies, cinema studies still has much to gain from a closer analysis of movement, performance, and passion within its own frame. Informed by (recent) performance and dance scholarship at the intersection of race by Jayna Brown, Jane Desmond, David Román, and Marta Savigliano, among others, my project unravels the representation of movement in terms of race, gender, and Hollywood film by taking into account the personal and communal negotiations of the dancing/performing body (Blanco Borelli 2008; Brown 2008; Desmond 1997, 1999, 2001; García 2008; Parédez 2009; Román 2005; Sandoval-Sánchez 1999; Savigliano 1995). *Dance and the Hollywood Latina* is thus interdisciplinary in both theory and method, combining analyses of texts and production practices with an archival method to produce a diversified discussion of racial representation in the United States. I am not, however, trained as a dance scholar; while I am attentive to choreography, my analyses more often focus on the depiction, use, and signification of dance in relation to the Hollywood Latina.

Latina + Dance = A Desiring/Desirable Body

The case studies of *La Cucaracha* and "Mural" help illustrate the larger foundational equation of passion and dance that constitutes the ideological continuum of the Latina body, as well as the paradoxical ways in which dance facilitates her sexualization and narrative agency. Neither example features a recognizable Latina star, but both exemplify the conventions that have become ubiquitous in the last hundred years of motion pictures. The short film *La Cucaracha* was produced to test and promote the then-nascent three-strip Technicolor process.[15] "Mural" on the other hand, is a thirty-second television and Web commercial for the "Sugar Free Dulce de Leche" Jell-O pudding product.[16] Both examples set up the formal categories that support my theoretical deconstruction of the myth of the dancing Latina.

Figure 1. The choreography in *La Cucaracha* consists largely of patterned movements and prioritizes the arrangement of colorful costumes over the skill of moving bodies. Courtesy of the Margaret Herrick Library, Academy of Motion Picture Arts and Sciences.

La Cucaracha is set in a Mexican cabaret, its vibrant Technicolor presumably motivated by the purportedly passionate characters who inhabit such exotic settings.[17] The twenty-minute film's protagonist is the feisty and jealous Chatita (Steffi Duna). Scorned by her hostile lover, Pancho (Don Alvarado), Chatita—clothed in a fiery, coral-red dress with a jealous-green shawl around her shoulders—attempts to foil Pancho's cabaret performance. Feeling rejected and defiant, Chatita disrupts Pancho's dance with his female partner by singing a version of the folk song "La Cucaracha" over the dancers' musical accompaniment. Enraged, Pancho abandons his partner and powerfully directs his movement toward Chatita; when she stands to meet his aggressive challenge, they begin to dance. Drums enter the musical score as the couple stares intensely at each other while dancing in unison. As they dance, bodies apart and arms up in the air, Pancho scowls but Chatita smiles in satisfaction: she finally has his full attention. When the dance ends, Pancho wraps her tightly in his red serape and rushes her to the corridor, where they are both swathed in a deep red light matching the serape. There, Pancho threatens, "You've ruined me, Cucaracha.

I'm going to kill you." Before he can attack, however, the lovers are invited to star as a dancing duo in Mexico City, and the film celebrates their turbulent union with a spectacular and colorfully choreographed finale on the cabaret dance floor.

The passion and knowing sexuality of the character Chatita are affirmed by her innate dance abilities and underscored by her vibrant costuming and (emotionally) abusive Latino partner. While the film's choreography largely consists of patterned movements and prioritizes the arrangement of colorful costumes over the skill of moving bodies (Higgins 2000, 365), dance propels the narrative and characterization: although Chatita is presented as a singer with no dance training, her naturalized abilities elevate the movement of the cabaret's star dancer, Pancho, and exceed the abilities of his professional female dance partner.[18] Chatita's ability to dance is motivated by her flared temper at Pancho's indifference and associated with her brilliant costume and ability to manipulate other male characters to get her way.[19] Duna's fiery-cool incarnation of Chatita is wholly charming; despite some overacting, the result is a headstrong yet vulnerable character. Yet Chatita's desirability and availability seem most correlative to the presumed inferiority of her Latino lover in the film. Although Chatita desires Pancho at all costs, his manner epitomizes the brutal affection of the Latin Lover stereotype (Berg 2002). Pancho's continual threats to Chatita suggest a sadomasochistic relationship, a kind of sexual deviance supported by the film's reference to the popular song "La Cucaracha."[20]

The equation of the Latina's symbolic value—Latina + dance = desiring/desirable body—was still being solidified when La Cucaracha was made, but seventy-five years later the association between "desire" and "Latina dancer" has become so evident that the Jell-O pudding commercial "Mural" uses this cultural knowledge to market its product in less than thirty seconds. "Mural" opens with a slender Latina enjoying an individually packaged dulce de leche–flavored Jell-O pudding. The Latin American–inspired gelatin dessert is so pleasurable that her tanned body begins to wriggle as her long, straight brown hair swings freely. The energy of her movement (and a taste of the pudding) animates three female figures from a nearby mural; the figures emerge from the wall as a live-action, dancing multicultural trio who mimic the Latina's seductive wiggle. The females' collective movement arouses the attention of the commercial's lone male figure, who is also on the mural. Magically, the animated man appears in the flesh. Although we never fully see his nonanimated face, he is marked as Latino by his dark hair, tanned skin, and white suit—clothing akin to the traditional Vera Cruz attire familiar to U.S. audiences thanks to Speedy Gonzalez

Figure 2. In "Mural," the anonymous Latin Lover pulls the Latina protagonist close. She responds with a "wiggle," indicating her pleasure in his powerful gesture. Her dynamic movements are enhanced by his static body and obscured face.

(Nericcio 2007). The Latin Lover pulls our Latina into a sexy dance duet as a male announcer's voice makes explicit what the layered images, movement, and sound imply about dulce de leche Jell-O: it is "pure desire." By commercial's end, the figures return to the mural and leave our Latina to enjoy her tasty treat—described by the announcer as a combination of "creamy vanilla pudding" and "intense caramel topping"—in private.

Whether feuding in *La Cucaracha* or feeding in "Mural," the Latina and her passion are expressed through dance because it is a distinct marker of her identification as Latina. The other ads for the Jell-O campaign, "Wiggle Room" and "Spa," use dancing, spunky women to sell pudding, but only "Mural" overtly links the product to a particular ethnicity and racializes the body movements of the commercial's cast. To put this racialization in perspective, consider how "Spa," which advertises dark chocolate Jell-O pudding by using a perky blond woman wearing dark brown, would read if the main character were a black woman.[21] Thus, the kinds of body/product associations "Mural" makes are particularly striking in terms of race and sexuality. "Mural's" sequential images of body and pudding reinforce the Latina's dancing as both racially and sexually motivated, especially when analyzed in tandem with the voiceover's narration and lyrics:

> FEMALE SINGER: Deep in my soul / Baby, It's meant to be / The wiggle in my heart / Is gonna set you free.
> CHORUS: Oooohh
> FEMALE SINGER: My wiggle / My jiggle
> MALE NARRATOR: Jello Sugar Free Dulce de Leche
> FEMALE SINGER: My wiggle will set you free / My jiggle / My wiggle
> MALE NARRATOR: Creamy vanilla pudding / Intense caramel topping
> FEMALE SINGER: It's gonna set you free
> MALE NARRATOR: It's pure desire
> FEMALE SINGER: My wiggle / My wiggle
> MALE NARRATOR: And just 60 calories
> FEMALE SINGER: My wiggle will set you free / It's gonna set you free
> MALE NARRATOR: Because every diet needs a little wiggle room.

Shots of drizzling liquids in white (vanilla pudding) and brown (caramel) flank and mimic the Latina's brown moving body as the female voice sings of wiggling and jiggling while the male announcer talks about vanilla and caramel (see fig. 3). The most sexually suggestive lyrics and announcements are layered over the racialized shots of (1) drizzling vanilla, (2) the dancing Latina, and (3) the drizzling caramel, which sinuously and sequentially appear in like movement. Here, we can imagine that the female singer simultaneously represents the dancing Latina and the pudding product. As the Latina, the lyrics use the promise of "wiggle" and "jiggle" to seduce the (male) lover whom she desires; as the pudding, the same jiggles and wiggles appeal to the female consumer. In either case, the presumably (white) female audience is expected to identify with the dancing Latina and desire her brands of pudding and exotic seduction.

Like *La Cucaracha*, "Mural" expects its audience to read the Latina's performance as both desirable and desiring. Although the Latina's bodily movements are continually juxtaposed with shots of pudding—positioning her as a tempting, perhaps even delicious, partner—she is clearly the dominant figure in the fantasy. Whereas Chatita made do with an emotionally abusive lover, "Mural" provides its Latina with a temporary (hallucinated?) Latino companion. Because the anonymous man in white is the only male figure to appear in the late 2008 Jell-O campaign, the Latina challenges gender norms while reinforcing racialized heteronormativity.[22] The jingle lyrics frame the Latina as a desiring woman, thus subverting the traditional equation of desiring male subject

Figure 3. The Hollywood Latina is a sinuous combination of vanilla/whiteness and caramel/brownness in this Jell-O commercial. *Clockwise, from top left*: the symmetry of the liquid mimics the Hollywood Latina's deliciousness and in-betweenness.

and desirable female object for its target female audience. Yet the presence of a male dance partner—in excess of the female backup dancers—suggests that hetero-normativity is an equally important signifier of Latina-ness. "Mural's" Latino dance partner functions as a prop, however: his anonymity and temporariness reinforce the Latina's dance as agency, narrative centrality, and desirability.

Although each short was composed for a different media venue at a different historical and technological moment, both *La Cucaracha* and "Mural" use the Latina in similar ways and to similar effect. In each example, the Latina's compulsory dance is the spectacle that entices the viewer in the service of its product, be it Technicolor film or pudding. In 2008 as in 1934, the narrative settings freeze the Latina in the past through formal choices like location, lighting, and casting: the Latinas are framed against Mission-style interiors—lit to evoke the warmth of the pre-electric era's candlelit glow—and partnered with seemingly Latino men who highlight the women's desirability and, more crucially, availability. Thus, the myth of the Hollywood Latina operates for both anonymous and brown female bodies.

In the chapters that follow on Dolores Del Rio, Carmen Miranda, Rita Hayworth, Rita Moreno, and Jennifer Lopez, I discuss how Hollywood film has negotiated national tensions surrounding nonwhiteness, Latin America, and gender/sexual equality at specific historical moments in the United States. Building on the terms and stakes outlined in the case studies of *La Cucaracha* and "Mural," I historicize and theorize each Latina's career, examining the Latina star's body within her specific cinematic era and according to her nation of origin or affiliation. Because each woman in this project illuminates the national stage differently and in different national-historical eras, each chapter illustrates the myriad ways in which race, gender, and sexuality were negotiated and restated through the dancing brown female body. Beginning with Dolores Del Rio and ending with Jennifer Lopez, *Dance and the Hollywood Latina* offers a cumulative picture of Latina stardom and the progression of the myth of the Hollywood Latina; however mobile, her image has remained in a state of flux as a result of the institutional practices of Hollywood and perceived racial identity within the United States.

To better untangle the multiple layers that inflect the myth of the dancing Latina and shift each performer's narrative in Hollywood, I first evaluate the national and cultural backdrop against which the screen Latina performs. The racist and heterosexist beliefs about gender, sexuality, and class that govern (nonwhite) female bodies are layered with the U.S.–Latin American relations or intra-U.S. policies about or against Latino/a populations within each historical period. With production largely concentrated in Southern California, Hollywood itself is a microcosm of this sociopolitical terrain.[23] The specific combination of these factors impacted the cultural power of the performer and the methods by which she achieved her agency and fame. With this in mind, I use archival materials—such as studio publicity, film reviews, and contractual negotiations—to contextualize the characterizations that composed each performer's career within the specific political and regional climate of her fame. Finally, I employ textual analysis to better identify the Latina's role in the service of a larger national imagery through formal film techniques like composition, costuming, and choreography. The chronological organization of this book locates each performer at a transitional moment in the nation's gendered, racialized, and sexualized history and allows for a comparison of Latina performers based on similar institutional frames like studio publicity practices, technological traditions, and genre conventions.

In chapter 2, "Dolores Del Rio Dances across the Imperial Color Line," I set up the myth of the Hollywood Latina. First, I identify the roots of the Latina mythology in the empire-building strategies of Spain and later the United States. I outline how the brown female body helped facilitate colonial power, from the Spanish conquest of the Americas to the United States' incorporation of the Southwest as a territory. By interrogating the symbolic figure of the "Spanish" woman, I clarify how discussions of Spanishness have masked the racist and class-based beliefs at the core of nation building and racialized hierarchies. Because the institution of Hollywood becomes a cultural force in Southern California, a space charged with the recent history of these imperial power plays, I show how the traditions of the Hollywood Latina are not divorced from assumptions about the availability and inferiority of brown women. I build on this analysis by showing how the technological development of sound impacted the Latina's representational role; as the musical boomed in the 1930s, the imperial relationship between the United States and Latin America further entrenched the Hollywood Latina's symbolic in-betweenness as a narrative tool. The chapter further charts Del Rio's career through the tensions surrounding the United States–Mexico border from the Mexican American War to Prohibition and the Depression.

Because Del Rio's Hollywood sets the stage against which each subsequent Latina will perform, chapter 2 develops some of the racial-national questions raised in the current chapter. The tale of the Hollywood Latina opens with Del Rio, the daughter of a purportedly wealthy family, dancing a tango in her family's parlor. Del Rio was discovered by a Hollywood director, and her persona was underwritten by her noble family narrative, yet her characters were women of ill repute (*Joanna*, 1925), noble yet exotic Others (a Pacific Islander princess in *Bird of Paradise*, 1932; and a Brazilian socialite in *Flying Down to Rio*, 1933), or tempestuous nightclub performers (*Wonder Bar*, 1934; and *In Caliente*, 1935). The class negotiations of Del Rio's career are particularly compelling because they tell how the studio insisted on linking her wealth to a Spanish (not Mexican) origin—a telling sign of the imperial tensions at the connecting point between the United States and Mexico in the 1920s.

In chapter 3, "Carmen Miranda Shakes It for the Nation," I focus on Miranda to highlight how the racial complexity of Latin America was immediately collapsed into an oversimplified and hyperexoticized version of the brown female body that exemplified the marketability of in-betweenness in the progression of the screen Latina's mythology. Within the U.S. frame, the social, racial, and cultural complexities of the Latina were disregarded in favor of familiar signifiers that highlighted the imperial position of the United States. As it further solidified its imperial position, the United States enacted its own reading of the brown female body regardless of her region of origin. This chapter shows, however, how the complexities of race that framed the Hollywood

Latina's national origin would play a significant—if subtle—role in the range of her characters and how performers from the Caribbean would face greater representational challenges than women from Mexico or Spain.

Chapter 3 also shows how, by building on the United States' hesitant relationship with Latin America, Miranda provided a crucial link between the United States and Brazil. As a Hollywood icon swirled in tropical fruit and Technicolor, Miranda was the Good Neighbor who taught the United States that Brazil was ripe for the picking. Her whirling celebrity spanned over two and a half decades—one decade in Brazil (1929–1939) and one and a half in the United States (1939–1955). While Miranda epitomized Latin America for her Hollywood audiences, she was in fact a Portuguese émigré who had embraced the style of disenfranchised black Brazilians. As a white woman living in Brazil, Miranda represented a commodified blackness; once she crossed over to the United States, she represented an amalgamated Latin American-ness. In both countries, her image fluctuated between the poles of racial representation. In the end, Miranda's costumed body, heavily accented English, and performative hips became a generic Latin American Other against which white Americanness could be measured—and from which she could never escape.

In chapter 4, "Rita Hayworth and the Cosmetic Borders of Race," I examine how Hayworth establishes racial mobility and its function in the mythological framework of the Hollywood Latina. With a focus on the problems specific to the domestic Latina body, I outline how assimilation was necessary for Latina performers aiming to become mainstream stars with leading roles and far-reaching careers. Also, I consider how, during World War II and the postwar period, the mythology of the Hollywood Latina functioned as a turning point for representations of female sexual identity for white women. At a transitional moment within the United States, Hayworth's career signals the challenges of mainstream representation that Latinas who followed would experience, especially Latinas unwilling (or unable) to meet the physical and nominal changes demanded by Hollywood.

I also outline the mechanics of cosmetic transformation and its role in Hollywood success, and explore the transformation of a Spanish dancer named Rita Cansino into Rita Hayworth and how her early history authenticated the exoticism that underscored her Hollywood career as a Love Goddess.[24] Like the contemporary performer Jennifer Lopez and Del Rio before her, Hayworth found that her career and popularity were predicated on a careful manipulation—and simultaneous semiotic representation—of whiteness and nonwhiteness. Hayworth combined the appearance of whiteness through hair color and name change with the performance of nonwhiteness through dance to cultivate a long career in Hollywood film. She embodied a persona that was exotic and sexual, yet simultaneously glamorous and all-American. The fusion of Hayworth's history as a dancer with her penchant for cosmetic transformation resulted in a complex persona at a transitional moment in the twentieth century—during and after World War II, a key period of national, social, and gendered restructuring in the United States.

The final two chapters show how Puerto Rican women have owned the latter half of the twentieth century and illustrate the kinds of negotiations required of contemporary Latina performers after two generations of Hollywood Latinas. Chapter 5, "Rita Moreno, the Critically Acclaimed 'All-Round Ethnic,'" marks an important shift in the iconic Latina through the Puerto Rican female body. Spanning the 1950s to the present, Moreno's career highlights domestic Latina representation during and after the civil rights movement and increased Puerto Rican migration to the mainland. As Hollywood began to incorporate the Puerto Rican woman into its cultural imagery, the frame began to shift her image toward the urban space of the city and blackness: the unresolved social and political tensions between the mainland United States and Puerto Rico were figured through the still-segregated landscape of New York City and embodied by the Latina's brown body. Yet the Hollywood Latina remained purportedly foreign regardless of her citizenship status.

Moreno's award-winning and vast multimedia career illustrates how one Latina actress used various venues—film, television, and theater—to push mainstream Latina representation beyond the limits of stereotype. Because Moreno's film opportunities remained limited after her Oscar-winning performance in *West Side Story*, she shifted her Hollywood career while openly critiquing the industry for the types of roles she was offered. Through the medium of television, Moreno fashioned roles that exceeded the limitations of Latina representation (*The Electric Company*) or playfully lampooned those popular expectations (*The Muppet Show, The Rockford Files*). Although Moreno worked hard to diversify the kinds of roles she played, the trajectory of her persona seemed to be forever marked by her role as Anita, the sassy Puerto Rican girlfriend of a juvenile delinquent. Moreno's career does not follow the traditional star path, but she is the most acclaimed performer in this study and has won an Academy Award, a Tony Award, and two Emmys; these awards, however, were for roles that largely reified the Latina myth through racialized sexuality or dance. By looking at the contradictions of Moreno's legacy, her influence on popular culture, and the negotiations necessary to facilitate her longevity, we can better understand her influence on later Latina mythmakers like Jennifer Lopez.

Dance and the Hollywood Latina concludes with chapter 6, "Jennifer Lopez, Racial Mobility, and the New Urban/Latina Commodity." Given the legacy of the Hollywood Latina, Lopez's multifaceted and multidemographic career is all the more impressive for its scope and use of the Latina mythology. Because of her variegated career (and the complications of contemporary cultural memory), I pay close attention to the formal aspects of her multimedia representations. From Lopez's television debut as a member of the hip-hop dance troupe the Fly Girls on *In Living Color* to her continued success in feature films and the pop music industry, Lopez's career is the direct result of a growing media interest in multiculturalism—or at least multicultural markets—on MTV (Music Television). Lopez emerged in media at the same time that black popular culture was becoming a viable and marketable aspect of mainstream culture. Her ability to maximize exposure in multiple arenas—film, music, fashion, and fragrance—illustrates the malleability of the Latina identity at the end of the twentieth and beginning of the twenty-first centuries. In this chapter I look at why Lopez's career is only possible now—as opposed to the 1950s or 1960s—and how the commodification of blackness through television and music and whiteness in Hollywood factors into this equation.

This final chapter marks the new era of the Latina body in mainstream media. As the 1990s and 2000s see the mainstreaming of black culture, the Latina body builds on the previous legacies of the Hollywood Latina to serve as a transitional body for a new multicultural market. Framed almost exclusively as an urban body, the Hollywood Latina reemerges as an apolitical entity framed by the dual lenses of Hollywood and television production (more specifically, through MTV). While the Hollywood Latina diversifies the cultural imagery through various media arenas, she also benefits from the multiplicity of meanings that these different venues provide, from film to music videos to clothing and cosmetics. Jennifer Lopez has arguably become the century's most successful Latina by mobilizing the myth through in-betweenness and racial mobility, but in the service of her own career and a new colonial force—the global market.

Because the dancing Latina's image is so ubiquitous, it is easy to overlook or dismiss her as a two-dimensional nonwhite female stereotype employed to seduce consumers. She is so visible that her own colonial and racial mythology—a product in and of itself—becomes invisible. Her titillating image compounds, carries, and disseminates a long narrative of colonization enacted through her brown female body. The dancing Latina is subject to the national and patriarchal variants of her era, a collective gaze that locks her performance within the colonizing frames of Hollywood. These narrowly defined roles largely serve to reify a gendered, racialized, sexualized, and nationalized Other against which the hegemonic ideal of the U.S. citizen is measured and visualized. But dance makes the Latina star a paradoxical figure. Her characters own a seemingly compulsive kinetic knowledge (regardless of the film's genre) that is limiting but also is an essential and invariable asset, regardless of the decade in Hollywood. These limited roles illustrate the dynamic ways in which Latina performers actively redefined their cultural marginality. By exercising the pleasure and power of dance, Latina stars redirected their kinetic energy into roles with more depth or, at the very least, more visibility than small character roles. Negotiating the pitfalls of Hollywood with deft footwork and untold falls, the Latina star strikes a balance: by wielding her body and its purported sexuality in familiar ways, she achieves agency in a career and nation that would otherwise exclude her and her movement. By mobilizing race and shaking her assets, the Hollywood Latina uses the myth to get paid.

CHAPTER 2

Dolores Del Rio Dances across the Imperial Color Line

Borders are set up to define the places that are safe and unsafe, to distinguish us from them.

—Gloria Anzaldúa

In *Wonder Bar* (1934), Al Wonder (Al Jolson) entertains a Parisian nightclub crowd with a song before the club's headlining dancer Ynez, played by Dolores Del Rio, takes center stage. Jolson augments his singing with his signature facial expressions and hand gestures. When the lyric recounts being "in the arms of a lovely Latin daughter," Jolson delivers this rather benign line while spreading his legs with his hands. This small gesture—hands parting, thighs open—effectively equates the lyric's "arms" with his pried-open legs; this juxtaposition between aural and bodily signifiers subtly transforms the song's "lovely Latin daughter" into a licentious character.[1] The small moment immediately sexualizes the only "Latin" female visible in *Wonder Bar*, Ynez/Dolores Del Rio, before she appears on stage for the awaiting diegetic audience.

As the first brown female star, Dolores Del Rio initiated the myth of the Hollywood Latina; her legacy frames the complex trajectory of Latina stardom in the United States. Del Rio's image—sexualized according to the complex and contradictory frames of race, nation, and class—produced the prototypical dancing Latina that later brown women were expected to emulate en route to stardom. As a Mexican performer popular during the overlapping and turbulent periods of Prohibition and the Great Depression, Del Rio, through her body, persona, and performance, complicated and mediated U.S. representations of whiteness and blackness; as a racialized and sexualized transnational figure cast amid the complex spatial-imperial tensions of Hollywood, Los Angeles, Southern California, the United States, Mexico, and Spain, Del Rio, with her so-called Spanish heritage, produced a crucial buffer for nonwhite representation during a period of racial and national tensions. Dolores Del Río established the myth of the Hollywood Latina and sparked the in-betweenness that enabled Carmen Miranda and later Latinas to develop their own careers.

Del Río emerged in Hollywood during the silent era, a period ruled by the blond female star; the few dark-haired stars at the time were Theda Bara and Pola Negri, women equally exoticized within the film frame or cast as vamps through publicity (Berry 2000, 103; Dyer 2004, 44; Negra 2001, 57). While the silent era allowed Del Río to maximize the racial ambiguity of her dark hair and fair complexion, she was cast in various ethnic roles whose characterizations and movements often carried sexual connotations (Carr 1979, 2–3). When Hollywood transitioned to synchronized sound films, Del Río's accented English limited her roles to those explicitly marked as foreign, but this aural marker of difference only reinforced what audiences had already surmised from these previous roles (Stoever 2007).

Del Río's silent film roles emphasized her body through dance, ethnicity, and overt sexualization—associations that began with her initial discovery in Mexico by a Hollywood producer named Edwin Carewe.[2] As the story goes, Carewe was traveling in Mexico when he saw Del Río dance a tango to entertain guests at a party (Beltrán 2005, 58; Hershfield 2000, 1–4; Rodriguez 2004). Soon after, Del Río debuted in Carewe's 1925 production of *Joanna*, in which she was cast as a vampish "woman of the world" who ruins the white female protagonist's reputation. *Joanna* provided the first in a series of silent roles that explicitly or implicitly cast Del Río in a sexually licentious context.[3] After *Joanna*, Del Río played a prostitute in *Resurrection* (1927) and unapologetically shared her love and body with two soldiers in *What Price Glory?* (1927). She was then cast as a fiery gypsy in *Loves of Carmen* (1927)—a role reprised by Rita Hayworth in 1953—and *Revenge* (1928), her final silent film. There, at the cusp of a new technological era in cinema, Del Río played a "fallen woman" in the silent-with-sound-sequences film *The Trail of '98* (1929) and a seductive Spanish dancer in *The Bad One* (1930) (*AFI Catalog*, s.v. *The Trail of '98* and *The Bad One*). Del Río was regularly cast as a dancer, prostitute, or woman with unconventional morals, and her presence implied a kind of racialized and sexualized difference that was often connected to white men.

Building on the racialized and sexualized history of her early work, Del Río erected the myth of the Hollywood Latina in the tradition of the colonized brown female body. She was able to surpass her Mexican origins by performing with an upper-class-ness—insistently framed by studio publicity as Spanish—that tempered her nonwhiteness in the United States. This emphasis on Spanishness masked the racist and elitist beliefs at the core of U.S. nation building and racialized hierarchies. By focusing on the films Del Rio made between 1932 and 1935, the period that fully transitions Del Rio to the sound period (largely via musicals), I show how her representational body helped establish costuming, hair, and dance as the emerging codes of the Hollywood Latina's in-betweenness. Focusing on the films *Bird of Paradise* (RKO, 1932), *Flying Down to Rio* (RKO, 1935), and *Wonder Bar* (First National/Warner Bros., 1934), I highlight how Del Rio's studio-cultivated Spanishness mirrored the social and spatial transformations of Los Angeles and Hollywood.[4] By emphasizing the role of dance and Spanishness in Del Rio's persona, I show how her image reified popular misconceptions about Latinos/as in the United States during a period of Mexican criminalization and marginalization in California—even as she carved a space for Latina performers in Hollywood.

IMPERIAL PAIRINGS AND CASTA PAINTINGS:
RACIAL MOVES FROM SPAIN, MEXICO, AND HOLLYWOOD

As the genesis of the Hollywood Latina, Del Rio is framed against the foundational mythology of the brown/Latina female body that informs her entry into Hollywood. I offer a brief cultural history of the brown female body's role in the colonization process, beginning with the Spanish conquest of the Americas and ending with the United States' seizure of Californian land. At each point, the brown female body functioned as a mediating body or imperial conduit—embodiments visualized in casta paintings, spatialized through locations such as Los Angeles' Olvera Street, or recorded and disseminated through Hollywood films.

Dolores Del Rio's arrival in Los Angeles in 1925 and her subsequent Hollywood career as a mediating body were framed by the imperial forces of Spain and the United States, racialized and gendered productions of power and space that framed the sociocultural development of Southern California (Almaguer 1994, 61; Appelbaum, Macpherson, and Rosemblatt 2003). Born in Durango, Mexico, Del Rio professed a Spanish-Basque heritage that bestowed on her the prestige of an elite class in Mexico. Meanwhile, her Hollywood debut coincided with the post-Revolutionary chaos that forced many Mexicans to seek employment opportunities in the United States (Marez 2004; Monroy 2001, 161). This influx of Mexican bodies exacerbated the U.S. perception of Mexicans and Mexican Americans as criminals or sexual deviants, either through media representation or literal police framings (Marez 2004). This recent history exacerbated the racial and class divisions that already operated within the United States and marked Mexico as inferior in both respects.[5] Southern California's initial attempts to distinguish itself from Mexico and Mexicans were heightened when the United States enforced Prohibition; as a liquor-fueled tourist industry developed south of the border, many Mexican cities gained reputations as "centers of vice and moral abandon" and intensified what many Anglo-Americans already imagined to be true (Tenenbaum 1996, 303). Los Angeles was particularly fraught with this racialized hierarchy of power, and the nation's frictions and tensions with Mexico were recorded and disseminated by the region's emerging film industry.

Since the Spanish Conquest, the constant within these colonial and national shifts has been the brown female body; Malintzin, born Malinalli Tenepal, was the first in a long line of brown women to bear the burden of cultural mediation and transmission in the Americas (Fuentes 1992, 111). The Indian lover of Hernán Cortés, Malintzin has been dually characterized as "mother of the first Mexican, the first child of Indian and Spanish blood" and traitor or La Malinche (Candelaria 2005; Fuentes 1992, 111, 117). As more Spanish men began to colonize the Americas, the colonized and converted Indian female body became the primary conduit for Spain's bloodline in the absence of Spanish (white) women—thus transmitting "white, male power" through the subordination of colonized and racialized brown women (McClintock 1995, 3).[6] Such Spanish male/Indian female unions colonized the New World with a population of racially mixed (mestizo) communities that were privileged in a caste system of Spanish, indigenous, and African intermarriages (Aldama 2005).[7]

As the marker of whiteness in the New World, Spanishness could only be achieved through the offspring of Spanish-Spanish or Spanish-Indian unions—relationships that implied Spanish men coupling with Indian women. In time, a Spanish man and Indian woman could produce Spanish descendents, whereas the offspring of Spanish-black and black-Indian unions could never be considered Spanish or white. This complex political, economic, and even romantic embrace of colonizer and colonized ultimately reified colonial power, and until the mid-eighteenth century, everything from speech to clothing to employment was officially determined by a person's caste (Aldama 2005; Appelbaum, Macpherson, and Rosemblatt 2003).

As if in preparation for its position as the Hollywood Latina, the brown female body's role in the colonization process was visualized and mapped through a series of paintings popularized in the New World during the 1700s. These paintings, known as casta paintings, outlined a structural hierarchy of race in the Americas. By chronicling the production of a so-called Spanish population in the New World, casta paintings arranged representations of heterosexual couplings according to their potential for producing whiteness: Spanish-Indian unions begat mestizas; mestiza-Spanish unions begat castizas; and castiza-Spanish unions purportedly produced offspring devoid of any Indian

blood and were eventually capable of producing so-called full Spaniards. When
and if depicted, Indian-black and Spanish-black unions appeared at the far end
of the paintings or in their own paintings altogether, representing the caste system's outer limits (Katzew and Los Angeles County Museum of Art 2004).
Beginning with the preferred sexual union of Spanish man and indigenous
woman, the Spanish bloodline's whiteness purportedly filtered out the child's
Indian heritage, generation by generation (Aldama 2005). The paintings depict
the role of Indian women in the post-Conquest regeneration of a Spanish population in the New World, with each mixed-heritage child displayed like an
exotic species of fruit.

As it had during Spanish colonial rule (1769–1821), the brown female body
facilitated the settlement of the southwestern United States after the nation
laid claim to lands now known as Texas, New Mexico, and California. As in
the New World, whiteness played a similarly crucial role in the nineteenth-
century development of a national identity within the United States, a racialized process fueled by Manifest Destiny, exacerbated by the Mexican American
War (1846–1848), and solidified by California's statehood (Almaguer 1994, 59;
Dyer 1997, 19). Although Mexico legally dissolved the caste system after winning its independence from Spain in the early 1820s, the social hierarchies
were harder to dissolve. Compared to laborers of Mexican or indigenous origins, wealthy Mexican families were considered privileged and white, illustrating the close connection among wealth, racial status, intermarriage, and local
concepts of miscegenation in the Southwest (Aldama 2005; Almaguer 1994, 4,
58, 62). As Anglo-American men from the United States began to settle in
(Mexican) California, they amassed both land and capital by marrying into
the wealthy and so-called Spanish families of the region (Almaguer 1994, 59;
Gonzalez 2000, 100; McWilliams 1946, 54). The daughters of these Spanish
families—however negligible or imaginary the family's actual connection
to Spain proved to be—were privileged mediums through whom power
alliances could be fostered for Anglo-American men in the absence of Anglo-
American women (Almaguer 1994, 59; McWilliams 1946, 50–54). The class,
gender, and racial specificity of these unions were crucial to this process, and
Mexican men seldom, if ever, married Anglo-American women, regardless of
their class or racial affiliation, whereas nonelite Mexican or mestizo women
were deemed unacceptable for marriage (Almaguer 1994, 60–62; McWilliams
1946, 50–55).

Transforming history into nature, the Hollywood Latina has similarly served,
like the flesh-and-blood brown woman on whom she was based, as a temporary partner in the service of imperial desires (Barthes 1972; Beltrán 2005, 64).
Whether the Latina was appearing as an elite Spanish señorita or a lowly

Mexican-indigenous woman of early Westerns, Hollywood's depiction of her brown female body signified all that could be claimed or conquered—an eager and sexualized visualization that reiterated the sense of entitlement that "white men in California [had toward] all of the bounty available in the new state" (Almaguer 1994, 60–61). Thus, the legacy of the brown female body as temporary imperial facilitator was deeply entrenched in the myth of the Hollywood Latina. Depending on her decade and class affiliation, the Latina performer was expected to embody either a temporary/transactional lover or a sexual deviant. Such expectations held true, even as the Production Code began to police representations of miscegenation. While explicit white-black unions were patently prohibited, white-Latina couplings remained an ambiguous or in-between exception so long as the narrative—in a kind of historical denial—did not depict evidence of their procreation (Courtney 2005; Hershfield 1998, 7).

Dolores Del Rio Performs a Spanish Fantasy Past in Modern Los Angeles

The early twentieth-century confusion or interchange of the terms "Mexican" and "Spanish" was a slippage laden with the imperial history of the region—a collapse that economically hierarchized both space and bodies along the lines of class, race, and nation. Like the Spanish-Mexican wives of U.S. settlers who facilitated the Anglo settlement of California, the term "Spanish" was applied to Mexican commodities as a means of whitening and improving their social cachet within the United States during a period of denigrating all things Mexican. As Los Angeles expanded from its rural roots to a key cultural and economic area of the United States, Anglo settlers became increasingly invested in reinventing the region's history around a Spanish fantasy (Kropp 2001, 36; McWilliams 1946, 80; Sánchez 1993, 71). As Phoebe Kropp (2001) has brilliantly shown, Los Angeles' racialized reinvention was exemplified by the refurbishing of Olvera Street, a thriving downtown center where Mexican families and merchants congregated. The area had been largely ignored by Anglo communities except as a "vice or health problem" until San Francisco society matron Christine Sterling helped spearhead the renovation project that changed the plaza into an image of a so-called Spanish past (Kropp 2001, 37).

The 1930s was a makeover period in Los Angeles, when Mexican culture was simultaneously denounced as part of a fixed colonial past yet renamed or reinvented as a consumer-friendly "Spanish" commodity for white tourists and Angelenos. The refashioning of Olvera Street—from a thriving Mexican American plaza into a Spanish-styled space catering to Anglo-American tourists—visually and symbolically demarcated the long-standing racial and class hierarchy that anchored Los Angeles to the Spanish side of the Spanish-Mexican distinction. All things "Mexican" functioned as the "contrasting image[s], idea[s], personalit[ies, and] experience[s]" against which the United States and Los Angeles imagined themselves, from city planning to Hollywood film (Said 1979, 2). Olvera Street was meant to highlight Los Angeles' metropolitan modernity and the supposed superiority of its Anglo community. When the *Los Angeles Times* declared the refurbished plaza to be "A Mexican Street of Yesterday in a City of Today," the real sting was that this "Mexican Street" required Europeanization before it was fully recognized as part of Los Angeles (Kropp 2001, 36; Saito 1998).

The relative ease with which a thriving Mexican plaza could be fossilized and appropriated highlights the relatively tenuous and temporary status that Latinos/as generally held and continue to hold in the United States. As a tourist space, Olvera Street required brown or Mexican vendors to perform the neutralized roles of "happy poor people," fully depoliticizing the plaza's origins as a community space (Kropp 2001, 46). This performance was literally temporary and of the past: Mexican vendors were expected to operate from mobile carts and wear peasant costumes, while Anglo vendors occupied the plaza's permanent structures and did not wear costumes (Kropp 2001, 43, 48). Dissent was immediately squashed, as exemplified by the literal whitewashing of David Alfaro Siqueiros's anti-imperialist plaza mural *Tropical America* in 1932 (Kropp 2001, 48–50). In the space of the real world, these performances and policing reiterated the perception that Mexican Americans were of the past and therefore had no present or future.

Although the Anglo investment in a Spanish fantasy past began with Helen Hunt Jackson's 1884 novel *Ramona* and its later film manifestations, Olvera Street made this public fantasy a physical reality—a symbiotic process that manifested the Spanish mission history each was supposedly re-creating (Kropp 2001, 39).[8] Kropp observes that Christine Sterling was shocked to find Olvera Street in "filth and decay," but it was because she was expecting to see the "beautiful little Spanish Village complete with balconies and senoritas with roses in their hair"—an image directly derived from the Hollywood screen's Latin lover narratives popularized by Valentino and Ramón Novarro in the 1920s (Berg 2002, 263; López 1991, 410). In fact, Olvera Street's reinvention was financed only a few months before Del Rio's version of *Ramona* appeared in theaters, during a period undoubtedly teeming with the film's publicity (Kropp 2001, 38). Both Jackson's novel and the films they inspired effectively romanticized the region with a "false [Spanish] past remembered as real," obscuring the actual Latino/a communities still living in the California region and greatly impacting the persona of Hollywood's first Latina star (DeLyser 2003, 887–888).

The popularity of *Ramona* as a novel and early film remake exemplifies how the cultural images produced in Hollywood were shaped by the national and imperial traditions of California and then widely dispersed to the rest of the United States. Both the novel and film focus on Ramona, a woman of white and Native American heritage who had been adopted by a wealthy and cruel Spanish ranch-mistress. Raised under harsh conditions, she eventually discovers her true ancestry and elopes with a young Indian named Alessandro. Ramona's new family life is cut short when her daughter dies and Alessandro is murdered. After suffering a nervous breakdown, Ramona is saved from despair by the kindness of her cruel guardian's son, Felipe. Although Hunt's novel was written to highlight the Anglo mistreatment of Native Americans, it was ultimately embraced for its white colonial image of the Spanish Southwest.

The tragedy and romance of Ramona's tale made her a powerful figure in the California imaginary, but Hollywood's incarnation of the fictional character made Ramona an icon of the racialized and gendered notions about the region. Early film versions of the novel cast fair-haired females like Mary Pickford (directed by D. W. Griffith, 1910) and Adda Gleason (1916) in the role of the Anglo-Indian heroine Ramona. Although Edwin Carewe was the third filmmaker to bring *Ramona* (1928) to the screen, and Del Rio may have been perceived as a more authentic choice for the role because of her ethnicity, the Southern California myth of a Europeanized Spanish/Mexican was preserved by Del Rio's fair complexion and upper-class persona, which kept the so-called lightness and desirability of Ramona consistent with Pickford's and Gleason's portrayals.

Like Olvera Street's Mexican vendors, Del Rio provided a racialized image of the past and embodied an impermanent, imperial fantasy for white U.S. audiences; unlike the vendors, her Spanish lineage racially mediated her body beyond the socially negative connotations of Mexicanness common in the 1920s and 1930s (Hershfield 1998, 6). To reconcile Del Rio's star image with the popular U.S. image of Mexico and Mexican Americans as inferior, Del Rio's off-screen persona was enhanced in terms of class and her family's Spanish heritage was emphasized.[9] Although Del Rio proudly self-identified as Mexican, studio publicity insistently framed her as "Spanish," a genealogical distinction that carried racial as well as class connotations (Monroy 2001, 163).[10] For the length of her Hollywood career, Del Rio's characters alternated between the wealthy exotic and primitive exotic, while studio publicity countered these roles with publicity that framed her as a "thoroughly modern woman" (Hershfield 2000, 22–23). The emphasis on Del Rio's Spanish-styled Mexicanness pioneered the transition that Rita Hayworth would later make from Spanish American to all-American, categorical adjustments that nudged the Latina female body up the privileged ladder of whiteness.[11]

Studios utilized the insistent if unconscious equation of whiteness, wealth, and Spain to facilitate the career of Del Rio, a Mexican woman of Spanish descent, so that eventually her persona was solidified into what I call "in-betweenness."[12] This in-betweenness buoyed Del Rio's persona through film narratives and publicity alike, as evinced in an *In Caliente* publicity stunt that stressed Del Rio's bi-leveled biography by way of a poem: "Dolores Del Rio / Dark Mexican rose / Whose exquisite loveliness everyone knows / Dolores Del Rio / the one in a million / Patrician Dolores whose blood is Castilian" (*In Caliente* Press Book 1935). As a "Dark Mexican rose" with a Castilian filling, Del Rio had a racialized identity that could be flexed at will and according to larger national/imperial needs as Hollywood helped the United States distinguish itself from its Latin American neighbors. Through this racialized and classed in-betweenness, Del Rio oscillated between the rungs of the nationalized hierarchies of class that attributed wealth and whiteness to Spain and poverty and nonwhiteness to Mexico. With her Spanish background firmly entrenched in her persona, Del Rio was granted the privilege of whiteness on a temporary basis, as Latinos/as were increasingly and paradoxically framed as historic, ripe for commodification, and a threat to the moral fabric of Anglo-Americans in Los Angeles and Hollywood (Marez 2004, 153; Sánchez 1993, 70–71).

Although Del Rio's Spanishness and in-betweenness expanded her possible roles, dance acted as a means of containing her racial ambiguity through a visualized difference—especially as Hollywood transitioned from silent to sound film. Despite the insistently upper-class affiliation affixed to her by the studios, Del Rio and her dancing body fulfilled the false expectations of Latina licentiousness operating in and outside of Hollywood. Her biography as a well-bred Mexican of Spanish descent was continually undermined by the seductive and fiery characters she played. Just as Carewe purportedly discovered Del Rio dancing for wealthy friends at a private parlor party, her film characters were frequently discovered dancing in bars and nightclubs.

Because no copy of the film exists, it is difficult to know if or how Del Rio danced in the film *Ramona*, yet it remains one of her most significant roles in the production of the Hollywood Latina. *Ramona* highlighted the racialized sexuality of Del Rio's earlier roles and seemingly bridged the sexualized white or white-ethnic roles of her silent period with the nonwhite or ethnicized dancing roles of her sound career. The Del Rio films made between 1932 and 1934 impacted her popular and academic legacy as a result of the formation of the musical genre and its use of Latin America as a backdrop during the period; these films also provide the foundation and framework of the Hollywood Latina—especially as technological developments and the Production Code impacted cinematic conventions through the spectacles of dance and dancing nonwhite bodies in exotic locales (Hershfield 2000, 34).[13]

Coupling: The Early Hollywood Latina and In-Betweenness

Del Rio's roles in the 1930s facilitated the cross-cultural romances at the center of musicals set in Latin America during the period, enacting U.S. fantasies of colonization and control through Hollywood couplings of white men and the emerging Hollywood Latina (Hershfield 1998, 8). In films such as *Bird of Paradise, Flying Down to Rio,* and *Wonder Bar,* the in-betweenness of the Hollywood Latina's body began to solidify. In each of these three films, Del Rio embodies a dancing desirability that must be liberated from brown men by white ones. While such romantic pairings—however temporary or taboo— underscored the privilege of Del Rio's body, they also illustrated the limits to which nonwhite female bodies could challenge the traditional black/white binaries of screen romance. As Del Rio signified a new kind of Latina body on screen, the off-screen Latina was often criminalized through sexualization in both Los Angeles and Hollywood. Curtis Marez has argued that this criminal- ization "promote[d] a fantasy of a hot Mexicana sexuality," a characterization that required the Latina to be romantically tamed by an assertive white male authority figure and a coupling that came at the expense of the Hollywood Latino (Marez 2004, 172–173). Marez identifies this sexualized and criminalized female figure as the "Mexican cantina girl" and defines her as a "sexually avail- able" nightclub performer whose "revealing costumes, sensuous performances, and . . . aura of sexual abandon" provide sexual titillation on screen (2004, 167). Paired with loathsome male Latino characters, these narratives reinforced the impression that brown women required white male saviors. By casting light- complected Latinas against dark-complected Latinos, a dichotomy of desirabil- ity was built to simultaneously reinforce a hierarchy of light nonwhite females with goodness and dark nonwhite males with danger in the Hollywood logic of racialization (Hershfield 2000, 40).[14]

The Del Rio musicals emphasized in this chapter were released in the period between the introduction of the Production Code in 1930 and its official enact- ment in 1934, a time period and process that link the representation of race, sex, and the body. The original version of the Production Code, an industry response to public outcry from religious groups in the wake of the Fatty Arbuckle sex scandal, debuted as a list of Don'ts and Be Carefuls the same year as *The Jazz Singer* (1927). This list of conditions, largely circulated among the studios, was eventually formalized as the Motion Picture Production Code (Hays Code). While the Production Code ultimately policed representations of sex and miscegenation, among other things, its simultaneous maturation with synchronized sound film and the musical genre made representations of dance a heavily regulated component of its doctrine. Intended to function as symbols for sex in Hollywood film, dance, costuming, and sexually suggestive gestures were regulated as part of the Code's investment in so-called decency (Thompson and Bordwell 1994, 160). Of particular concern were dancing females and their potentially revealing costumes, since their scantily clad, mobile bodies continually threatened to be indecently exposed.[15]

By focusing on racialized sexuality as encoded by costuming and bodily movement or placement, we see that the examples of *Bird of Paradise*, *Flying Down to Rio*, and *Wonder Bar* highlight how Dolores Del Rio's body was reiterated as a body in between whiteness and blackness. In *Bird of Paradise*, Del Rio's in-betweenness is cast toward the darker side of the white–nonwhite spectrum. With the Latina Del Rio cast as a Polynesian princess, Del Rio's body paradoxically enables the onscreen interracial romance while the narrative polices this representation by aligning her with the figure of the tragic mulatto. In *Flying Down to Rio*, the costume and choreography of the film's primary dance sequence reinforce the levels of racial and sexual difference assumed across the representational spectrum of whiteness, brownness, and blackness; although Del Rio's body is tellingly absent from this procession, the establishment of these codes reinforces her position as a Hollywood Latina. And in *Wonder Bar*, studio publicity affixes Del Rio's in-betweenness, highlighting how her career would forever frame the imagined racialized sexuality of the Hollywood Latina as dancing somewhere between primitivism and refinement—regardless of whether that Latina could in fact dance.

In 1932, Del Rio was cast as a desirable nonwhite Other in King Vidor's RKO film *Bird of Paradise* (Hershfield 1998, 3–15). Del Rio's character, the light-skinned Island princess Luana, is caught in an interracial romance with an Anglo-American sailor named Johnny (Joel McCrea). Set on a series of unspecified South Sea islands, the film depicts the tragic courtship of Johnny and Luana. After witnessing her sensuous charms during the course of a mating ritual dance, Johnny pursues Luana despite the fact that she is already betrothed. Luana encourages Johnny's advances, ignoring the fact that her father, the village king, has forbidden their association. When Luana is taken to meet her future husband ("the native prince"), Johnny follows and rescues her from the arranged marriage. Their bliss is cut short, however, when Johnny falls ill and Luana realizes she must sacrifice herself to save both Johnny and her people from an unstable volcano.

Bird of Paradise begins from the perspective of Johnny and his all-white male crew as they happen upon an island and its inhabitants—an ethnographic

frame of reference that highlights the imperial dichotomies of lightness/
darkness, modernity/primitivity, monotheistic/polytheistic, and rationality/
irrationality at the thematic center of the film (López 1991). Although Luana's
self-sacrifice ends any chance for a long-term cross-cultural relationship in the
film, the possibility of their union is emphatically denounced from both sides
of the film's racialized spectrum. While Johnny's shipmates argue that inter-
cultural unions are possible in the modern age of 1932, the captain notes that
Johnny would "break his mother's heart" if he married Luana; this declaration
underscores the island king father's prohibition of the union, thus present-
ing interracial romance as a "universal problem, forbidden by even the most
primitive societies" (Hershfield 1998, 8).

While *Bird of Paradise* allows Luana to serve as a temporary object of white
male desire, her designation as "islander" puts Del Rio's body on the outskirts
of the Hollywood Latina's in-betweenness. No matter how light Luana's skin
appears to be or what we know of the woman playing her, the character's relationship with Johnny is derailed by her death. This narrative trope aligns the
Pacific Islander characterization with blackness, most specifically with the
tragic mulatto, a character that King Vidor (director of *Bird of Paradise*) had
popularized three years earlier in his film *Hallelujah!* (1929). As with the tragic
mulatto, Luana's death at the end of *Bird of Paradise* serves as a kind of penance
for her racially sexualized transgressions; by embodying a dancing, desirable,
and racially ambiguous woman, both Luana and Del Rio epitomize the forbidden temptation for white men (Bogle 2001, 9, 31). As the only light-skinned
female islander character given significant screen time, Luana embodies physical features that seemingly negate the complexity of Pacific Islander representation in the course of the film; indeed, the analysis of Pacific Islander
representation is frequently overlooked in discussions about Del Rio in *Bird of
Paradise* (Desmond 1999).[16]

In the film, the two dance sequences function simultaneously as moments
of sexual foreplay and demarcations of racialized and sexualized Otherness. As
Luana, Del Rio wriggles and writhes at the center of the frame; every scantily
clad step and twist signifies temptation. The first dance sequence occurs immediately after Luana has rescued Johnny from drowning, highlighting how the
agency of the brown female body can paradoxically challenge the traditional
power dynamic of male heroism while reifying the sexualized and colonial
expectations of white male entitlement to the nonwhite female body. In the
second dance sequence, Luana reluctantly performs for the native prince until
purportedly rescued by Johnny from the fate of a brown mate. This scene
underscores the film's endorsement of Johnny's sense of entitlement toward
Luana's racially sexualized body.

Figure 4. In *Bird of Paradise* (1932), dance becomes a mating ritual. Islanders gyrate (*top row*) while Dolores Del Rio as Luana (*bottom row*) dances with wild abandon before Joel McCrea as U.S. American Johnny.

When Luana appears at the center of the first ritualized dance circle, the choreography and framing of her body are very different from those of the surrounding dancers, a formal choice that highlights the racially sexualized connotation of the performance and Luana/Del Rio's special role in the frenzy. After Luana saves Johnny from drowning, he and his crew join the village members for a feast. As male villagers begin to eat with voracious appetites in the foreground, an elaborate dance ritual begins in the background. At first, the dance largely consists of village women wriggling their hips and arms; the camera often captures these movements from extremely low angles, highlighting the sway of each hip and curve of each buttock. Although most characters dance in place with deeply bent knees, gyrating pelvises, knee sways, and slowly rotating bodies, Del Rio as Luana is more erect. Her body is typically framed in long and medium shots at less drastic angles. When Luana's body is shot from a low angle, the composition emphasizes the upper body's ecstatic movement as suggested by Del Rio's facial expressions and flailing arms. While we often see Luana's hips swaying back and forth, the low-angle shots of her body do not include her hips until a key shot at the end of the dance frames Luana's writhing body and buttocks in profile as Johnny admires her from behind.

The first sequence equates dance with native movement and frames it as an exoticized and eroticized "mating ritual" (Hershfield 1998, 8). The islander women are the focus of the first dance; their frenzied hip and arm movements, choreographed to a mounting percussive beat, increasingly excite the drumming men. When the dance beat peaks, the men hurriedly carry the women off into the night, presumably to their huts to have sex.[17] One by one, each woman is carried off until only Luana remains. After she collapses from exhaustion, Johnny attempts to carry her off but is told that she is promised to the prince of a neighboring island. This moment in the film marks Johnny as an outsider and Luana as a privileged body; while he cannot consummate the ritual because he does not fit in, she is taboo for anyone except the native prince. When Johnny later goes undercover to rescue Luana from the fate of betrothal in the second dance sequence, he infiltrates the prince's prenuptial dance ceremony by putting mud on his body and mimicking the new village's dance gestures (see fig. 5). Because the film closely aligns dance with native bodies, the audience is expected to believe that the island's only blond man is sufficiently concealed by a few hand gestures.

In the second sequence, dance is confirmed as a racialized precoital act by correlating arousal with intensified bodily movement, an equation so suggestive that it caused concern among U.S. censorship boards. When Johnny finds Luana to rescue her, she is already dancing before the plump and dark-complexioned prince. Her sad and uninspired movements obviously underwhelm the prince—until she spots Johnny. At that point, her performance is immediately enlivened, arousing the prince and literally igniting a ring of fire around her dancing body. As the prince begins to dance around Luana's ring, the islander crowd bow their heads to avert their gaze from this precoital moment, and by the time the prince looks up from his dance, Luana has been stolen from the ring by Johnny. The sexual connotations of these dance scenes were so alarming in the United States that they overshadowed the film's explicit nudity during an underwater swimming sequence with Luana and Johnny. Several state censorship boards restricted the dance sequences, yet no U.S. board objected to or censored the shots of Del Rio "swimming half-naked underwater" (*AFI Catalog*, s.v. *Bird of Paradise*).

These dance sequences highlight the contradiction of Del Rio's agency and the "hyper-performance" of sexualized movement that was expected of her as a result of her in-betweenness. While dance was and continued to be a signifier of Del Rio's "Latina-ness," it proved overwhelmingly racialized by Luana's character, which was seemingly more nonwhite due to her Pacific Islander

Figure 5. *Top row:* In *Bird of Paradise*, dance serves as Johnny's cover as he attempts to rescue Luana from marrying an islander prince; after seeing Johnny, Luana dances with an intensity that literally ignites a ring of fire. *Bottom row:* Increasingly aroused by Luana's incendiary dance, the island prince begins a dance of his own.

affiliation. Despite the glimmers of intelligence and strength that the character Luana exhibited by saving Johnny's life and teaching him how to live off the land after their escape, Del Rio explicitly banned such roles from her contract when she moved to Warner Bros. from RKO. Perhaps sensing that such islander characters would pose a significant threat to the (racial) trajectory of her career, Del Rio insisted that her Warner Bros. contract explicitly state that she would not be required to portray "the part of a native girl or in a South Sea Island type of picture without [her] express consent" (Del Rio–Warner Bros. Studios contract 1934, 2).[18] As South Sea islander types, Del Rio's characters were incapable of living happily ever after with their romantic white male leads. Although later characters such as Belinha in *Flying Down to Rio* or Ynez in *Wonder Bar* proved to be less independent than Luaná, Del Rio's decision to avoid such roles because of a specific kind of racialization marks her ownership of her career at the expense of Pacific Islander characterization.

In *Flying Down to Rio*, Del Rio's character is once again the object of Anglo male desire. The aristocratic Brazilian Belinha (Del Rio) and Anglo-American

Roger (Gene Raymond) meet in a Miami hotel where Belinha is a guest and Roger the bandleader. After hotel management warns Roger about his reputation as a gigolo, he and the band are fired when Belinha proves too tempting for Roger to ignore. Searching for work, the band is hired by Roger's Brazilian friend Julio at a Rio de Janeiro resort; unbeknown to Roger, Belinha is betrothed to Julio, and her father owns the resort. Despite Roger's playboy ways and Belinha's engagement, the duo begin a turbulent romance en route to Rio. Meanwhile, two of Roger's band members—Fred (Fred Astaire) and Honey (Ginger Rogers)—visit a Rio club to scope out their musical competitors and discover a dance called the Carioca in the process. When it becomes clear that the hotel is in danger of financial ruin, Roger, Fred, Honey, and the band save the day with an ingenious aerial show complete with scantily clad women dancing atop the wings of airborne planes. The film ends when Julio, learning of Roger's love for Belinha, relinquishes his claim to her hand and dramatically exits the film by parachuting from Roger's plane.

While Belinha's elite status makes her racialization and sexualization less overt than Luana's, *Flying Down to Rio* nonetheless builds on the equation of exotic locales with racialized and sexualized movement as formalized by *Bird of Paradise*. Early in *Flying Down to Rio*, Del Rio boasts to her Miami friends that she can have any man she desires; when she wins Roger's attention with nary the bat of an eye, one companion asks, "What do these South Americans got below the equator that we haven't?" This sexually suggestive statement foreshadows "The Carioca," a dance number choreographed by Hermes Pan.

"The Carioca" (another term for "Brazilian") depicts a racialized evolution of passion through a progression of white and nonwhite bodies and crucially collapses the codes of dance, race, and sexuality "south of the equator." Despite the fact that Del Rio is conspicuously absent from "The Carioca," the number marks her in-betweenness through the racialized and sexualized conflation of body, movement, and costume. The core movement of "The Carioca" couples male and female dancers with their foreheads touching, but each iteration of the dance—white, "Latin," and black or Afro-Latino—is depicted as more revealing and risqué than the last. By encoding white, brown, and black versions of the same movement as increasingly more erotic and revealing, the film's progression of dance/passion is equated with bodies that are increasingly racialized as darker than the last (Kinder 1978, 40).

"The Carioca" is introduced when Fred and Honey witness it performed on the dance floor by the competing venue's elite yet ambiguously nonwhite Brazilian patrons. This group of wealthy and light-complected Brazilians, dressed in evening gowns and tuxedos, dance the Carioca with a smoldering intensity; the expression on their faces and the determination of their movements lead

Honey to blushingly and suggestively remark that she "can tell what they're thinking about" from the balcony. When Fred pulls Honey to the dance floor so they can try out the dance, the bandleader offers them the stage. Dancing atop a rotating stage of seven white pianos, Fred and Honey re-create the basic movement of the Carioca but chastely omit its supposedly implicit sensuality or sexual intensity. The Fred-Honey version of the dance is instead embellished with intricate footwork and a complex series of turns, a technically proficient performance that glamorizes the Carioca but seems to lack that certain something suggested at the start of the scene. When Fred and Honey comically bump foreheads midway through the dance, their clumsiness signals a kind of sexual ineptitude—an ineptitude not shared by the groups of brown and black dancers who subsequently take the stage.

The first chorus line to follow Fred and Honey features the codes of Latinness, such as fair complexions, dark hair, and costumes cobbled together from Hollywood versions of Latinness. While the female dancers simultaneously wear signifiers of Spanishness (hair combs) and Brazilianness (bead necklaces), it is the sheerness of their flowing Mexican-style folk skirts that highlights the supposed sensuality of their bodies. The transparent skirts enhance the female dancers' bare legs and black-clad buttocks, especially when captured turning in and out of the camera's low-angled frame. Despite the fact that these bodies move less dynamically than Honey and Fred, they appear more sensational and nonwhite, especially in comparison with Honey's blond hair and her body demurely clothed in a long opaque gown. Although the "Latin" choreography is primarily composed of formations across the floor, the representation of these supposedly brown moving bodies is necessary to transition from the white to the black version of the Carioca.

"The Carioca" number concludes with a black ensemble, whose members' bodies literally vibrate across the floor in a dance that is progressively more vivacious, dynamic, and sensual than the previous three performances (Freire-Medeiros 2002, 54). As they take the stage, the black dancers are serenaded by the African American singer Etta Moten. Dressed in a baiana costume, Moten, in an English-language song, informs the audience "how to be a Carioca."[19] The flamboyant bodily movements and increased pace of the editing of the black group suggest that their version of Carioca is even more extreme than the blush-worthy dance that opens the scene. If the core Carioca move has its partners touch foreheads, the black version of the Carioca requires its female dancer to achieve this forehead-to-forehead stance by arching backward and meeting her male partner's forehead as he leans forward.

Del Rio's final RKO film, *Flying Down to Rio*, is perhaps her most famous—a distinction no less attributable to the film's solidification of a racialized and

Figure 6. In *Flying Down to Rio* (1933), a dance called the Carioca is all the rage. Each racialized group (*clockwise from left*) exhibits its own version of the dance, moving from the "authentic" Carioca to the gliding gestures of Honey and Fred (Ginger Rogers and Fred Astaire) to the contortions of the black chorus dancers.

sexualized hierarchy through dance as it is to the inauguration of Astaire and Rogers as a dancing duo. The film, through "The Carioca," was one of the "first and last U.S. musical[s] about Rio to incorporate black performers in the cast," suggesting just how problematic blackness was to imagining Latin America for U.S. audiences in the 1930s and 1940s (Freire-Medeiros 2002, 41). As black representation decreased in Hollywood films about Rio, light-complected performers like Carmen Miranda increasingly embodied the highly commodified aspects of black Brazilianness (fashion, song, and movement) through the more mainstream-acceptable in-between female body. By solidifying the formula that demarcated the degrees of racialization and sexualization in films set in Latin America, "The Carioca" and *Flying Down to Rio* were crucial to this transition.

Del Rio's absence from *Flying Down to Rio*'s two large-scale musical numbers ("The Carioca" and the aviation finale) curiously calls her dance skills into question. Despite her supposed dance training and initial discovery as a tango dancer, Del Rio does not have the same range as the rest of the dancers in the cast. She only dances within the diegetic space of the dance floor, first with

Roger in a Miami nightclub and then with Fred in a Rio nightclub. Belinha's dialogue-laden tango with Fred is the more dynamic of Del Rio's dance scenes, but her dance abilities are thoroughly overshadowed by the lesser-known performers Astaire, Rogers, and the "Carioca" chorus lines. Despite Del Rio's limited dance scenes, *Flying Down to Rio* adds to the image of the dancing Latina in Hollywood film.

(Racially) Framing the Dance

As studios adjusted to the new sound era, Del Rio's persona was increasingly and explicitly framed by racialized and sexualized dance performances, especially while she was under contract at Warner Bros., home of Busby Berkeley and Al Jolson and the studio behind *Wonder Bar* (López 1991, 410). As the musical became the favored genre, it was increasingly associated with Busby Berkeley dance sequences and the large-scale spectacles of scantily clad, blond female bodies in motion that he produced. Del Rio's musicals of this period often included dance scenes directed by Berkeley—including the uncredited dance sequences in *Bird of Paradise (AFI Catalog, s.v. Bird of Paradise)*. As Del Rio's early silent-era seductress roles (French, Russian, or any woman with an aura of "foreignness") decreased, they were replaced by the oversimplified and exoticized dance roles—like Luana and Belinha—in the sound era (Berg 2002, 263). As we shall see with publicity for *Wonder Bar*, Del Rio's actual dance abilities were ultimately less important than the idea that she was a natural dancer—an important facet of her depiction as the in-between body of yet another racialized musical.

Advertising for the film *Wonder Bar* offers two final examples of Del Rio's in-betweenness as utilized by Warner Bros. Using two promotional articles, written by the studio as press publicity about the film, I show how Del Rio's body functioned as a crucial figure of racial mediation and how dance operated as a signifier of exoticism and hypersexuality in the process. By analyzing the advertising rhetoric used to contextualize still images of Del Rio's dancing body, we can see how the Latina myth was marked through excessively passionate bodily movement and gestures that were racialized as natural and primitive.

In the film *Wonder Bar*, Al Wonder (Al Jolson) runs a Parisian nightclub of the same name. Al is in love with the club's dancer Ynez (Del Rio), but she loves only her dance partner and gigolo, Harry (Ricardo Cortez). After Harry becomes involved with the wife of a wealthy bar patron, Liane, he attempts to finance his and Liane's escape to the United States by selling her expensive necklace. When Liane's husband begins to investigate the missing jewelry, Al remedies the situation by convincing Liane to stay with her husband and pretending to buy the necklace from Harry. Al hopes to woo Ynez in Harry's absence, but things turn ugly when Ynez discovers that Harry plans to leave without her. Blinded by passion, Ynez stabs and kills Harry on the dance floor during their signature dance performance, "The Gaucho." The choreography, which involves Harry whipping at Ynez as she writhes on the floor, is so violent that the stabbing appears to be an elaborate finale and the club audience cheers while Harry lies dying on the dance floor. To save Ynez, Al makes Harry's murder look like an accident. Despite Al's best efforts, he finally admits defeat when Ynez finds comfort in the arms of the club's bandleader (*AFI Catalog*, s.v. *Wonder Bar*).

Because the film is set in a European nightclub, *Wonder Bar*'s publicity transfers the exoticism previously connoted through locales such as the Pacific Islands or Brazil directly onto Del Rio's body. One article written by Warner Bros. to advertise the film, titled "Gaucho, Exotic New Dance Invented for *Wonder Bar*," illustrates how deeply ingrained dance was to the Latina myth by crediting Del Rio and Cortez with the dance's choreography. According to the article, the Gaucho number was originally intended to be a French "apache" tango (*Wonder Bar* Press Book 1934b). As Marta Savigliano has noted, the apache enacts an exaggerated and brutal encounter between a pimp and his impoverished prostitute, movements that are strikingly similar to those performed by Del Rio and Cortez in the *Wonder Bar* dance (Savigliano 1995, 111).

Whether or not the film uses an apache dance, it is significant that the publicity article credits Del Rio and Cortez with the choreographic shift as the supposed result of an impromptu dance improvised during their lunch break. The ethnographic language used in the article approximates a wildlife encounter: all is quiet on the set when the director and crew happen upon the two Latinos as they enact a "strange and elusive" dance, later identified as a "swell tango" or a "half apache, half tango." According to the article, the director "watch[ed] from the shadow of the set, while [Del Rio and Cortez] danced on, unnoticing and unconcerned. He watched them—and so did the returning company, standing their distance, silent and intent, making no sound to break in on the dance" (*Wonder Bar* Press Book 1934b). Where *Bird of Paradise* used an ethnographic lens to frame its visual narrative, this article asks us to conjure an image of what purportedly happens when two Latinos are left alone in the same room by positioning us with the hiding crew, anxious not to disturb the dancing creatures in their native habitat. Ironically, this essentialist and exoticizing narrative is disrupted by Ricardo Cortez's biography and the press book itself. Born Jacob Krantz, Cortez was not in fact Latino but had changed his name to "take advantage of the public's fascination with 'Latin Lovers'" (Hershfield 2000, 38). On the same press book page as "Gaucho, Exotic New Dance Invented for *Wonder*

Bar" appears another publicity article stating that Del Rio complained of dizziness after a series of spins, an odd grievance for a trained dancer, which suggests that Del Rio was not as skilled a dancer as her films and publicity claimed (*Wonder Bar* Press Book 1934a).[20]

Wonder Bar's sensationalist imagery illustrates how studio publicity reinforced the colonialist tendencies of Hollywood in terms of race, gender, and sexuality. The film's narrative hinges on the club's patrons confusing the diegetic violence of the stabbing with the staged violence of the Gaucho; similarly, the film's advertising contextualizes and sells *Wonder Bar* to mainstream audiences by framing Latinos as passionate and dangerous creatures. When the publicity article ultimately names the origin of the Gaucho's "wild, weird, and elusive steps" as the "restless, gypsy race, half Indian, half Spanish descent, that roams over the pampas," its pseudo-ethnographic language reinforces the iconography of the campaign at large, which depicts the film's Latino male as a sexually violent threat to the passionate, yet vengeful, Latina (*Wonder Bar* Press Book 1934b).

Although the article "Gaucho, Exotic New Dance Invented for *Wonder Bar*" helped shift the connotations of an exotic locale to the Latina body itself, the layout of another publicity piece makes Del Rio's in-betweenness a primitive yet literal borderline between blackness and whiteness through its use of text and image. Titled "On with the Dance," this publicity article was intended as a special Sunday feature for distribution in local newspapers and surreptitiously promotes *Wonder Bar* under the guise of a historical look at the evolution of dance (*Wonder Bar* Press Book 1934c). By visually juxtaposing black and white dance styles, the article presents the history of dance as an evolution from primitive to civilized movement. The racial polarization of this narrative is anchored by a series of images organized according to whiteness, blackness, and in-betweenness. Whereas white performers are depicted in tuxedos and gowns, the featured nonwhite performers (save Del Rio) appear in blackface or loincloths. Although these white and nonwhite representations are nearly equally distributed within the article's layout, costuming and captions frame the white bodies as overwhelmingly more refined than the nonwhite bodies. At the center of these images rests the article's largest and most prominent image, an enlargement of Del Rio and Cortez midstep. In this still from the Gaucho, the bodies of Del Rio and Cortez literally border the racialized images of a photograph of white people in tuxedos on the left and "modern dusky maidens" (female performers in blackface) on the right. The opening text of the article contextualizes the "white" photograph, stating that this "fashionable Waldorf-Astoria crowd" honors Franklin Delano Roosevelt's birthday by dancing "merrily in a midnight rendition of the Virginia Reel." The upper-class associations of this racialized image are echoed at the bottom of the article, where another white, tuxedoed body appears in the figure of Hal Le Roy, a popular 1930s tap dancer and the article's second largest image. As we shall see, the "modern dusky maidens" and Del Rio are contextualized through other means.

Like the visualized hierarchy of the casta paintings, the article "On with the Dance" frames Del Rio as a mediating body between civilizing whiteness and primitive nonwhiteness. The text supports the connotation of these visuals by explicitly developing a narrative history about the supposed refinement of dance from its primitive beginnings. The images illustrate this evolution, showing how the "crudest form of rhythm" has been refined in France, where "national dances [are] brought to Paris, polished and perfected."[21] The article states: "Dancing, which among primitive people was practiced to express joy or grief—to excite the passions of love and hate—to placate vengeful gods—or to foster homage or worship—has degenerated or improved (as you will), into a pastime. Music, though not an essential part of dancing, almost invariably accompanies it—even in the crudest form of rhythm—it's beaten on a tom-tom." The discussion of "crude" rhythms develops into a section titled "Savage Dance Survivals" about the "rude, imitative dances of early civilization." Detailing how every "savage tribe" from "Australian Bushmen" to "tribes of Northern Asia" dances in one way or another, the article uses words like "rude," "savage," and "imitative" to create a kind of dance history lesson at the expense of non-Western dances and dancers. Although the article concludes that some of these so-called primitive dances have been purportedly civilized by nations like France, the last sixth of the article ultimately identifies Spain as the "true home" of dance due to "the gay, irresponsible nature of the people," before transitioning its dance history lesson into an explicit advertisement for the film (*Wonder Bar* Press Book 1934c).

Although Del Rio's image sits squarely between the article's depictions of whiteness and blackness, she is in fact closely aligned with the primitive passion affiliated with the other nonwhite images that pepper the page. In contrast to the tuxedoed white bodies, the article's depiction of nonwhite bodies is presented through one photo of female performers in blackface and a series of three line drawings depicting so-called primitive bodies. A diagonal arrangement of three line-drawing panels appears below the U.S. photo; each line drawing exemplifies one of the so-called primitive dances mentioned in the article. The nonwhiteness of these framed bodies—captioned as Polynesian, Indian, and South Sea islanders—is indicated by the shading of their illustrated faces. The figures are depicted as primitive and potentially hostile; some appear in loincloths, and many more hold spears, clubs, and torches to suggest a link between primitive dance, nonwhite bodies, and violent passion. Further, the scene described at the opening of this chapter shows how the actions of Al Wonder (played by Al Jolson) enhanced the division of whiteness and non-whiteness through an emphasis on racialized sexuality. Known as a blackface performer, Jolson hoped to make *Wonder Bar* his comeback film for Warner Bros. Yet *Wonder Bar* is the only Jolson film that features blackface without including a single black performer in its cast (Knight 2002, 68). This significant omission amplifies Wonder's suggestion that the "lovely Latin daughter" of his song is sexually open and available, a gestured innuendo that collapses the full weight of this racialized sexuality onto Del Rio's body—the only Latin and only nonwhite body in the entire film.

The form and content of the primitive line drawings of "On with the Dance" undercut the glamour and sophistication of the central Del Rio–Cortez image and enhance the violent and racialized embrace of a second, illustrated image of Del Rio and Cortez. The illustration echoes the aesthetics of the line-drawing series and shows Cortez holding Del Rio with his hand on her hip while brandishing a whip about her body; in turn, Del Rio's raised fist clutches a dagger aimed at his heart. The illustration was frequently used in the *Wonder Bar* press book and was often identified as the "Tango Del Rio." Because this small line drawing sits atop the article's first paragraph and is nearly embedded in the title line, its prominence in the layout of "On with the Dance" contradicts the glamorous image of Del Rio–Cortez and reiterates the efficient yet subtle ways that desire, danger, and primitive nonwhiteness were conflated through depictions of nonwhite bodies.

By physically mediating the lines of whiteness and blackness in *Wonder Bar*'s advertisement, Del Rio's body delineates the film's "Waldorf-Astoria crowds" from its "dusky maidens" by representing elements from both sides of the racial equation (*Wonder Bar* Press Book 1934c). A medium-sized photo from the Busby Berkeley waltz number "Don't Say Goodnight" highlights Del Rio's in-betweenness. Placed in the lower half of the article's layout, the photo shows Del Rio and Cortez standing in the foreground, against a chorus of blond-wigged women. Del Rio, wearing a white gown and with her arms presented, is the only dark-haired female dancer among them. The women mirror Del Rio's posture, but their hair color and costuming are distinct: their gowns are black on top and white on bottom. Del Rio "complicates this black-and-white motif . . . [because] she is neither a blonde woman nor a dark haired man. . . . She is a racial and national other masquerading as a racial and national other" (Hershfield 2000, 46). As the star, Del Rio in the foreground highlights both her screen significance and her difference due to the excessive blondeness of the bodies featured in the dance and publicity photograph.

Shortly after *Wonder Bar*, the prominence of Del Rio's Hollywood roles began to dwindle and she eventually returned to Mexico.

Although the benefits of Del Rio's in-betweenness were exhausted in Hollywood by the late 1930s, the remainder of her career in Mexico and (on occasion) in the United States remained marked by the myth of her career. In 1942, Del Rio returned to Mexico to "choose [her] own stories, [her] own director and cameraman" (Bodeen 1976, 288). She was welcomed as a star and became a prominent figure in Mexico's cinematic Golden Age. Between 1946 and 1954, Del Rio was nominated for five Ariels—the national film award of Mexico—and won three. Yet she continued to embody a racialized and sexualized myth built around a colonial history. As Mexico began to emerge from the shadow of U.S. and Hollywood imperialism, the dancing and racialized sexuality of Del Rio's Hollywood persona made her a perfect symbol of redemption for its national cinema. Characterized as the redeemed Fallen Woman, Del Rio found that her Mexican screen persona and cinematic success were not divorced from the exotic nightclub performers and Othered women whom she played in Hollywood films (López 1994, 262). As the ever-suffering maternal star in women's films, she symbolically repented her past as a Hollywood exotic. Eventually, Del Rio's Mexican roles enabled a sort of Hollywood rebirth. Though cleansed by her Mexican melodrama roles and industry awards, echoes of her early Hollywood roles remained. In the John Ford film *The Fugitive* (1947), Del Rio played Maria Dolores, the Latin American Indian mother of an illegitimate child. In the film, which was shot on location in Mexico, Maria Dolores helps a rogue priest escape by distracting his pursuers with her dancing body.[22] Thirteen years later, the myth of her racialized sexuality and bodily movement would again be invoked when she played the mother of the hypersexualized rock-and-roll figure Elvis Presley (playing a half Native American character) in *Flaming Star* (1960).

Throughout Del Rio's Hollywood career, she was racially sexualized and reified as an in-between body through the rhetoric of Spanishness. While I have been attentive to Del Rio's filmic difference, my goal is not to reify whiteness as normative but instead to identify the dialogue of power possible and visible through Del Rio's ambiguously racialized representation. As one of the first (and one of the few) exoticized female performers to sustain a multidecade career in Hollywood, Dolores Del Rio proved that Mexicans, Mexican Americans, and (white) Americans were drawn to her image in the United States (Sánchez 1993, 174). Del Rio's professional decisions—to refuse roles, limit her character types, and leave the United States—were powerful moves that effectively "subvert[ed] and negotiat[ed]" the systems of representation (Hershfield 2000, 52; Savigliano 1995, 69).

Dolores Del Rio's career highlights the potential for Latina agency and negotiation through Hollywood film, but it also sparked the myth of the Hollywood Latina as a racialized and sexualized mediator in Hollywood film. While Del Rio's success and multidecade career do not diminish the fact that she was the prototypical Hollywood Latina, her paradoxical trajectory illustrates the complex matrix of race, gender, sexuality, and nation that has continued to operate symbolically in mainstream Latina representation. However limited Del Rio's roles, her career greatly impacted the star trajectories of each Hollywood Latina who followed, especially those closely aligned with cinematic whiteness like Rita Hayworth and Jennifer Lopez. Dolores Del Rio's career thus set the mold for the myth of the Hollywood Latina and showed how dance and in-betweenness could become lucrative—if double-edged—codes of her representation.

CHAPTER 3

Carmen Miranda
Shakes It for the Nation

Carmen Miranda: You do not understand me when I'm talking?
Charlie McCarthy (Edgar Bergen): No. I understand you better when
*   you're not talking.*

—*The Edgar Bergen/Charlie McCarthy Show* (1941)

Carmen Miranda is a Hollywood icon—a swirl of tropical fruit and Technicolor, the Good Neighbor who taught the United States that Brazil was ripe for the picking. Her whirling celebrity spanned over two decades: one decade in Brazil (1929–1939), and nearly fifteen years in the U.S. spotlight (1939–1955). While Miranda epitomized Latin America for her Hollywood audiences, she was in fact a Portuguese émigré. In Brazil, Miranda was a white working-class woman who embraced and commodified the traditional black styles of Brazilian music and performance; in the United States, however, this complexity was reduced to an amalgamated Latin American-ness that helped the United States negotiate its own racial and national hierarchies.

As the opening epigraph from the Edgar Bergen/Charlie McCarthy radio program suggests, Miranda's U.S. audiences did not prioritize her speech ("Ventriloquism, Carmen Miranda" 1941); in the United States, as in Brazil, her allure was widely read and interpreted through her exoticized body. In both countries, Miranda embodied an in-betweenness; her body, image, and persona existed between the representational poles of blackness and whiteness. But Miranda's in-betweenness served Brazil and the United States in radically different ways, unifying one nation through a hybridized sonic sameness and the other through an exoticized visual difference. In Brazil, Miranda bridged the gaps of race and class and united the nation through samba, an African-based Brazilian musical form that established Miranda as a recording and radio star early in her career. The image of Miranda's white working-class female body performing traditionally black music provided an early symbol of national unity in Brazil, even though she did not appear in many films before going to Hollywood. In the United States, Miranda continued her musical career, but her celebrity was heavily dependent on her spectacular physical appearance as a light-skinned woman bearing an excess of Latin American emblems. Miranda's colorful costumes, heavily accented English, and performative body parts (hips, arms, and eyes) became a generic, if exaggerated, Latin American Other against which white Americanness could be defined.

Miranda's flamboyant in-betweenness—as a Latin American fashion icon, dancer, and performer—helped the United States negotiate its own domestic tensions around race, gender, and nation by commodifying and compartmentalizing in-betweenness.[1] Unlike many of the women in this volume, Miranda displayed an in-betweenness that initially benefited from whiteness (in Brazil), but ultimately she was not white enough (in the United States); in effect, her Hollywood career was aligned more closely with blackness, preventing the greater access to narrative opportunities that whiteness afforded. While Miranda's style was quickly co-opted by white women (and men), its black roots were increasingly obscured in the United States and insistently framed as solely Latin in U.S. publicity (a precariously racialized position not unlike that of Jennifer Lopez in later years). Unlike Rita Hayworth, Rita Moreno, or Jennifer Lopez, with their more heavily choreographed legacies, Miranda was an untrained dancer and rarely danced with a partner or traveled across the floor. Yet she was associated with constant movement, especially of her hips, hands, and eyes—gestures that largely incited others to dance. As a shining screen star of the 1940s, Miranda, through her U.S. career, exemplifies how in-betweenness and movement were transformed into a generic yet marketable commodity known as the Hollywood Latina.

By popularizing a so-called Latin style in film, music, and fashion during the 1940s, Miranda facilitated the U.S. importation of an exotic nonwhiteness as though it were a raw material like coffee or sugar. Although Hollywood's emphasis on Miranda as a wholly Latin American figure erased the black roots of her performance style, her presence helped mediate the commodification of blackness within U.S. popular culture. Subtle repercussions of the Afro-Latino/a lineage and transgressions of Miranda's image and movement arose, however, and the particular sexualization of Miranda's restricted representation in Hollywood film illustrates the complex hierarchies of class, race, and gender operating within both the United States and Brazil. Although Miranda's profits from live appearances, film roles, and musical recordings with Decca allowed her to dance all the way to the bank, her short but spectacular

Hollywood stardom had little professional range or mobility beyond her shim-
mying hips. While her physical movements were clearly considered among her
assets, in this chapter I focus less specifically on the types of movements
Miranda performed in her films; instead, I am interested in the way that representations of her body were conflated with movement itself as part of her
racialized and sexualized iconography.[2]

"Would You Like My Hips to Hips-no-tize You?"

As a Latin performer in the 1940s, Miranda was able to access Hollywood in
ways that black performers in the United States could not. Still struggling for
integration in mainstream Hollywood films, most black performers found
their limited welcome within the space of the musical (Knight 2002). Miranda
became a darling of the Hollywood musical, appearing first on Broadway and
then in Hollywood films largely set in Latin America.[3] As Miranda's exoticism
was fawned over, the United States could disavow its own black-white racial
tensions with an increasing focus on its Good Neighbors.

Miranda's debut at the 1939 World's Fair began Hollywood's whirlwind
affair with Latin America (and its "soft primitive" form of ethnic nonwhiteness
[Desmond 1999, 12]) as the United States accelerated toward a second world
war. Her arrival in the United States was lauded as a discovery, and she was
then treated like an international commodity, quickly ushered from one
nationalized stage to another. After debuting at the Brazil Pavilion of the New
York World's Fair, Miranda became the feature attraction of a revue titled
The Streets of Paris (1939). Produced by the theater kings the Shubert brothers,
The Streets of Paris sought to lure fair patrons back to Broadway with
Miranda's unlisted performance of "Sous American Way" (Roberts 1993, 3).
The performance was such a sensation that the Shuberts were credited with
finding the "torrid, infectious, undulant Carmen Miranda," terms that were
later used to describe Rita Hayworth. Miranda was a cure for lagging box office
profits in the face of the World's Fair ("She Saved Broadway from the World's
Fair" n.d.). With Paris, France, as a framing device, the revue legitimized an
otherwise hodgepodge collection of performances by capitalizing on the mystique of France as a center of culture and taste.[4]

Once *The Streets of Paris* proved Carmen Miranda could attract audiences in
the United States, she was offered a featured role in her first Hollywood film,
Down Argentine Way (1940). Miranda's cinematic debut was the first in a series
of Technicolor film musicals set in or themed around Latin America and developed by Twentieth Century-Fox (Freire-Medeiros 2002; Sandoval-Sánchez
1999, 38). Cast as a nightclub performer, Miranda lifted her performance from

her six-minute routine in *The Streets of Paris*. The cameo opened a floodgate of opportunity and signaled Miranda's star potential: to accommodate Miranda's schedule, Fox shot her scenes in New York, perhaps sensing that she would become one of the studio's (and Technicolor's) biggest stars (Basten 1980; Solberg 1995). The film was well received by critics, especially "the exotic and exciting Carmen Miranda," who could "sway [her] hips" in full "Technicolor regalia" (*Variety* 1940).

Miranda's increasing appeal in the United States required a generic Hollywood Latina-ness that did not sit well with Latin American audiences. Appearing in "south of the border" films set in locations like Argentina (*Down Argentine Way*), Brazil (*That Night in Rio*, 1941), and Cuba (*Weekend in Havana*, 1941), Miranda was all too frequently cast as part (or all) of the local color (Roberts 1993, 8). While *Variety* erroneously praised Miranda's Portuguese songs for lending "an authentic Argentinean note" to *Down Argentine Way*, the film was quickly censored in Argentina and Brazil for mangling Latin American geography and culture. Although such boycotts spurred significant Production Code Administration reforms regarding films set in and exported to Latin America, the results were not always successful.[5]

As happened with discourses about black female performers like Josephine Baker, public discussions were usually fixated on the movement and exotic excess of Miranda's body. Her vivacity, exaggerated headdresses, platform shoes, bare midriff, exposed legs, and animated hands and eyes easily fulfilled the light-skinned, tropicalized stereotype of Latin American women desired and upheld within Hollywood. Words like "barbarous" and "savage" were used to describe Miranda's body and performance style, and she was regularly compared with exotic animals in the popular press (Sandoval-Sánchez 1999, 39). Publicity often described her movement as a flurry of enticing and seductive gestures, a narrative reflected by studio biographies even toward the end of her career:

> What it is that Carmen has is difficult to describe; so difficult, in fact, that dramatic critics have grown neurotic in their attempts to get it into words that would make sense. Nevertheless, it must be attempted again. First, there is the impact on the eye of Carmen's costumes, always barbaric and brilliant, but nearly always covering her thoroughly with the exception of a space between the seventh rib and a point about the waistline. Second, what the male spectator hopes she means with a flicker of her eyes is easily visible at the distance of one kilometer. In case anybody has missed the point, Carmen develops the idea with her singularly expressive hands.[6]

The passage positions Miranda's body and its movements as a spectacle aimed at arousing male desire, even as this desire renders the subject neurotic.

According to the biography, even dramatic critics were rendered incapable of coherent thought because of their own carnal responses.

A closer analysis of the texts suggests that the true power of Miranda's bodily performance (her solar plexus) is both obscured and framed by the "barbaric and brilliant" costuming she wore. The excess of color, fabric, and sequins that adorned Miranda's costuming left only the smallest region of her flesh exposed, enhancing the sensuality of the tiny sliver of belly described by the biography as "the space between the seventh rib and a point about the waistline." Because Miranda's costuming invariably covered the more common points of costuming emphasis for women in films (bustline and hips), the top of Miranda's belly became a fetishized focal point. That very space between the rib and waistline is more than an erogenous zone; the solar plexus is also the center of a dancer's balance and a singer's breath. Obviously drawn to its nakedness, the critics and spectators might overlook it as the source of her charisma, channeled from her belly, transmitted through her voice, and united through her body as a spectacular performance of excess.

Unlike Del Rio, Hayworth, or Lopez, for Miranda dance was largely located and contained in the sinuous movement of her eyes, hips, and hands. The gestures of these body parts belied Miranda's otherwise modest costuming, purportedly revealing her true sexual nature with every flickering eye or "singularly expressive" hand. In the quoted studio biography, the critic watching Miranda waits for a gesture or signal that she is a willing participant in his fantasy. Words, ironically, betray the writer. Even the description of Miranda's clothes—"barbaric and brilliant"—exposes the paradox of Miranda, of her in-betweenness. While the term "barbaric" exoticizes Miranda (connoting a primitive lack of control), the word "brilliant" simultaneously hints at her radiance and her intelligent movement. Her expressions are so vibrant, so evident that her supposed desire—what "she means with a flicker of her eye" and underscored by her hands—can be seen from miles away.

Miranda's body was so sensuous, so powerful that it was regularly scrutinized by the Production Code Administration (PCA), whether for her costume or simply for her expressive performance style. At the height of Miranda's fame in the early 1940s, the PCA was the gatekeeper of so-called good taste. Beyond its usual policing of sexuality, the PCA also regulated costuming and dance—and sometimes both simultaneously. Additional importance was placed on how the costume functioned during a dance; the code explicitly forbade "costumes intended to permit undue exposure or indecent movements in the dance."[7] Most costumes modeled for the Production Code tended toward cabaret costumes or other suggestive apparel, such as women's nightgowns, but Miranda regularly modeled her own costumes for the PCA to determine their decency.[8]

By 1944 Miranda was one of the highest-paid female performers in the United States, but this financial success belied her intense and variegated labor. Miranda was so financially successful because she often performed nightly shows at multiple clubs, while also appearing as a radio and film performer (Gil-Montero 1989, 89–90). Further, Miranda's contract with Shubert entitled him to half of her earnings, so she was forced to work twice as hard for her worth.[9] Yet Miranda was proud of her success and even boasted about her fortune to Hedda Hopper, one of Hollywood's premier gossip columnists. In one telegram to Hopper, Miranda outlined not only her financial worth but also her frequent travel and the momentum of her career as a performer—from Miami to Chicago to Hollywood.[10] In time, Miranda worked enough to buy herself out of her contract with the Shuberts (Gil-Montero 1989, 90).

Shifting from the cultural to literal frame, Carmen Miranda was filmed and publicized as if she were constantly in motion. In musical numbers, the shot composition that framed Miranda was determined by the height of her turban and the swing of her moving hips: the lower edge of the frame often began below her hips, while its top edge soared above her head to contain the height of her increasingly outlandish turbans. For example, Miranda's third Hollywood musical, *Week-End in Havana* (1941), opens as an advertisement for Cuban tourism. The first shots depict postcards of Havana and quickly dissolve to a colorfully clad band performing.[11] The camera pans to Miranda, the focal point of the scene, posed with arms erect in front of her body to begin and end the musical number. A hallmark of Miranda's publicity photos, her ever-erect arms and lifted eyes created a constant sense of movement even while still. This pose is so iconic that it—along with a bowl of fruit on the head— completes the characterization in parodies of Miranda.

There are relatively few shots in Miranda's opening sequence of *Week-End in Havana*, but each frames her body in telling ways. The first shot is wide, framing Miranda—colorfully dressed in a bright pink-, white-, and blue-striped skirt, midriff shirt, and flowery headdress—from her ankles to the top of her hat. When the camera pushes in on Miranda, it reframes her figure from torso to hat, accentuating the exposed parts of her body: bare shoulders, exposed midriff, naked lower arms, expressive hands, and hips. Miranda's costuming enhances the sway of her hips, which appear exposed through triangular cutouts on each side of her skirt. While Miranda sings her first verse, her eyes and hands are within this frame. When the band changes to the chorus, the camera pulls out to reveal Miranda's dance step in a wide shot. Her movements are contained and do not extend beyond a few square feet. She completes three three-point turns and shifts her weight from foot to foot, in a series of ball changes, toward the band stage right. Her arms and skirt are in constant motion, twirling about her. The shot finally cuts to a medium frame, where it remains for the remainder of the song. Miranda's singing—"con movimientos"—tells of beautiful girls, while her ever-moving hands enunciate their feminine shape with gestures outlining an hourglass.[12]

The shots and the dance gestures that compose Miranda's cinematic dance performances enunciate the importance of her exposed body and its movement. The continual presentation of Miranda's body in wider frames made her ever-moving body a figure of entertainment, not identification (as also occurred with the framing of Jennifer Lopez). Rarely captured in a close-up and largely viewed from afar during her performances, Miranda was never granted the framing of a leading lady (Ovalle 2007). Like Latin America itself during the Good Neighbor policy days of Roosevelt and World War II, Miranda was a temporary turn-on, an "ideal partner with whom to shack up for a night" (Mandrell 2001, 31; Pike 1995, 112). Miranda fulfilled the U.S. desire for escapism in a most spectacular way. Alberto Sandoval-Sánchez's research on Miranda and the Latin recording craze of the 1940s asserts that Latin rhythms provided U.S. audiences with a sense of "escapism, exoticism, and potential for fantasy ... after the Depression and during WWII"; these rhythms, however, were often conflated with a sense of "primitivism, liberation of the instincts and the body, and pervasive sexuality" (Sandoval-Sánchez 1999, 31–32).

Caught in the frame, Miranda's moving body invoked the myth of the Hollywood Latina—in this case as an in-between female conduit for the consumption of nonwhite and Latin American culture. In spite of Fox studio's insensitivity to Latin America and the limited characterizations it offered Miranda, its film catalog represents a contradictory period of progress for nonwhite performers in mainstream Hollywood film. Sean Griffin's work on racial integration in musicals has shown that Fox musicals, largely based on the vaudeville format, have often been overlooked by academia in favor of the more lauded musicals that integrated these numbers into the plot (Griffin 2002, 22).[13] But it is precisely the nonintegrated, vaudeville format that enabled nonwhite performers—like Carmen Miranda and the tap-dancing duo the Nicholas Brothers—to exert some control over their choreography and representation (Griffin 2002, 28–29). Conversely, the nonintegrated musical format conveniently enabled nonwhite musical performers to be edited from films released in the more racist, southern parts of the United States without losing narrative elements (Bogle 2001, 121; Knight 2002). At such a juncture in racial representation, Miranda's in-between body became all the more alluring; as an ambiguously nonwhite female performer, Miranda's power and agency were fully tied into her affiliation with blackness, whereas her visual identification was seen as white—or, more crucially, nonblack. To understand the full complexity of Carmen Miranda's role in the U.S. media, however, the full lineage and legacy of her movements and fashion must be considered.

MERGING WHITENESS AND BLACKNESS
IN BIOGRAPHICAL BRAZIL

Before Miranda became the toast of Hollywood, she began her career in Brazil, where she was first inspired by blackness and mediated through whiteness. In the Portuguese-colonized Brazil, Miranda's whiteness stemmed from the Portuguese lineage of her body, while her association with blackness was rooted in her working-class origins and affinity for samba music. The result was an in-betweenness that facilitated a professional and performative hybridization of race and class. Miranda's hybridity was initially represented through her musical sound and eventually through her image and style of movement.

Miranda's whiteness arguably maximized her appeal as a samba singer and helped foster a national culture in Brazil (Davis 2000, 184).[14] Latin American historian Darién J. Davis has illustrated how Carmen Miranda's popularity emerged alongside the first presidency of Getúlio Vargas (1930–1945). At the time, Vargas attempted to foster a unified national identity for Brazil that "presumably overcame racism" (Davis 2000, 183). To accomplish this feat, the government channeled the myth of racial equality through popular culture, specifically through samba music. To effectively intersect and unify the so-called classes of this racially divided population, Vargas's administration sought a symbol that would reach and appeal to various communities. Miranda was the perfect artist to facilitate his goal; with both public and governmental support, she enjoyed a soaring popularity, and soon she became the white face of black Brazilian samba (Davis 2000, 184).

In *Brazilian Bombshell*, the only English-language biography of Carmen Miranda, Martha Gil-Montero describes Miranda's rise to fame in Brazil and the United States as a dream of upward mobility come true.[15] Born Maria do Carmo Miranda da Cunha in Porto in 1909, Miranda migrated with her family to Brazil around 1910. Her father sought a more prosperous life yet struggled to make ends meet once in Rio (Gil-Montero 1989, 12–13). The family initially lived near the docks, a rough neighborhood described by Gil-Montero as "a raucous meeting place for sailors and prostitutes," and Maria enrolled in a Catholic convent school for disadvantaged children (Gil-Montero 1989, 14–15).[16] By 1925, the da Cunha family had relocated to another part of Rio and opened a boardinghouse. The boardinghouse relied on the labor of family members, and Maria left school to work at home and as a milliner's assistant (Gil-Montero 1989, 17). She eventually began to perform around town as a singer, and in 1928 her career accelerated when she met Josué de Barros, the first in a long string of musical collaborators and mentors (Gil-Montero 1989, 20). With Barros's help, Maria debuted in 1929 as Carmen Miranda, an alias chosen to hide the recital's publicity from her father. Although she had begun her career by singing tangos, Miranda gained both popularity and success when she began to sing sambas. Within a year of her publicized debut, Miranda became the first singer in Brazil to receive a radio station contract and was soon crowned the Queen of Carioca and "Ambassador do Samba" (Davis 2000, 188).[17]

Miranda's status as a white woman in Brazil helped facilitate the mainstreaming of black music as a national form. Her persona was an "exaggeration of black and popular rhythms" that gradually developed into a humorous and satirical repertoire; over the radio, her "unique character and delivery" broadened the popularity of samba beyond the working class (Davis 2000, 184). Though it was still considered inappropriate for a woman to sing on the radio, Miranda's racial affiliation with "the urban elite and the state" enabled her to challenge societal norms (Davis 2000, 184, 188). Her visibility and agency as a musical performer grew because she had greater access to mainstream media than a black performer of either gender.

Despite her gender and working-class background, Miranda was a privileged member of Brazil's racialized society (Davis 2000, 184). In Brazil, Portugal's enforced hierarchy of colonization and slavery had ensured white privilege and the systematic subordination of black and nonwhite people since 1550. As Brazil became Europe's primary source for sugar, the lucrative yet labor-intensive crop was increasingly dependent on slavery, and Portugal began to import African slave labor. By the late 1800s, Brazil was the second largest slave importer in the New World—second only to Cuba (Klein 1988, 40).

Brazil abolished slavery in 1888 and began to reposition itself as a racially equal democracy, a process that ultimately emphasized cultural (or literal) whitening. To facilitate a sense of racial equality, Brazil reimagined its social hierarchy as a class-based, rather than a race-based, structure.[18] This national ideology denied the existence of racism within Brazil, and by 1920 the term "race" was eliminated from the census.[19] Yet Ben Bollig clarifies that racial equality in Brazil was false and involved treating black Brazilians "*as if they were white*" (Bollig 2002, 162). Organized around the needs of its "white ruling elite," Brazil addressed the so-called problem of blackness by attempting to hybridize the racial identity through whiteness. Interracial marriages were encouraged among the population to produce "an overall whitening of the Brazilian population," while immigration from European countries was actively encouraged (Jensen 1999, 277).

As Brazil egregiously attempted to deracialize itself through whiteness, Miranda's performance of in-betweenness as a kind of hybridization of blackness proved to be the perfect instrument for this national project. To manufacture a stronger sense of nationhood in the 1930s, the Vargas administration capitalized on Miranda's potential for mass appeal. As a working-class Portuguese descendent who gravitated toward the Afro-Brazilian sounds of samba in racially complex Brazil, Miranda was the hybrid performer capable of distributing a traditionally black musical style to upper-class, white audiences on a national scale. Over time, as Davis points out, Carmen Miranda's white body and black musical style became "the embodiment of Brazilian popular music" in the service of national unity—just as it later would be in the United States (Davis 2000, 186).

Even after Miranda began to use the samba sound, she had yet to incorporate the image and movements associated with Brazilian blackness into her performance. What came to be known as the "Carmen Miranda style" was inspired by the fashion of Brazil's diverse African slave descendents in Bahia (Coelho 1998, 90). While Miranda's childhood in Lapa—a "bohemian district" known for its samba and nightclubs—had made her intimately familiar with the look and sounds of Brazil's Afro-Brazilian cultural lineage, it was her collaboration with Dorival Caymmi, a "dark-skinned" biracial man from Bahia, that purportedly inspired Miranda to adopt the baiana style (Coelho 1998, 96, 35; Gil-Montero 1989, 51). Caymmi's ode to the look and allure of women of his region, "O que é que a bahiana tem?/What Does the Baiana Girl Have?" introduced Miranda to the possibilities of baiana style and movement during her work on the Brazilian film *Banana da terra* (1938) (Coelho 1998, 35, 93; Gil-Montero 1989, 55).[20] Miranda's collaboration with Caymmi, begun only a year before her departure for the United States and at the end of her Brazilian career, would have a lasting impact on her persona, career, and in-betweenness.

With *Banana da terra*, Carmen Miranda debuted the look and moves that would ultimately become her trademarks. Trained as a seamstress and milliner, Miranda exaggerated and maximized the baiana style to create a signature look that complimented her body: she enhanced her petite frame with a turban, used European influences to devise platform sandals that created the illusion of height, tightened the skirt to highlight her hips, and added a surplus of large necklaces and a midriff shirt to further amplify her style (Coelho 1998, 97–101). From a performer's standpoint, the grandeur of this modified baiana style worked well on stage: the colors and fabrics flattered Miranda's eye color, complexion, and body shape while simultaneously enhancing her stage movements and presence (Gil-Montero 1989, 57).[21] By developing her own style, Miranda wrested the traditional control that men have had over the look of women's bodies—either as spectators, "framers of women's movement," or fashion designers (Coelho 1998, 40; Savigliano 1995, 98). The film also marked the moment that dance and sensual movement became key features of Miranda's performance style. The grand gestures of Miranda's active hands and hips became the focus of her movement and enhanced her colorful style.[22] Caymmi is often credited with instructing Miranda on these energized baiana gestures; simultaneously, he benefited from his collaboration with Miranda by breaking into the music industry as a dark-complexioned man (Coelho 1998, 96, 93; Gil-Montero 1989). The baiana look, carefully described in Caymmi's song, firmly affiliated Miranda with this national icon, one of the only representational female "types" identifiable in Brazil (Davis 2000, 187; Gil-Montero 1989, 55–56).

While the baiana makeover was indeed a mark of Miranda's agency as a female performer, her use of Afro-Brazilian style and movement to create a mode of sensual expression cannot be divorced from the larger arenas of the politics of race, gender, class, and the body. Reception and critique of Miranda's use of the baiana style in Brazil provide a good snapshot of the centrality of whiteness and the marginality of blackness in the nation's cultural discourse (and beyond). Despite the popularity of her new look, the Brazilian elite, who often looked to Europe as their fashion center, considered her use of the baiana style to be both risqué and tacky (Coelho 1998, 91, 95; Gil-Montero 1989, 56). While the Brazilian contours of racism were expressed along racialized class lines rather than racialized hypersexuality as in the United States, the Brazilian elite's discomfort with Miranda's embrace of a so-called lower-class style highlights the racial and social tensions that Miranda negotiated in the latter half of her career (Coelho 1998, 95, 187).

For the most part, gender and class transgressions have been prioritized over race in the two most widely circulated English-language biographical explorations of Carmen Miranda's career.[23] For example, biographer Gil-Montero credits Caymmi as the source of Miranda's gestures, but emphasizes her agency at the expense of the racial and gender politics involved in the partnership with Caymmi, a black man who enabled Miranda's incorporation of a black Brazilian style. When Gil-Montero observes "it is true that Dorival [Caymmi] taught her how to move her hands, but Carmen perfected the gestures and involved her whole body in a pursuit of self-expression," she seemingly disconnects Miranda's self-expression from her performance of a black dance form (Gil-Montero 1989, 55). This emphasis on self-expression is in keeping with the long tradition of appropriating nonwhite dance forms as quasi-acceptable outlets for white sexual or sensual expression, a practice Marta Savigliano has studied extensively through the Argentinean tango (Savigliano 1995, 127). But whereas Gil-Montero at least acknowledges Caymmi's contribution to Miranda's career as well as his status as a black man in Brazil, Helena Solberg, in her documentary *Bananas Is My Business* (1995), seemingly disregards the role of race in Brazil in favor of gender and class transgressions in the United States. Solberg, who identifies herself as a member of the Brazilian elite, offers in her documentary an interesting and subjective view of Miranda's career and life. Although Solberg is primarily fascinated by Miranda's racial negotiations with the Hollywood blond ideal, she does not engage whiteness itself and seemingly ignores the complex racial negotiations Miranda epitomized in Brazil.[24]

A TROPICAL STYLE FOR A DIVIDED NATION

At a time when tensions between U.S. blacks and whites were intensifying, Miranda's in-betweenness enabled the transmission of black styles and culture through a white body under the code or guise of Latinness. Because Miranda adopted the baiana style immediately before visiting the United States, it is important to identify how her mediation of black fashion and movement facilitated the style's commodification for whites in the United States.[25] The success of Miranda's career marks the moment when the Latin body—in this case, Brazilian—mediated blackness and black style to the point that white U.S. audiences could commodify, compartmentalize, and accept it. Jane Desmond offers a similar example of the cultural necessity of in-betweenness through the figure of the iconic Hawaiian female. As Hawaiian performance became more popular in the 1930s, the representational Hawaiian female body was purposefully cast as not too light and not too dark as a means of embodying "an important racialized subtext" of difference. Desmond observes:

> Hawaiians are portrayed as neither black nor white. The significance of this presumed racialization in the visitor's imaginary is that it helps to manufacture and "authenticate" at the bodily level a sense of "exotic" difference while escaping from the tendentiousness of the black/white dichotomy that most powerfully frames racial discourse and fuels discord on the mainland [United States]. The resulting soft primitivism proffers a gentle, sensuous encounter with difference, different enough to be presented as "alluring" but not threatening, of which the hula girl's body is metonymic. (Desmond 1999, 12)

Like the iconic Hawaiian female, Miranda's body provided a nonthreatening difference that could be identified, desired, and commodified for U.S. audiences eager to taste the exotic while disavowing the racial discord in their own backyard. Miranda proved that black culture, as raw material, could be more easily imported and commodified if it were worn on or mediated through a so-called culturally nonthreatening body. This association with blackness, however, was quickly erased as part of her Hollywood persona—a crucial aspect of in-betweenness that ultimately serves the needs of hegemonic whiteness at the expense of nonwhite culture.[26]

Miranda's entry into the United States coincided with the nation's emergence as an imperial power, particularly in relation to Latin America. For many, Miranda embodied the Good Neighbor and was conceivably Brazil's most important cultural export to the United States (Enloe 1990; Freire-Medeiros 2002; Roberts 1993; Sandoval-Sánchez 1999; Walters 1978). Despite Miranda's years of success and celebrity in Brazil, her "discovery" has largely been credited to Broadway producer Lee Shubert and ice-skater-turned-Hollywood-star Sonja Henie. As the story goes, both Shubert and Henie visited Rio in 1939 and attended one of Miranda's nightclub performances. Shubert, a very shrewd theater owner and producer, was scouting new talent for Broadway; presumably, Henie was his companion on the trip. Although the details of Miranda's early interactions with these Americans are (even by biographical accounts) vague, both Henie and Shubert found Miranda to be an appealing entertainer. Henie admired Miranda's dress, while Shubert eyed Miranda's performance.[27]

Miranda's body enabled a style traditionally worn by black women to be transported to the United States and "revolutionize fashion with its so-called Latin style" (Gil-Montero 1989, 55–56). While Miranda appropriated the baiana style and made it her own, her light skin and migration from Brazil enabled securely white stars like Sonja Henie to desire and adopt this increasingly generic Latin fashion (Negra 2001, 88). In 1940, *Modern Screen* pondered Miranda's influence on Hollywood fashion and vice versa. After Miranda praised Hollywood as a fashion mecca for international women, the interviewer responded in kind:

> To interrupt Miranda, briefly, and asking her Sous' American pardon, quite a few women are turning toward Miranda as toward Mecca, too, come to that . . . for the heavy scarlet mouth make-up she affects has certainly been picked up by the New York debs and has since cut a crimson swatch from coast to coast. . . . the "bahiana" costume she introduced to Nors' America has become a Thing. . . . Lana Turner has one, Kay Frances, Alice Faye, Vera Vague . . . the turbans, great hunks of gold and great chunks of jewels the size of rocs' eggs, barbarous, exciting, melodramatic.[28]

Although Francis, Faye, and Vague owned their own "bahiana" costumes, the interviewer continues to rely on inflated and marginalizing terms to describe

Miranda's style as both "barbarous" and "melodramatic." However mainstream the look became, it was still considered Latin—a reality assisted, no doubt, by the fact that many of these fashions were literally marketed on Miranda's body. To sell turbans at stores like Saks Fifth Avenue, casts were made of Miranda's face, and these heads were occasionally affixed to mannequins that featured Latin fashions in department store windows (Gil-Montero 1989, 84; Stam 2004, 85). In addition, Miranda's body was simultaneously used to sell South American–inspired North American fashions to South American women, exemplifying her status as a mediating body. As "silent Good Neighbors," the mannequins traveled Latin America (including Havana and Rio), all the while flying Pan American Airlines and wearing Bonwit Teller fashions.[29]

Miranda's adoption of the baiana style and its sweeping success in the United States epitomize the commodification of a nonwhite sensuality, especially as Miranda's look became one of her most identifiable traits in Hollywood. Miranda's costume packaged the perceived exotic passion of nonwhiteness for white consumption. As Miranda's star ascended, however, the popularity of the baiana style was increasingly disassociated from the blackness of both Bahia and Caymmi. By the beginning of the end of her career in 1950, the origin of Miranda's turban was rewritten as simply Latin, if that. In a publicity article titled "Carmen's Success Goes to Her–Hat," one studio attributed Carmen's success to her fashionable chapeaux, while fully revising the history behind the style. Distributed by MGM to publicize *Nancy Goes to Rio* (1950), the article states:

> It was the Miranda head which first started the turban rage which caromed from Carmen's native Rio to the States. Like most innovations, it was inspired by accident. "It was all because I had spent the day swimming," Miss Miranda explains. "Then I was asked to go out dancing. My hair was a mess. I went to my wardrobe and pulled out a scarf. I twisted it around my head. It didn't look so bad. Then I decided to pep it up with some sequins. When it was finished, I slicked back my hair and wrapped the scarf around turban-style." (*Nancy Goes to Rio* Press Book 1950)

Although Rio is mentioned, this narrative completely removes the baiana traditions of Miranda's style, despite the fact that this history was acknowledged early in her career, as seen in *Modern Screen*'s inclusion of the term "bahiana." Further, the 1950 publicity article erases Miranda's working-class roots by associating the moment of inspiration with leisure activities like swimming and dancing rather than with the style of former African slaves as modified by a milliner's assistant.

Hair has played a significant role in the star trajectories of the women presented here, and Miranda is no exception. In the twentieth century, the color and style of a Latina performer's hair have been directly related to her access to lead roles and stardom. Because the color, style, and texture of an actress's hair often determines whether she will be cast in a leading, supporting, or ethnic role regardless of her race, hair becomes a crucial marker of racial representation for in-between women. Most simply, the closer to blond, the greater a performer's chances of being cast as white and thus the better her chances of achieving a mainstream or leading role. As Shari Roberts has highlighted, the blondeness of performers like Betty Grable, Alice Faye, and Viviane Blaine indicated their stardom, and they were invariably cast as the leads to Miranda's supporting characters (Roberts 1993, 4).

While Dolores Del Rio's dark hair set the trend for exotic beauties of the 1930s and Rita Cansino lightened her hair to become Rita Hayworth in the 1940s—it is the *absence* of Miranda's hair that arguably expanded and restricted the scope of her career. Because Miranda's hair was largely hidden beneath the turbans that she became so famous for, its absence pushes her farther from the realm of whiteness; unlike some of the other Latinas in this study, Miranda's supposed lack of hair prevented her from readily modifying it to access the cosmetic markers of whiteness that facilitated mainstream representation in Hollywood.[30] In fact, one archival publicity short film, featured in Solberg's *Bananas Is My Business*, highlights the cultural anxiety around Miranda's tresses. At one point in the film, Miranda seems keen to prove that she actually has hair and asks the male host, "You don't believe I have any hair, do you?" When the interviewer asks for proof, Miranda removes her turban and the shot cuts to show Miranda revealing an impossibly full head of beautifully coiffed blond locks. As if disproving a myth, Miranda tosses and shakes her hair while saying, "See, it is my own hair. I like it very much." In either a moment of self-consciousness or institutional critique, she admits that blond is not her "natural color" and states, "They bleach it in Hollywood. They change the color of my hair. But I have a lot of fun. But don't forget, people, I make my money on the bananas. You know that. I make my money on the bananas. [Concluding by way of a joke:] So very glad to 'bleach' you" (Solberg 1995).[31] The sustained emphasis by publicity and the print media on Miranda's excessive turbaned décor seemingly necessitated an explicit address of Miranda's hair by this short film. While Miranda presented blond locks, her continued lack of hair and overly prominent turban subtly yet solidly linked her representation to cinematic blackness. The only other characters who regularly hid their hair with turbans or hats during this period were maids or housekeepers, who in the 1940s were predominantly played by black actresses. The absence of Miranda's

Figure 7. In *Bananas Is My Business* (1995), director Helena Solberg includes film footage of Carmen Miranda being interviewed about her hair. When the interviewer asks to see proof that she has hair, Miranda shakes her blond coiffure for the camera.

hair thus spoke more fully to her nonwhiteness than the public could admit; by continually concealing her hair, Miranda was forced to hide any hint of black roots that may be hidden there, a disavowal of nonwhiteness (especially blackness) that became increasingly apparent in the late 1940s and early 1950s.

Even before Technicolor accelerated its appeal in the 1940s, Latin America had a certain allure as an exotic background and frame for Hollywood musicals and racialized sexuality. As I observed in my analysis of Dolores Del Rio, the 1933 musical *Flying Down to Rio* (set in Rio) succinctly summarized the hierarchy of racial representation and sexuality in the musical number "The Carioca" (The Brazilian). The fictitious Brazilian dance style of Carioca, choreographed by Hermes Pan, presents a progression of passion in dance form. After the dance is established by upper-class Brazilian characters, Rogers and Astaire enact a tamely glamorous (white) version of the Carioca. Following this duet, a series of nonwhite dancers (racialized by both costuming and performers' skin colors) perform the Carioca with increasingly sexualized movements—first through performers codified as brown and then as black.[32]

Although Miranda was not featured in the film, *Flying Down to Rio* is significant because it was "the first and last U.S. musical about Rio to incorporate black performers in the cast" (Freire-Medeiros 2002, 54). The passions seemingly evident in this black version of the Carioca are punctuated by the inclusion of African American singer Etta Moten; dressed as a baiana, she instructs the audience "how to be a Carioca," against an "Afro-Cuban rumba" instead of a Brazilian samba, as black performers dance (Coelho 1998, 92).[33] Because this appearance epitomizes the lure and conflation of Latin rhythms—and marks the beginning of Hollywood's omission of black bodies from later representations of Rio—*Flying Down to Rio* illustrates how problematic blackness was for the imagining of Latin America in the United States during the

Figure 8. *In Flying Down to Rio*, African American singer Etta Moten, dressed as a baiana, instructs the audience through song on "how to be a Carioca," while the chorus of black dancers performs.

1930s and 1940s. From this point on, it would be all the more important to have a Latin female body mediate blackness for white consumption.[34] Carmen Miranda's 1939 arrival in the United States made her the embodiment of commodifiable blackness through fashion, song, and movement at the exact moment that black bodies were excluded from the Hollywood imagining of Brazilian and, by extension, Latin American landscapes.

MIRANDA'S MOBILE ICON AND THE LEGACY OF FLAMBOYANCE

As a white Brazilian woman, Miranda embodied an in-betweenness that produced a paradoxical distance between blackness and whiteness both in Brazil and the United States. Through the lens of Hollywood, however, her display of Latin American dance and fashion coupled with the sexualized expectations that follow U.S. representations of Latin American women resulted in a truncated star trajectory that enhanced the racialized spheres of U.S. representation. Despite her impressive income, Miranda was not imagined as part of the U.S. power elite because—whether white Brazilian or black—she was a foreigner from Latin America and ultimately a novelty performer within the United States. The paradox of this in-betweenness—between Miranda's ambiguously racialized position and performance in the United States—is exemplified by two cinematic moments: her reception as a nonblack body in *The Gang's All Here* (1944) and her framing as a nonwhite body in *A Date with Judy* (1948).

The complex social and cultural disavowal of blackness in the 1940s seemingly allowed Miranda to be welcomed as white—or at least, nonblack—within the United States, highlighting how her in-betweenness was determined as much by reception and censorship as by narrative and cinematographic framing. Despite her use of the baiana style and her depiction as a Latin American body, Miranda personified a difference that was ultimately divorced from blackness—even in racist pockets of the South. As a nonblack performer surreptitiously carrying markers of blackness, Miranda, in Busby Berkeley's *The Gang's All Here*, was welcomed to the screens of Georgia in 1944. The film, one of the most-cited examples of Miranda's Hollywood career because of its cinematic and choreographic extravagance, features Miranda as a Brazilian nightclub performer in which the excess of her body literally expands from her head to a giant matte-painted extension of her famously fruited turban.

Despite the exoticization of Miranda's body in the film, the response of Atlanta film censor Zella Richardson to *The Gang's All Here* highlights the complexity of Miranda's in-betweenness (Bernstein and White 2007, 176n38). In a letter to MGM studios, Richardson thanks the studio for a film that—"at last"—did not feature black performers. Although the letter does not explicitly mention Miranda, her omission from this correspondence underscores how her Latin American-ness was a nonissue in terms of nonwhiteness and might have actually been read as white. The letter states:

> I had the real pleasure of sitting thro the very pleasing picture THE GANG'S ALL HERE and of enjoying the MANY comments such as—"At last the Producers have realized that white people CAN be entertaining without having to inject Negroes" and "Thank the Lord one picture without niggers"—Yes, I'm quoting. . . . It is the same old squawk. We cannot understand the desire to exploit these [black] people, and who to us represent paganism at its height, when they are doing their natural things, and the acts of monkeys when they are aping the white folks. That's the way we feel, and I guess we will always feel that way so I will just continue to cut out the most objectionable parts and WALK OUT with hundreds of others on the rest. (Richardson 1944)

Richardson's letter exemplifies the racist reviewing process that policed film distribution in local theaters across the nation. While many theaters simply cut the scenes that featured black performers so as to avoid "offending" their audiences, many films were simply rejected based on the inclusion of black bodies within the frame (Bogle 2001, 121).

Although Miranda's in-betweenness enabled her to share a few onscreen kisses with white male co-stars, something largely out of range for black actresses in Hollywood, her nonwhiteness was ultimately reiterated by the fact that she was never successfully cast as a romantic lead, and her roles became little more than a version of the sexualized Other. In the 1948 film *A Date with Judy* (1948), Miranda was cast as the "other woman" in an otherwise delightfully generic MGM musical. Based on a radio program about the love life of a teenager named Judy, the film finds the heroine in the midst of her first lover's quarrel, causing her to lose her faith in boys and men. Meanwhile, Judy's father (Melvin) decides to learn to rumba as a surprise anniversary present for his wife. When Judy's insecurities cause her to suspect that her father is having an affair, she mistakes his dance instructor Rosita (Miranda) for the other woman.

While the film makes several jokes at the expense of Miranda's well-known, sexualized persona as a Latin American dancer, it is the way that the film conflates Miranda's body with a so-called vulgar dance and illicit sexuality that is most telling of her representational status in Hollywood.[35] Rosita does not enter the narrative until forty-one minutes into the film, although her presence is the plot's linchpin.[36] Her first job in the film is to explain the basic principle of the rumba: "It's just a matter of a little wiggle here and a little wiggle there. All you have to do is to get the right wiggle at the right place at the right time. Everything will be fine. I'll show you." This explanation is accompanied by a sinuous wiggling of her hips in a medium wide shot. Though fully emphasized in the composition of the shot, the film suggests that the motion of Rosita's hips is too risqué when Melvin makes eye contact with the camera and closes the shades of his office window. By breaking the fourth wall with Melvin's look, the scene indicates an understanding between the white male character and the film audience, suggesting that we all know how embarrassingly powerful Miranda's—not Rosita's—wiggling hips can be.

The equation of wiggling hips, embarrassment, and concealment suggests that Rosita's, and Miranda's, exhibition is too sensuous and therefore shameful to "normal folks" as embodied by the white family at the film's center. This scene's equation of dance, sexuality, and Rosita's/Miranda's body is reprised when Judy surprises her father at the office and Melvin tries to hide Rosita in a closet. Rosita's indignant response—that her profession "is an honorable one"—is met with further suspicion when her skirt gets caught in the door and seemingly confirms Judy's suspicions that her father is having an affair. Miranda made only two more feature films after *A Date with Judy*, so although

Rosita's/Miranda's profession may have been honorable, it was definitely expendable (Roberts 1993, 4).

As Miranda's career came to a slow halt, her in-betweenness proved to be a source of professional agency and frustration because she was never able to surpass the limitations of her style or of the supporting, comedic roles that required some form of dancing. Already restricted in the kinds of roles she was considered for, Miranda found her options further reduced as Hollywood's enthusiasm for an exotic, international Latin American fantasy declined and the fantasy became integrated into the larger U.S. cultural sphere (Roberts 1993, 3).

In Hollywood, the more fixed Carmen Miranda's image became, the more her iconicity became a space for gender and sexual play. Her legacy as a flamboyant performer exemplifies the limitations and power of her in-betweenness. In the United States, the complexity of her Brazilian identity was gradually dissolved in favor of a depoliticized, "Euro-Brazilian" performance and persona organized around gender and sexuality (Coelho 1998, 192; Mandrell 2001, 35). While Miranda's untimely death from a heart attack suggests that such a fixed image was too much to bear, the icon and movement generated by "Carmen Miranda" remain transgressive symbols—as much then as now.

Despite the racialized sexuality that was affixed to Miranda's image, her in-betweenness may have opened other spaces for the expression of gender and sexuality. The ambiguity of Miranda's persona carved out a space for parody that allowed performers—from professional entertainers to housewives and (amateur) drag queens—to take on the aura of the Other. During World War II, for example, Miranda was the female celebrity most frequently impersonated by GIs, heterosexual and homosexual alike (Mandrell 2001, 35). While many impersonations reduced her persona to a bowl of fruit on the head, and parodies ranged from tributes to cruel reductions—by Mickey Rooney, Jerry Lewis, Bugs Bunny, Lucille Ball, and herself (she often lampooned her own look)—her legacy lives on.[37] Even Rita Moreno, at the age of nine, "donned a fruit salad chapeau" while performing at a bar mitzvah in New York (Twentieth Century-Fox ca. 1956). Unfortunately, such parodies can overshadow Miranda's contribution as a symbol of female strength during the World War II era. As white women entered the labor force, Miranda's exotic appearance provided an easy-to-adopt look for women eager to "spice up" their work uniforms with "colorful floral scarves . . . bright red lipstick and costume jewelry" (Berry 2000, 126).

The strength and longevity of Miranda's iconic image exemplifies the power of her meteoric rise and her skill as a performer. Her posthumous popularity exceeds her bright but brief time in the Hollywood spotlight. As World War II came to a close, so did her stardom—an indication of the deep correlation between Miranda's image and Hollywood's promotion of escapism. Her complex Brazilian persona was collapsed into a two-dimensional image of brightly colored fabric, fruit, and faux mispronunciation in favor of an exotic Hollywood image against which the United States could idealize its notions of cultural citizenship and whiteness during World War II. Miranda's hybridization of Brazilian blackness and whiteness became a highly commodifiable form of Latina representation that paradoxically paved the way for later Hollywood Latinas such as Jennifer Lopez. Unable to break from her oversimplified characterization in musical films, Miranda overextended her body to outperform her own flamboyant style. But she lives on, from the top of her turban to the tip of her platformed toe.

CHAPTER 4

Rita Hayworth and the Cosmetic Borders of Race

You are not one woman, but many. And never the same.

— Juan (Tyrone Powers) to Doña Sol (Rita Hayworth)
in *Blood and Sand* (1941)

Now they all know what I am, Johnny!

— Gilda (Hayworth) to Johnny (Glenn Ford) in *Gilda* (1946)

Rita Hayworth, like Carmen Miranda, lives on as a Hollywood icon, but few remember her as one of the industry's most successful Latina actresses. While Miranda's stardom was in transit from Brazil to the United States, Rita Hayworth was transitioning from an ethnic starlet to a mainstream Love Goddess. Born Margarita Carmen Cansino to a Spanish father and American mother of English/Irish descent in New York City, Rita was discovered as a teenager by Hollywood film producers in the Mexican nightclub where she danced professionally. Although she eventually changed her name (and look) from Cansino to Hayworth, Rita's Hollywood sex appeal and stardom were underwritten by her racialized lineage, despite a full glamour makeover at Columbia Studios. Rita's celebrity history illustrates how the myth of the Hollywood Latina has facilitated the gradual proliferation of sexuality and sex appeal as marketable and mainstream qualities of white women in Hollywood film.

The mechanics of Hayworth's transition from ethnic Spanish dancer to all-American Love Goddess illustrates how cosmetic manipulation and transformation established racial mobility as a key function of the Hollywood Latina's mythological trajectory in the United States. In this chapter I pay close attention to Hayworth's transition from minor to major performer through the careful and simultaneous manipulation of semiotic representations of whiteness and nonwhiteness. By combining the cosmetic codes of whiteness with the supposed dance gestures of nonwhiteness, Hayworth displayed a racial mobility that can be charted through the evolution of her look and dance performances in terms of racialized and sexualized representation. As a Cansino, Rita found that dance was an expected and compulsory part of her racialization as an ethnic dancer or cantina girl in Hollywood; as Hayworth, dance primarily functioned as a measure and limit of her characterization. When Rita was paired with Fred Astaire in *You'll Never Get Rich* (1941), her sensual dance style was reborn as a talent unexpected from an all-American girl. As Rita Hayworth emerged from the Cansino molting, her transition to Love Goddess was accomplished through war-themed Hollywood musicals.

Hayworth's career and popularity were predicated on her fulfillment of racial mobility through the careful manipulation and simultaneous semiotic representation of whiteness and nonwhiteness. Unlike Carmen Miranda, whose attempts at racial mobility were ultimately limited by her exoticism and "foreignness," Rita facilitated her semiotic simultaneity through her name change and gradually Anglicized hair color. Through dance, Rita's persona retained a kind of racialized exoticism and sexuality that was simultaneously glamorous and all-American. Hayworth's dance history and cosmetic transformation produced a complex career that helped symbolically transition the depiction of female sexual identity in the United States from the prewar to postwar period of the twentieth century. Although Hayworth's body and persona were effectively whitened, the mythology of her Latina body helped mediate her success through a multitude of national frames—from Mexico to the United States and from Spanishness and Irishness to all-Americanness.

In this chapter I use film and studio publicity to analyze the role of cosmetic manipulation, choreography, and characterization in Rita's transition from Cansino to Hayworth; in so doing, I illustrate how the Hollywood Latina's in-betweenness became racially mobile in a period of the reconstruction of U.S. national identity during and after World War II. While Rita Hayworth's stardom was based on ambiguously racialized embodiments of strong and sexual female characters, she managed to produce mainstream films that shifted depictions of female sexuality beyond prostitution or amorality and were as popular with women as with men (McLean 2004, 117). Despite the emphasis on her sexualized representation, Rita's image was significantly less exaggerated than the Latina body made famously visible by Carmen Miranda in the early 1940s. While the trajectory of Rita's persona resembled some aspects of Dolores Del Rio's career, Rita's Spanish lineage was ultimately more malleable than that of Del Rio due to her U.S. birth, American accent, and willingness to follow the trajectory of whiteness during a period of significant assimilation within the United States (Jacobson 1998, 92, 96; Quigley 2009, 65, 73–74). Ultimately, Rita's career marked the zenith of the Hollywood Latina until Jennifer Lopez's debut many decades later.

Rita's discovery in Mexico as well as the recurrence of Latin American locales in her dancing films highlight how racial and sexual ideologies were continually conflated and naturalized into her persona. Studio publicity—however unreliable—provides concrete examples of the ways in which Rita's persona was both racially mobile and couched within the larger mythology of Latina performers in the United States. Adrienne L. McLean's comprehensive and complex study of Rita's career, *Being Rita Hayworth: Labor, Identity and Hollywood Stardom* (2004), remedies the usual oversights of Hayworth biographies by providing a critical and contextual approach to her career.[1] Perhaps most significant to this chapter is McLean's assertion that Rita's contemporary audiences were fully aware of her origins as Rita Cansino, an important fact that most biographers overlook or assume was fully erased with her name and hair changes. Further, McLean's analysis does not dismiss Rita Hayworth as a manufactured image of dyed hair and dubbed singing; instead, McLean impressively outlines Rita's stardom as the product of a lifetime of labor to highlight her often-overlooked agency as a performer and her professional discipline as a dancer and actor.[2] This history has been erased over time, however, so Rita Hayworth is rarely remembered as Latina, and those who know of her Cansino origins often believe she was Mexican.[3]

Rita's professional career began when she was a young child. Her father, Eduardo Cansino, was a famed Spanish dancer and her mother, Volga Haworth (Rita's mother's maiden name, on which Hayworth is purportedly based), was a vaudeville performer. The Cansinos moved often to accommodate Eduardo's dancing career; in 1927, the family moved to Los Angeles so that Eduardo could transition into film-related dancing (Billman 1997, 251; Leaming 1989, 11). In California, Eduardo choreographed some of the live performances that preceded feature films, and in 1932 Rita debuted as one of the Spanish dancers in a live number that opened the screening of *Back Street* (*AFI Catalog*, s.v. *Back Street*; Parish 1972, 220).[4] Rita's performance apparently encouraged Eduardo to re-form the Dancing Cansinos with his fourteen-year-old daughter (Leaming 1989; Parish 1972).[5] From 1932 to 1934 the team found steady work performing along and across the United States–Mexico border in towns like Agua Caliente, at venues such as the Foreign Club in Tijuana, and on the *Rex*, a notorious gambling boat off the coast of Santa Monica, California (Kobal 1978, 44; Parish 1972, 220).

Rita's tenure as a Spanish dancer aesthetically provided her with a higher class of exoticism within the racial and social hierarchy of United States–Mexico border clubs. As we witnessed with depictions of Dolores Del Rio, the United

States' privileging of Spanish culture at the expense of Mexican culture and history was as much about class as racial or imperial affiliations. To ensure that her fair skin and dark hair would visibly fulfill U.S. idealizations of Mexico in the 1930s, Rita darkened her hair to a "glossy black" and pulled it into a tight bun while performing along the border (Kobal 1978, 49; Leaming 1989, 16).[6] The Dancing Cansinos' reputation, coupled with Rita's look, enabled the duo to regularly book nightclub engagements. After Rita was discovered by a Hollywood producer named Winfield Sheehan in a Tijuana club co-owned by Twentieth Century Films' cofounder and amusement park pioneer Joe Schenck, she was signed to a Fox Studios contract to serve as a "Latin type" in the vein of Dolores Del Rio (Leaming 1989, 19; Schatz 1988, 44, 177).[7]

It is compelling that the cultural weight of Rita's origin story has largely been disregarded, as though it was perfectly normal that a young American female performer would be discovered as a Spanish dancer in a Mexican nightclub owned by Hollywood moguls at the end of Prohibition. Nightclubs along the Mexican side of the United States–Mexico border were mostly co-owned by and catered to wealthy Americans, a financial arrangement built on the lucrative pleasure industry of liquor, bars, nightclubs, and casinos (Proffitt 1994, 198; Tenenbaum 1996, 303). Located at the intersection of the United States and Mexico, these sites often featured dancing Latinas; by indulging the pleasures of an Anglo-American male clientele operating from a wholly U.S. perspective, these dancers further defined and differentiated Latina bodies as readily available objects and commodities of first world tastes (Savigliano 1995, 85). Like Olvera Street in Los Angeles, the manufactured border spaces served to help U.S. tourist-consumers assume and sustain a sense of cultural superiority through the exhibition of exoticized nonwhite bodies (Savigliano 1995, 89). Disempowered by the Great Depression (1929–1939), U.S. national identity at the very end of Prohibition (1929–1933) became increasingly dependent on distinguishing itself from Mexico, and the border became a source of panic and confusion—especially in Los Angeles (Kobal 1978, 45–51).[8]

Rita's discovery at a border club in the 1930s helped establish her association with sin, sexuality, and dance.[9] Those privileged enough to cross the border recreationally, as nightclub patrons, sought a romanticized and exoticized venue for liquor, gambling, and (though more discreetly) prostitution, and many border clubs even advertised themselves as modern "Sodom and Gomorrahs" to (white) U.S. audiences (Lorey 1999, 46–47). Such associations ultimately framed Mexican border towns as "center[s] of vice and moral abandon," but Hollywood also played a role in fueling Mexico's negative image (Tenenbaum 1996, 303; Lorey 1999, 46). Film narratives, and the moguls and stars who frequented these establishments, helped reinforce the sinful connotations with

Mexico that continue to linger in the U.S. cultural imagination (Lorey 1999, 46–47). Rita Cansino's career was beginning in the wake of Del Rio's roles in *Bird of Paradise* (1932) and *Girl of the Rio* (1932), films that conflated racialized sexuality with dance or exemplified the dubious representation of Mexican cantinas and the dancing girls who worked there (Kobal 1978, 49; Marez 2004, 167, 172).[10] As Del Rio's career began to wane, Rita Cansino's early roles capitalized on her history as a nonwhite nightclub dancer: her Fox screen test was a minor dancing role in *Dante's Inferno* (1935), a film choreographed by Eduardo Cansino, and she was soon cast in *Paid to Dance* (1937) as an "underpaid dance hall hostess" (Parish 1972, 221; Ringgold 1974, 89).

The function of Spanishness in Rita Cansino's racial mobility toward whiteness in the borderland space of Southern California highlights both the malleability and marketability of this racialized and nationalized identification (Berry 2000, 113). It is remarkable that both Del Rio and Cansino were identified as Spanish in the early part of the twentieth century, despite the fact that Rita was born a native English speaker in New York and Del Rio was born a native Spanish speaker in Durango. As Sarah Berry has argued, the Spanish female body often functioned as the "most idealized and assimilable form of nonwhiteness possible" in the 1930s, a purported racial versatility that proved useful to Hollywood and the emerging cosmetics industry as they attempted to woo white female audiences (Berry 2000, 112). By grooming Rita to project a stylized version of Spanish seduction, Fox Studios perpetuated Spanishness as an "ethnically acceptable alibi" for depicting passionate female sexuality while capitalizing on its increasingly marketable properties toward the end of the 1930s (Berry 2000, 95–98, 113).

Building on her early history as a Spanish, dancing Cansino discovered in Mexico, Rita became the first racially mobile Hollywood Latina through a combination of this exoticized dance history and a progressively whitened appearance. As she became a Hayworth, Rita increasingly transgressed the racialized and sexualized limitations of Hollywood typecasting for Latinas as she exceeded the puritanical sanctions placed on mainstream representations of white female sexuality and autonomy during the 1930s and 1940s. For Rita to reinvent female sexual representation through racial mobility, she reinvented her look through Irishness.

The Cosmetics of Transition, or Building a Star from the Name Up

While the Spanish look and label were intended to mediate Rita's career in the way they had done for Del Rio, Rita's racial mobility—her transition

Figures 9 and 10. The fair-skinned, dark-haired Spanish look popularized by Dolores Del Rio (*left*) was utilized by Rita Cansino (*right*) before she became Rita Hayworth. Courtesy of the Margaret Herrick Library, Academy of Motion Picture Arts and Sciences.

toward whiteness—was ultimately negotiated through her affiliation with Irishness. Unlike the other women in this study, Rita's Spanish lineage is categorically European and not Latin American, but her discovery in Mexico reiterates how Latina-ness, Spain, and Spanishness were amalgamated in Hollywood.[11] For Rita to succeed as a mainstream actress in the 1940s, her transition to Americanness required a more significant cultural and cosmetic transformation toward whiteness, even as the underlying ethnic markers of her Spanish and Irish difference lingered in her characterizations. Because Rita's representation already relied on the semantic whitening of Spanishness, her transformation from Cansino to Hayworth was afforded by the liminal—but no less racialized—white status of Irishness. Just as the exotic "dark lady" roles that Rita Cansino performed in the Del Rio tradition were played out through casting and appearance, so too was Rita's emergent and tenuous whiteness organized and conflated through labels like Mexican, Spanish, or Irish (Berg 2002).[12]

Rita's transformation from Cansino to Hayworth was an economic decision made by a studio looking for a marketable star commodity, but it was not a magical makeover, nor did it occur overnight. As Rita's contract came to an end at Fox, the limitations of her Spanish exoticism and dance talents became evident. As a result of regime change at Fox, Rita lost her chance to star in the 1936 version of *Ramona*, a remake of Del Rio's most famous character and a telling example of how much she was expected to follow in Del Rio's footsteps (Parish 1972, 222). Although Rita eventually signed with Columbia Pictures in 1937, studio head Harry Cohn was looking for a future star to empower his studio's stock in Hollywood, and an ethnic starlet—with a limited range of possible characterizations—did little to improve the studio's opportunities for profit. As a result, Cohn ordered Rita to change her last name to Hayworth, a modification that improved Rita's star potential but not her visibility.

Like Dolores Del Rio and Carmen Miranda, Rita was marked as nonwhite by her Spanish surname and dark hair. By becoming Hayworth, Rita was nominally de-ethnicized, yet her most significant transformation would again involve her hair. To expand beyond the limitations of so-called ethnic roles and reach a mainstream audience, Rita needed a physical makeover that began with the usual starlet regimen of diet, fashion, and photo opportunities. But Rita's most significant transformation to Hayworth began when Helen Hunt, Columbia Studios' hair stylist, dyed Hayworth's dark hair an auburn hue (Ringgold 1974, 87). Raven hair—even for white actresses—often meant second-caliber or ethnic roles, a fate exacerbated for a woman recently surnamed Cansino. While blondes carried the cultural cachet of cinematic Americanness, Hollywood was already brimming with blond hopefuls (Roberts 1993, 4).

Auburn hair was a good business decision because it distinguished Hayworth from a crowd of starlets, but the decidedly American and unambiguous whiteness of blond hair may have been out of Rita's reach because of her Cansino history (Dyer 2004, 44; Roberts 1993, 4). Various biographers have noted how auburn-red hair "brightened" Rita's face, a process and rhetoric that cannot be overlooked in terms of whiteness, lighting practices, and Hollywood stardom.[13] This brightening process was more than a matter of hair color; Rita's hairline and face were painfully resculpted over the course of two years through electrolysis. Unlike the cosmetic modifications of Joan Crawford and Marilyn Monroe, however, Hayworth's transformation was uniquely conducted in full view of the public through studio publicity (McLean 2004, 33).[14] Because the labor of Rita's star production was so public, her ethnic history precluded her from becoming a blond star; instead, her red hair enabled a kind of sexualized and independent persona.[15]

Although Rita Hayworth was initially cast in cursory roles in second-tier Columbia Studios Westerns, her career trajectory was changed by three films that seemingly announced her makeover and piqued Cohn's interest (Ringgold 1974, 32). Howard Hawks's film *Only Angels Have Wings* (1939), the Warner Bros. film *Strawberry Blonde* (1941), and Twentieth Century-Fox's *Blood and Sand* (1941) each emphasized the connection among Hayworth's persona, hair color, and star commodity status. While the black-and-white films *Only Angels*

Have Wings and *Strawberry Blonde* signaled the beginning of Hayworth's red-haired persona, it was effectively colorized with the Technicolor film *Blood and Sand*. Beyond announcing her ethnic revision in these films, Hayworth's work for Warner Bros. and Twentieth Century-Fox signaled Columbia's coming of age as a studio and illustrated to Cohn that he finally possessed a star desired by other studios.

Only Angels Have Wings, widely considered to be Hayworth's breakthrough role, is set in the ambiguously South American harbor of Barranca, a "mythical location constructed out of the most recognizable, and hence most offensive, of cultural stereotypes" (Maltby 2003, 519). We are introduced to the locale and its inhabitants through the point of view of the female protagonist, Bonnie Lee (Jean Arthur); Bonnie's blondeness marks her as an overtly U.S. American woman, and she immediately attracts the attention of two homesick American pilots.[16] After accepting their invitation to dinner, Bonnie finds herself among a band of pilots working for a low-rent airline run by Geoff Carter (Cary Grant). When one of her new pilot friends dies before her eyes, Bonnie is compelled to stay in Barranca and eventually falls in love with the hardened Geoff. Eventually, Geoff's misogyny is revealed as the fault of a woman named Judy (Hayworth) when she arrives in Barranca with her husband, a blacklisted pilot named Bat McPherson (Richard Barthelmess). By the end of the film, Bat and Judy are redeemed, and Geoff confesses his feelings for Bonnie with the help of a two-headed coin (*AFI Catalog*, s.v. *Only Angels Have Wings*).

The emphasis on hair as a means of identifying Bonnie's nationality, characterization, and narrative agency is underscored when the film seemingly addresses Judy/Hayworth's makeover at a crucial plot point of the film. The film begins from Bonnie's perspective, and her blondeness signals both her Americanness and the intention for audiences to identify with her. Through Bonnie's eyes, we are introduced to the town and its locals, who appear as crowds in the street until we happen upon an overcrowded club and witness local couples dancing. Before Hayworth's character appears, Bonnie is depicted as the only American woman in Barranca; as the only blonde, she remains centralized as the most desired woman in the film. While the introduction of Judy and Bat is diegetically tense, the audience initially connects this tension to Bat's past. It is not until Judy and Geoff have a moment alone that we realize their own tension: though they were once in love, she is now the source of his distaste for women. We learn this history when Judy enters Geoff's office and asks if he likes her hair. In a seemingly extradiegetic moment of dialogue, Geoff responds: "I thought it looked different." Though the film is in black and white and what looks "different" about Judy's hair is never mentioned, the scene signifies Hayworth's reentry into Hollywood as a siren with a makeover.

In between blond (white) and raven-haired (nonwhite), Hayworth's newly dyed red hair helped "brighten" or racially mobilize her image toward whiteness while retaining the ambiguity of her past through ethnic characterizations and exotic locales. While the expansion of Rita's roles beyond Cansino's bit-part dance characters and two-dimensional vixens was slow, the fact that Hayworth's hair was refashioned as auburn or red and not blond or brunette symbolized that her representational ascent required a kind of racial ambiguity. As *Strawberry Blonde* hit theaters, Hayworth's in-betweenness became an asset to studio publicity because it marked her character's alluring danger as the "luscious siren" who was paradoxically "naughty but oh so loveable" (*Strawberry Blonde* Press Book 1941). After Hayworth's stint as a "strawberry blonde"—a woman with "light red hair with golden glints"—Hayworth emerged as a more palatable Other in *Blood and Sand*; in this film, her hair was deepened to the "coppery red" color that it would remain for nearly all of her career (Ringgold 1974, 32; *Strawberry Blonde* Press Book 1941).

Because Hayworth's transformation was a public process that mirrored larger shifts in terms of whiteness, gender, and sexuality, the symbolic function of her red hair in *Strawberry Blonde* and *Blood and Sand* highlights the tenuous racial status of Irishness in the United States and the importance this identity played in facilitating the public articulation and performance of white female sexuality. As the symbolic marker of a white ethnic group still heavily racialized within the United States, Hayworth's red hair framed her as a transitional body—in terms of race/ethnicity, female sexuality, and the prewar to postwar era.

While Rita's maternal Irish lineage largely explains the choice to "brighten" her image with red and not blonde hair, her transition also capitalized on the recent assimilability of Irish descendents. The early to mid-twentieth century heralded the tenuous incorporation of Irishness into the legal and cultural fold of whiteness after decades of racism directed toward Irish immigrants (Dyer 1997, 51; López 1996, 37–38; Negra 2001, 28; Roediger 2005; Rogin 1996, 56–57). As a transitional figure herself, Hayworth, through her public transformation, did much to facilitate such inclusion in mainstream media—if only symbolically through her red hair and Irish character names—but Irishness itself remained distinctly outside Americanness for many years thereafter (Jacobson 1998). In the wake of Hayworth, even Marilyn Monroe's character in *Gentlemen Prefer Blondes* (1953) joked about the tenuous status of Irishness by saying, "I'm American except on my mother and father's side—they're Irish."

As a redhead, Hayworth was increasingly cast as a white—not a dark—exotic, a transition evident in the names of her characters. As Cansino, Rita was credited simply as a dancer in *Dante's Inferno* (1935) and *Professional Soldier* (1936). In *Charlie Chan in Egypt* (1935), her character was named Nayda, whereas in subsequent roles in *Rebellion* (1936), *Meet Nero Wolfe* (1936), *Old Louisiana* (1937), and *Human Cargo* (1936) she was given the Latina names Paula Castillo, Maria Maringola, Angela Gonzalez, and Carmen Zoro, respectively. As Hayworth, however, Rita immediately appeared as Judy MacPherson in *Only Angels Have Wings* and as Patricia "Patsy" O'Malley in *Music in My Heart* (1940). With a few notable exceptions,[17] Rita's screen names were further aligned with American whiteness after this brief period of transitional Irish-aligned roles. As her star rose, Hayworth was cast as Rusty Parker in *Cover Girl* (1944), Rosalind "Roz" Bruce in *Tonight and Every Night* (1945), Terpsichore/Kitty Pendleton in *Down to Earth* (1947), and Elsa "Rosalie" Bannister in *The Lady from Shanghai* (1948). Of course, Hayworth was simply cast as Gilda in *Gilda* (1946).

Rita's evolution from dark-haired señorita to all-American strawberry blonde was a story of upward mobility, an assimilation process that procured more and better roles after her name was changed to something with a "good old American ring."[18] For a nation in the early stages of transition, it is perhaps no surprise that Rita's visual transformation became a major selling point of publicity for films like *Strawberry Blonde*. Warner Bros. advertised *Strawberry Blonde* by penning and nationally distributing features to newspapers and magazines that highlighted Hayworth's transformation from Spanish to American: "Rita Hayworth dyed her brunette Spanish locks to play the title role, thereby creating a new fad for hair stylists. . . . Several weeks after the conclusion of *Strawberry Blonde*, Rita Hayworth was still strawberry blonde. She says she liked it and intended to stay that way" (*Strawberry Blonde* Press Book 1941). Similar articles continued to invoke Rita's Spanish origins, maintaining it as a significant facet of her persona and making the labor of Americanization both visible and cosmetically attainable. For McLean (2004, 45), the visibility of this transformation affirmed that Hayworth's rise to fame was an incredibly "American" process.

By emphasizing Rita's cosmetic transformation, social mobility, and work ethic, studio publicity simultaneously capitalized on the nation's recent cultural acceptance of cosmetics and the inclusion of women in its workforce (Delano 2000; Peiss 1999, 192–196). Attentive to an increasing market of (white) female laborers, publicity for films like *Strawberry Blonde* portrayed Hayworth as a hard worker, and she was applauded for her ability to go "through the entire picture without forgetting her lines or missing a cue"—reportedly as a result of her "nightly [study sessions] with a dramatic coach" (*Strawberry Blonde* Press Book 1941). While rehearsal and preparation might be expected from a performer professionally employed since the age of fourteen, the studio's attention to Rita's hard work and diligence carried the added symbolism of assimilation and gender equality at a time when women were increasingly being recognized for their contributions beyond the home.

The privilege of Hayworth's Spanish-Irish lineage in the assimilation process becomes more apparent when her career trajectory is compared with the careers of Carmen Miranda, Rita Moreno, or even Dolores Del Rio. Despite the Americanization of Hayworth through name, hair, and work ethic, the lingering residue of her early racialization and sexualization was never lost. Hayworth's true ethnic alignment was signaled in other ways—from specific dance performances to films set in Argentina, Mexico (en route to Shanghai), the Pacific Islands, and Spain. Although many films of this period were set in Latin America due to World War II, the impact of these locations and films carries an additional weight on Hayworth's body.

From Cansino to Hayworth: Location, Characterization, and Racialized Sexuality

Because hair color and style so readily tell us about a female performer's characterization, Rita's emerging redhead status highlights her in-betweenness and marks 1937–1941 as a period of transition in her racialized and sexualized persona. Cast in her "first leading role in a major production" in *Strawberry Blonde*, Hayworth is positioned by the film and its publicity as a strawberry blonde—a tenuous blonde akin to a "brunette with a blonde temperament, [or] a blonde with a red-headed temper" (*Strawberry Blonde* Press Book 1941). In the film, Hayworth's character (Virginia Brush) is presented as the temptress who lingers in the male protagonist's memory until he discovers—many years later—that she is in fact a "querulous, complaining woman who makes life miserable for her husband [Jack Carson] despite his wealth" (*Strawberry Blonde* Press Book 1941). Like the film's plot, the film's publicity makes Hayworth's duality—or in-betweenness—a key factor of its narrative. The ambiguous hair color of both Virginia and Rita seems to signal the unknown dangers posed by her character and persona, respectively. One publicity article written specifically to be of interest to women notes that gentlemen might prefer blondes of all kinds, but compared to the platinum, peroxide, golden, natural, or dirty blonde, the strawberry blonde's in-betweenness was the "most dangerous" and threatening to gentlemen across the nation. This slippage between the hair color and temperament of the character and actress is enhanced by another publicity article quoting Hayworth's pleasure in her new look, saying: "The first time I looked in a mirror and saw myself with light red hair with golden glints, I felt positively wicked." Although Rita is quoted as saying that "blonde-ness suits [her] real disposition better," it was not to be; shortly after *Strawberry*

Blonde, Rita's hair was darkened and her persona confirmed with *Blood and Sand* (*Strawberry Blonde* Press Book 1941).

The Technicolor film *Blood and Sand* makes the symbolic meaning of Rita's hair color all the more explicit when she is recast as a Spanish woman. The film centers on the rise and fall of a married matador named Juan (Tyrone Power), who gradually loses his talent after being seduced and abandoned by a wealthy socialite named Doña Sol (Hayworth) (Ringgold 1974, 123).[19] Although the high-profile film marked Rita's emerging cachet in Hollywood, it also cemented her persona as a "coppery" haired Spanish temptress in a movie that aligned this (hair) color with passion, seduction, betrayal, and death.[20] In multiple ways, the color red signifies Doña Sol's "hot-blooded sexuality." As a hair color, it directly contrasts the pious characterizations of Juan's dark-haired Spanish wife and mother. As a prop, it is the color of the bullfighter's cape that Doña Sol uses to seduce Juan. In terms of costuming, it is the color of Doña Sol's dress when she dances in a cantina with another bullfighter to make Juan jealous. And when Juan meets his tragic fate, red is also the color of his blood left in the sand as another matador takes his place in the ring.

To highlight the spectacle of color in *Blood and Sand,* Twentieth Century-Fox's publicity department stressed its symbolic significance and quoted director Rouben Mamoulian to emphasize this feature. In one publicity article, titled "Bright Colors Fascinate Men Says Mamoulian" (*Blood and Sand* Press Book 1941a), the director notes the importance of red in the film's primary seduction scene. According to the article, Doña Sol's seduction of Juan takes place amid hues of red that thematically link the couple's passion to the bullfighter's cape in the ring. While certainly color-coded, the seduction scene is not as passionate as the publicity piece suggests. Instead, the scene is one of manipulation: Doña Sol sings Juan to sleep at her home because she knows that his wife is waiting up for him. Red—whether in her hair or on her body—signifies Doña Sol as an embodiment of passion.

Hayworth's performance as the "fiery temptress" Doña Sol captured America's attention and secured her identity as a redhead, proving the significant impact that hair color can have on a female performer's roles and persona (*Blood and Sand* Press Book 1941b). Her triumph in *Blood and Sand* became evident when many red-haired look-alike starlets appeared in Hollywood after the film's release (Ringgold 1974, 91). In fact, it was another actress's commitment to her hair color that made the role available to Hayworth in the first place. Carole Lombard, originally considered for the role of Doña Sol, refused to become a redhead for the part because it had taken time to cultivate her "blonde bombshell" persona and she did not want to disrupt it for *Blood and Sand* (Ringgold 1974, 123). With *Strawberry Blonde* and *Blood and Sand,* Hayworth was well on her way to becoming a leading lady. Roles like Doña Sol were the scaffolding of her full development as a sex icon until another 1941 film—*You'll Never Get Rich*—reintroduced her as an all-American dancer.

LEADING MEN: CHOREOGRAPHING HAYWORTH'S WARTIME SEXUALITY

Despite Rita's extensive dance training, it was not until *You'll Never Get Rich* that she captured Hollywood's imagination as an all-American musical performer and became a racially mobile Hollywood Latina. Rita found that, as a Cansino, dance primarily measured and limited her characterization as an ethnic performer. The press book for *Blood and Sand* (1941b) comments on Hayworth's ascent from mere dancer by remarking that "for several pictures, she did nothing but dance. After changing her name to Hayworth, she decided to carry on the Haworth tradition and devoted her time to acting . . . [in the tradition of her] English acting family, famous for its Shakespearean interpretations." Whereas Rita Cansino was once expected to perform dance numbers, Rita Hayworth was deemed worthy of moving beyond that limitation.

Before the making of *You'll Never Get Rich*, various modes of publicity heralded the end of Hayworth's dance career in favor of an acting career, a concerted disavowal of dance that attempted to break the nonwhite typecasting held over from her Cansino years (McLean 2004, 37). During the early years of cinema, dance in film had a relatively low status. Beyond Fred Astaire, Ginger Rogers, and a handful of musical celebrities or dance directors, dance was often denigrated or utilized as spectacle, as an ethnic signifier, or it was easily dismissed. Technically proficient dancers were not the standard, and the best-known dance director of the period, Busby Berkeley, primarily employed women for their aesthetically pleasing faces and legs rather than their dance skills. Rita's dance skills were simply a facet of her Otherness as a Hollywood Latina until Astaire—who knew the Cansino family from his days as a vaudeville performer—highlighted her training in *You'll Never Get Rich* (Mueller 1985; Ringgold 1974, 128–129). *You'll Never Get Rich* changed the function and type of dancing that Rita performed on screen. Unlike *Blood and Sand*, in which Hayworth's character Doña Sol performs a brief dance that is contextualized and sexualized within the space of a cantina as a means of inciting jealousy, in *You'll Never Get Rich* Rita's dancing was integral to the film and did not solely mark her racialized difference or sexualized characterization.

Hayworth's racial mobility was facilitated by her partnership with Fred Astaire because he legitimized her dance abilities and helped redefine her sexuality as more American and (slightly) less threatening to the movie-going public.

Paired with "dancing's elegant gentleman," Rita was now cast as an all-American girl named Sheila Winthrop in *You'll Never Get Rich* (Billman 1997, 66). While *Only Angels Have Wings, Strawberry Blonde*, and *Blood and Sand* had developed Hayworth as a siren, *You'll Never Get Rich* lent a tinge of domestication to her characterization. As Sheila, Hayworth's in-betweenness was refurbished as a kind of representational tension somewhere between virgin and siren; this characterization utilized her racially mobile semiotic whiteness and performative nonwhiteness to cultivate a kind of sex appeal that soon became a key part of her musical persona.

You'll Never Get Rich frames the reluctant romance between a chorus dancer named Sheila (Hayworth) and her choreographer, Bob (Astaire). Sheila fancies Bob, but Bob resists romance. Mr. Hubbard, their mutual boss, complicates matters by attempting to woo Sheila with an engraved diamond bracelet. Sheila refuses the boss's gift and advances, but Mrs. Hubbard discovers the abandoned evidence. Because the wealthy Mrs. Hubbard threatens to divorce and financially ruin her husband if he cheats, Mr. Hubbard lies: he says that he is simply helping Bob to woo Sheila, and then forces Bob to pursue Sheila on his behalf. The ensuing mishaps sour Bob's and Sheila's feelings, and Bob enlists in the army.[21] When the two reunite, Bob begins to woo Sheila in earnest and organizes a militaristic dance show finale—the "Wedding Cake Walk"—in which the performing couple exchange binding marital vows without Sheila's knowledge.[22]

Beyond its relatively benign narrative, *You'll Never Get Rich* adjusts the conventions of the classic musical genre by creating a new type of "musical female" role for Hayworth. According to traditional critical analysis of Hollywood musicals, the musical male performer courts his love interest through dance (Altman 1987; Feuer 1993).[23] Dance functions as a symbolic copulation: by teaching the musical female to dance, the musical male awakens his female partner's sexuality. This sexual awakening is fulfilled when the musical female gains the ability to dance. Often, a musical siren intervenes to complicate the narrative, testing the musical male's fidelity to his love interest. The siren appeals to the musical male's weakness—his sexual appetite—and she is often characterized as a dancer who requires no tutelage, a perfectly tempting partner. For her own pleasure, the siren attempts to seduce the musical male, but he triumphs and proves worthy of the virginal, musical female. The musical male is thus rewarded with domestication, gaining a legitimized social position through marriage (Altman 1987, 28–58).

You'll Never Get Rich, however, plays with this musical formula by hybridizing both virgin and siren figures through Hayworth's character: Sheila is both the protagonist's love interest and the other woman. By 1941, Astaire's female partners were all measured against Ginger Rogers, whose onscreen romantic partnerships with Astaire were characterized as inevitable, long-term, and rooted in a previous friendship.[24] Astaire's professional break from Rogers caused audiences to pine for their reunion, but *You'll Never Get Rich* provided an opportunity to appease them by reintroducing Hayworth as a dancer. Dancing in the Astaire style (both ballroom and lyrical) repositioned Hayworth as a mainstream musical performer, completing the cosmetic and nominal refashioning that had already transpired according to the dictates of whiteness. This style of performance propelled Hayworth's career toward the mainstream and away from the margins of Spanishness and Irishness, but her evolving Americanness would remain paradoxical since her persona retained an exoticized sexuality. The domestication process of the musical is ultimately never complete because Hayworth's persona symbolically reversed the musical female's gender norms and made her a knowledgeable partner.[25]

The beginning of *You'll Never Get Rich* uniquely stresses that Hayworth/ Sheila already possesses the dance technique worthy of a partnership with Astaire/Bob, an adjustment to the genre that heralds Hayworth's hybridized musical female and foreshadows a new wave of female sexuality through dance performance. Two dance scenes in the film signify these differences: the "Rehearsal Duet," a challenge dance sequence that opens the film, and "So Near and Yet So Far" by Cole Porter. The "Rehearsal Duet" scene introduces Sheila as a chorus dancer and establishes her desire to attract the attention of her choreographer, Bob. As the company rehearses the "Boogie Barcarolle," Bob reprimands Sheila for dancing one count behind the rest of the company; because the routine incorporates elements of tap, the error is both audible and visible. When Bob pulls Sheila aside to review the steps, the tutorial becomes a challenge duet between the two characters. Despite Bob's position of power, the scene's subsequent dialogue between Sheila and another chorus girl makes it clear that Sheila's missteps are deliberate and designed to catch Bob's attention. By manipulating Bob, Sheila initiates the duet and fulfills her desire to dance with her supervisor while undermining his rank for her pleasure.

The pairing of Rita Hayworth and Fred Astaire reverses the gendered power structure of the genre and choreography tropes typical in Astaire musicals. As our first glimpse of Hayworth's character in the film, "Rehearsal Duet" proves that she is a "capable and confident dancer" who surpasses Astaire's other musical partners in terms of her skill and sexually assertive persona (Mueller 1985, 190).[26] By reintroducing Hayworth as a dancer (worthy of Astaire) in a scene in which she leads the dance, the film signals the emergence of a hybridized musical female capable of an assertive yet wholesome sexuality—what McLean calls exhibiting the "paradoxical" elements of "eroticism and decency" (McLean 2004, 63). The film was a turning point for Hayworth: as a screen siren able to

Figure 11. In *You'll Never Get Rich* (1941), Sheila Winthrop (Rita Hayworth) tricks choreographer Bob (Fred Astaire) into dancing with her, then admires him while midstep in the "Rehearsal Duet."

motivate male characters, her persona retained a narrative agency that produced compelling leading roles.[27] The power of the choreographic reversal is exemplified by a shot from "Rehearsal Duet" that shows a rehearsing Sheila looking at Bob as he leads the company, unaware of her amorous gaze.

Hayworth's appeal as Astaire's partner ultimately banked on her racial mobility, employing the codes of whiteness and nonwhiteness to produce a sexual persona that was both desirable and desiring. To help explain the function of this simultaneity, McLean explicitly addresses the impact of Hayworth's ethnic background:

> Hayworth is able to express her feelings of frustration, anger, jealousy, and fear (and also *joy*) not by attempting to merge with other ethnic or racial groups [like Bette Davis in *Jezebel* (1938)] but because she is already herself "nonwhite." This all is certainly true of her musicals, as well as *Gilda*, and helps to explain the presence of Hayworth numbers utilizing types of music and dance often characterized as torrid or hot—stereotypically modes of "nonwhite" expression—in virtually every film, generic musical or not, that Hayworth made as a star at Columbia (the notable exception being *The Lady from Shanghai*). (McLean 2004, 52–53)

Like her ability to express anger, jealousy, and joy, Hayworth's ability to express desire is directly related to her ethnic prehistory and the perceived lack of self-control that comes with being a Hollywood Latina. Because contemporary audiences were familiar with Hayworth's origin story, they were consciously or subconsciously privy to the logic behind explicit and implicit references to her ethnic background through dance.

The coalescence of Hayworth's sexual allure, narrative/choreographic power, and ethnicity is fully visible in the Cole Porter rumba "So Near and Yet So Far,"

Figure 12. In *You'll Never Get Rich*, Sheila's manipulating undulations lead Bob
into "So Near and Yet So Far" (*left*); he later highlights this movement in the
choreography by framing her hips with his arms and gaze (*right*).

the second *You'll Never Get Rich* dance performance in which Hayworth leads
Astaire. In his meticulous analysis of Astaire's musical career, John Mueller
highlights "So Near and Yet So Far" as particularly noteworthy because it
uniquely features a female partner leading Astaire into the choreography
(Mueller 1985, 194). Mueller observes that "having the woman manipulate *him*
into the dance is a witty reversal of the usual procedure in Astaire duets"
(194–195). Because Mueller states that Ginger Rogers is the superior Astaire
partner, his appreciation of Hayworth in "So Near and Yet So Far" is all the
more remarkable. Mueller comments that Hayworth is the one female partner
capable of leading Astaire, although he does not explicitly state why. Instead,
the meaning is implied by his commentary: Hayworth's "enticing" hips and
torso—especially their "undulations" (a word he uses twice)—beckon Astaire
to follow her lead from his static starting position while her "arms seem naturally to embellish the choreography" of this so-called rumba (Mueller 1985,
194).[28] These undulations are so hypnotic that, when Astaire finally leads
Hayworth, the first few phrases of the dance involve Astaire framing the iso-
lated sway of her hips with his arms and gaze.

  While Astaire lent Hayworth a touch of domestication, studio publicity for
You'll Never Get Rich capitalized on the sexual side of her in-betweenness, as
reflected in a risqué publicity photo published in the August 1941 issue of *Life*.
Released one month before the film, the photo featured Hayworth in a lace
negligee posed atop a tousled, satiny bed. Although seemingly at odds with the
boy-meets-girl narrative of *You'll Never Get Rich*, the photograph's sexual
allure underscored the film's military theme by catering to an audience of
young men gearing up for war. The image made Hayworth one of the first and
top-ranked World War II pinups; its massive popularity established Hayworth
as a sex icon (*Variety* 1987).[29] Hayworth's iconographic sexuality reinforced the

virgin-siren tension of her persona. Thanks to her racial mobility from Spanish girl to all-American Love Goddess, what had once originated as a signifier of her ethnic difference as a Hollywood Latina now pioneered a new breed of American female sexuality.

The mainstream allure of Hayworth's sexuality gained popularity with young GIs during the war and was enhanced upon their return. *You'll Never Get Rich* ushered in a wave of war-themed musicals or films with musical numbers starring Hayworth, including *Tonight and Every Night* (1945), *Gilda* (1946), and *Miss Sadie Thompson* (1953). Though war is never explicitly addressed in *You'll Never Get Rich*, the mise-en-scène features marching troops, guns, and guardhouses, while the finale, "The Wedding Cake Walk," shows Sheila and Bob exchanging vows atop a wedding cake shaped like a tank (Mueller 1985, 187, 196). Just as the finale linked the public and private spheres of war and domesticity, Hayworth's visibility helped the nation rearticulate the concepts of work and womanhood that had been in effect during the war effort. With a persona that fused both Americanness and sweet sexual agency, Hayworth exemplified the simultaneity of labor and cosmetic femininity advertised during the period (McLean 2004, 54, 55).

After *You'll Never Get Rich*, Hayworth's cinematic male partners helped articulate her sexual persona and vice versa. This state of affairs was most obvious with leading men like Gene Kelly and Glenn Ford. While the success of *You'll Never Get Rich* ensured that Hayworth and Astaire were partnered again in *You Were Never Lovelier* (1942), it was Columbia's first Technicolor musical, *Cover Girl* (1944), that highlighted her stardom and star-making potential (*AFI Catalog*, s.v. *Cover Girl*).[30] The film *Cover Girl* established Kelly as a musical performer, and it was the first film that allowed him to contribute a significant amount of choreography (Roman 1996). Unlike Astaire, with his white-tie-and-tails, upper-class ballroom persona, Kelly developed athletic and working-class characterizations and often appeared in white socks and loafers, with an onscreen tendency toward uniforms. Kelly was invested in the virility of dance and aimed "to dance like the man in the streets," as indicated by the 1958 *Omnibus* documentary he directed titled *Dancing: A Man's Game* (Barzel 1997; "Gene Kelly, Anatomy of a Dancer" 2006). As a hybrid musical female, Hayworth enhanced Astaire's stardom through her brand of sexuality, while seemingly propelling Kelly's cachet—not unlike what Jennifer Lopez would do for George Clooney fifty years later.[31]

It was, however, Hayworth's collaboration with the choreographer Jack Cole that firmly established her sexualized persona in films like *Tonight and Every Night*, *Gilda*, and *Down to Earth* (1947). Although Cole's sexually expressive choreographic style was unpopular with film censors, his movements anchored many prominent female celebrities in the 1940s and 1950s and were designed to highlight their assets and bodily vocabulary (Billman 1997, 79). Cole's collaboration with Marilyn Monroe in films like *Gentlemen Prefer Blondes* (1953) and *Some Like It Hot* (1959) epitomizes his reputation.[32] Although Hayworth and Cole were briefly united on the set of *Cover Girl*, it was the film *Tonight and Every Night* that featured the choreographic sensuality that landed Hayworth the title of Love Goddess.[33] While the moniker was officially bestowed on Hayworth in a 1947 *Life* magazine article titled "The Cult of the Love Goddess," the article itself attempted to discredit Hayworth as an actress and performer and epitomized her lifelong struggle to achieve agency as a performer within the larger industrial constraints of Hollywood (McLean 2004, 57–63).

Tonight and Every Night takes place in a musical theater during the German air raids on Britain from 1940 to 1941. A *Life* magazine reporter has come to investigate the story that this particular music hall never missed a performance during the Blitz. The film, a generic musical, is set in England and centers on the gradual romance of an Englishman named Paul Lundy (Lee Bowman) and an American woman named Rosalind Bruce (Hayworth). Paul is a Royal Air Force aviator in pursuit of Rosalind, a musical performer whom he meets after her performance at the club. The club's largely nationalistic musical numbers feature brash lyrics such as, "We're going to win. C'mon grin. Therein lies our might." Despite some unique performances and moments of reflexive humor, the primary performance of the film is arguably "You Excite Me."[34]

Cole's controversial choreographic style coupled with Hayworth's training and ethnic background cultivated her legacy as both a sexual woman and an object of desire. "You Excite Me" exemplifies the sensuality of Hayworth's collaboration with Cole, especially in its evocation of racialized difference through samba movements choreographed to heavy percussion. Unlike the more "American" appropriation of the jitterbug number, "What Does an English Girl Think of a Yank?" the rhythms of "You Excite Me" read as more exotic—both through movement and mise-en-scène.[35] "You Excite Me" blends various styles of so-called foreign signifiers—from Middle-Eastern-esque props to the vaguely Latin American costuming—as visual reinforcements for the themes of temptation and excitement at the core of the song's lyrics and performance. The seductive intent of this number is so strong that the song becomes the film's motif for desire. Both the dance and lyrics incurred intervention from movie censors, one of the seemingly few indications that the story is based on the true tale of a burlesque venue whose dancers never missed a show during the war because men continued to come to see naked women, whatever the war conditions (Loney 1984; Ringgold 1974, 153–154).

The exotic sensuality of "You Excite Me" established the cornerstone of Hayworth's Love Goddess persona as articulated by her siren-virgin persona and enhanced by the film's narrative, setting, and choreography (Billman 1997, 92; Ringgold 1974, 154). The language of the song—in terms of both lyric and movement—supports the agency and power of Rosalind as an active subject: she is simultaneously desired (by presumably male audience members watching her on the cabaret stage) and desiring (as indicated by the lyrics of the song). Singing "You excite me / You lead me on and I pursue," Hayworth exudes the kinetic energy of quick and intense body bends, leaps, and shakes, which highlights the physical intensity and power of her performance. She is indeed a Love Goddess, one whose movement seduces from the screen.

Unfortunately, control of this desire is lost when Rosalind leaves the stage. While the dance of "You Excite Me" suggests that Rosalind is a desiring subject, the song is continually repeated during the film as a signal of male desire for her. In terms of dance and performance, "You Excite Me" challenges the usual position of feminist film studies by highlighting the (female) dancer's power to hold the (male) spectator's gaze with the willful use of her own body (McLean 2004, 118–119). In this sense, Hayworth's character declares and exhibits her own desire through song and dance in "You Excite Me." While reverse shots denote the aviator's desire by way of his agape mouth, shots of Rosalind suggest that she looks right at him while singing. The cinematography and narrative of this scene encourage us to witness Hayworth's performance from the aviator's point of view: we enter the club with him and sit with him as the performance begins. It is Rosalind, however, who demands our attention when she declares her passion in his direction, thus preventing an oversimplified evaluation of her as only an object of desire.

Tonight and Every Night's intertwining of dance and war frames Rosalind and Hayworth as simultaneously desirable and dangerous. After Rosalind's initial performance of "You Excite Me," the film uses the song to cue Paul's desire in the real world rather than Rosalind's and suggests that her true sexual agency is limited to moments of dance performance. The performance initially highlights Rosalind's agency, but the song's reprisal undermines her power by making her the object of desire. Before Rosalind falls in love with the aviator in the latter half of the film (one of the plot's more contrived moments), she is an independent and headstrong woman, but the film's war theme and generic romance ultimately temper and disrupt this self-assuredness until the end of the film.[36] At one point, Paul literally uses a recording of "You Excite Me" to indicate his amorous intentions when he tricks Rosalind into joining him for a private dinner in his room. The film's constant comparisons between Rosalind's body and war underscore this contradiction of her power. We are introduced to Paul as he passes the theater with his aviator friends; upon seeing Rosalind's marquee picture, Paul states that he and his crew have found their "target" for the evening. When an air raid forces the cast, crew, and audience into the base-ment shelter after "You Excite Me," Paul attempts to woo Rosalind by declaring that she frightened him: "You did a little bombing tonight yourself, you know. That dance you did . . . It's not only unfair, it's practically illegal." Rosalind's cool response—"I hope I didn't hurt anything vital"—suggests why she was so popular during the war. Men desired Hayworth as a pinup with a cool demeanor, while women imagined themselves in her sexually powerful and desirable likeness; in fact, women composed a large percentage of Hayworth's audiences, defining what McLean calls "women's musicals" (2004, 117).

There *Never* Was a Woman Like Hayworth!

After World War II, Hayworth's film performances were more fully organized around the ideals of nation and gender and seemingly obscured her remarkable career in terms of racialized sexuality. When Hayworth's persona peaked with *Gilda* in 1946, her role in World War II went beyond GI pinup to something less tangible but no less lasting: an idealized representation of American woman-hood for a generation of U.S. soldiers and a nation recuperating from war. While this period may seem to represent a period of less racially sexualized screen roles, closer inspection highlights how Hayworth's racial mobility could not ultimately obscure the trajectory of her persona in terms of intertwining codes of racialization and sexualization.

The film noir *Gilda* is a love-hate-love triangle set immediately before and after the end of World War II. A down-and-out gambler, Johnny (Glenn Ford), is taken in by a wealthy but crooked casino owner named Ballin (George Macready). Johnny becomes Ballin's ever-ready right-hand man—until Ballin returns from a business trip with a wife, the beautiful Gilda (Hayworth). As a result, complications in Johnny and Ballin's relationship develop, but the fact that Johnny and Gilda were once married remains hidden to all except them. As Gilda and Johnny engage in equally cruel games of jealousy and punish-ment, Ballin fakes his own death to escape the Nazis after extorting money from them. Despite a series of increasingly torturous emotional games, Gilda and Johnny finally acknowledge their love and reunite after Ballin is actually killed.

The picture's location was to have been the United States, but it was switched to Argentina after the Production Code Administration opposed gangster representations in U.S. cities (Stanley 1945). Gangsters and love tri-angles were deemed more acceptable against an Argentinean backdrop. To explain the location switch, one Columbia press book for *Gilda* suggested that

Latin America provided a temporary—although inferior—substitute for war-ravaged Europe:

> Europe, still in the throes of post-war upheaval, isn't the proper setting for escapist films. Thus, the love duets that formerly flourished in the continental playgrounds have been moved to Mexico and South America, where life is gay—gay as it hasn't been in Europe. Now, the background is Argentina and Uruguay, where a gal like the one that Rita portrays can still get silk stockings without difficulty, and rare metal cloths for evening dresses. No need to worry about rationing below the border—tires are fine, and a bottle of Scotch can be shown without getting a snicker from audiences. (*Gilda* Press Book 1946a)

Although backdrops like Argentina served the needs of the U.S. film industry, articles such as these presented Latin America as an undeserving place. The same article goes on to suggest that Latin America and Mexico unwittingly and illegitimately benefited from the recent conclusion of the world war. Under the subheading "Free Ads for Mexico," the publicity piece states that "Mexico is getting more than its share of free advertising these days." The feature concludes by remarking: "The Pan-American Chambers of Commerce are undoubtedly feeling pretty good these days. You would, too, with a billion dollars worth of publicity dumped in your lap *for nothing!*" (*Gilda* Press Book 1946a). This last sentence, the final one in the article, underscores the economic and cultural tension between the United States and Mexico.

The tension between the United States and Mexico—regarding something as seemingly benign as a film location—suggests that Hayworth's racial mobility was especially important to her success in this period and was continually highlighted in publicity. Hayworth's hard work to become American in the public eye was symbolically rewarded with dramatic and high-profile films like *Gilda*, but like Del Rio's Mexican persona after she had achieved U.S. fame, Hayworth was expected to continually echo elements of her past. Despite the fact that Hayworth had already collected a goodly number of seductive leading roles by the time of *Gilda*'s premiere, the film was publicized as yet another turning point in her career by the studio and press. Columbia proclaimed *Gilda* as Hayworth's "first important dramatic role," a distinction implying that her previous dance work—and history as a dancing ethnic—was inferior or, at the very least, something of the past. Yet the studio quickly stressed that Hayworth "sings and dances, too! Stunningly gowned, swaying to throbbing Latin rhythms and softly rendering a torchy tune, Rita brings down the house" (*Gilda* Press Book 1946d). By juxtaposing Hayworth's new dramatic turn with her dancing and Spanish past, the studio renewed her status as an in-between figure.

Arguably Gilda, Hayworth's most provocative character, and the film memorialized Hayworth both in popular memory and in film studies with the defiant mock striptease, "Put the Blame on Mame." At the time, however, Columbia considered the film's most seductive number to be a rather tame samba that occurs later in the film—a dance that has been nearly forgotten in critical analyses of the film. As generations of audiences and scholars have begun to forget Hayworth's origins, "Put the Blame on Mame" may seem more compelling because Hayworth's sensuality—evoked through the removal of a pair of gloves and necklace—is disguised as a racially or ethnically neutral image; without the prehistory of Cansino fresh in mind, the fact that Hayworth dances for her own pleasure as much as for ours may seem all the more remarkable (Dyer 1978b, 96–97). At the time, the samba may have seemed more "torrid" because it unmasked Hayworth's ethnic history within the space of one performance (*Gilda* Press Book 1946c, 1946g).

The tension between the sameness of Hayworth's Anglicized persona (however sexual) and the difference of her racialized past effectively and fully recasts Hayworth as a femme fatale. In "Resistance through Charisma: Rita Hayworth and *Gilda*," Richard Dyer compellingly argues that film noir women are "unknowable" and therefore fatal. He adds that Gilda does not fit this bill because we know the star Hayworth and consequently know Gilda (Dyer 1978b, 92–93). Even though Rita's transformation from Cansino to Hayworth occurred in plain sight, this transition from Other to American provides the unknowability that her stardom seemingly dispelled (Dyer 1978b, 92–93). Like Ballin's sword disguised as a walking stick, *Gilda* underscores the fatality of this unknowability. When Johnny and Ballin propose a humorous toast to the sword in Gilda's presence, they determine the weapon to be female because it appears one way and then, "before your very eyes," becomes another. Because the men have shared both the sword and Gilda, this dialogue highlights Gilda's unknowability despite her hypervisibility.

Gilda was not a traditional femme fatale, yet this aspect of her characterization was manifested through a direct association of Hayworth and her character with the war. Gilda does not appear in the film until a newspaper headline spirals into the film frame declaring "Germany Surrenders," and Johnny casually mentions in a flippant voiceover: "By the way, about that time the war ended." The scene that follows introduces Ballin's bride to Johnny and the audience to Hayworth. Studio publicity made this connection between Gilda/Hayworth and the war even more distinct. One *Gilda* studio publicity piece, disseminated by the *New York Times*, directly compared Hayworth's body to a

Figure 13. A publicity photo featuring *Time* magazine makes explicit the connection between Rita Hayworth, dance, and male members of the military. Courtesy of the Margaret Herrick Library, Academy of Motion Picture Arts and Sciences.

military tank, while Hayworth's likeness was purportedly affixed to an atom bomb, which was then christened "Gilda" (*New York Times* 1945, 1946; Leaming 1989, 129).[37] As a literal bombshell, Hayworth, with her sex appeal and ethnic masquerade, was made synonymous with mortal danger and warfare (Smith 2006, 75, 78).

Since *You'll Never Get Rich*, Hayworth's growing fame had become inextricably tied to her dance performances, her roles in (post)war films, and her popularity with GIs. The intertwining importance of dance and military men to Hayworth's career was echoed by publicity suggesting that *Gilda* included musical sequences to appease a "host of GI's who requested that she be allowed to display her shapely gams in some torrid dance routines" (*Gilda* Press Book 1946f). While it is difficult to know whether such publicity-disseminated desires were true, the fact that the studio felt compelled to stress this point is striking and speaks to the fact that audience members— especially those returning from war—were encouraged to feel a shared sense of control over their favorite 1945 pinup's first 1946 performance (*Gilda* Press Book 1946b).

Despite her rebellious performance of "Put the Blame on Mame" and her characterization of Gilda in general, the brand of unknowability that Hayworth brought to the role was ultimately contained and reprimanded by studio publicity featuring Glenn Ford, an actor recently discharged from Marine duty. Ford's studio publicity emphasized his return to Hollywood after active duty, and he embodied the disciplinary element of the studio's publicity campaign (*Gilda* Press Book 1946c). On a semiotic level, Ford's depiction of Johnny in the publicity for *Gilda* seemed an attempt to tame Hayworth's persona by way of punishing Gilda. Three studio advertisements emphasized a masculine, militarized persona, pitted against Hayworth's Gilda, to present a progressive representation of Ford/Johnny as hypermasculine, even though Johnny is routinely emasculated by Gilda, who defies him and calls him "pretty" (Dyer 1978b). The first pose depicts Gilda as the prototypical femme fatale: she either lounges on a couch or stands alone against a dark background while smoking a cigarette. The second series features Gilda at Johnny's feet with the accompanying tagline that underscores her unknowability: "Now they all know what I am." The third series features a static image of Johnny slapping Gilda, a pose that proved so effective it was reiterated in every studio campaign for films that paired Glenn Ford and Rita Hayworth—from *Gilda* to *The Loves of Carmen* (1948) and *Affair in Trinidad* (1952). The tensions symbolized by Hayworth/Gilda's transgressions and Ford/Johnny's containment were even echoed in the press books for *The Lady from Shanghai*, especially when Hayworth's early associations with Mexico were disavowed.

THE LADY FROM SHANGHAI, OR SHANGHAIED BY MEXICO

In *The Lady from Shanghai* (1948), Hayworth is symbolically castrated by being stripped of both her hair and mobility. Like Glenn Ford's characters and the publicity images in *Gilda* and *The Loves of Carmen*, Hayworth's persona and character in *The Lady from Shanghai* seemed to be similarly reprimanded by director and costar Orson Welles. *The Lady from Shanghai* is unique to Hayworth's persona for many reasons. First, her famous locks are shorn and dyed blond. The film is also a "notable exception" in Hayworth's star career at Columbia: she sings but does not dance in the film. As Adrienne McLean has noted, Welles's canonization as a film auteur has made this otherwise atypical depiction of Hayworth one of the predominant components of her academic representation (McLean 2004).

The Lady from Shanghai relies an interlocking series of racialized and ethnic representations that underscore the intended ambiguity of its film noir script—not least of which is Hayworth's racial mobility toward white American

Figure 14. There *never* was a woman like Gilda. The image of Glenn Ford slapping Rita Hayworth (*inset*) was repeated in each of their subsequent films together, from *Affair in Trinidad* to *The Loves of Carmen*. Courtesy of the Cinematic Arts Library, University of Southern California.

blondeness. Soon after an Irishman named Michael O'Hara (Welles) flirts with a mysterious woman named Elsa Bannister (Hayworth), he must save her from a group of thugs. To thank Michael for saving his wife's life, Arthur Bannister (Everett Sloan)—a slightly built criminal lawyer with a mighty reputation— offers to employ Michael on his yacht, which Michael reluctantly accepts.

En route from San Francisco to the Mexican coast, Michael slowly realizes the Bannisters' lives are laden with dysfunction, mistrust, and deceit, but he cannot help but fall in love with Elsa. When he discovers that Elsa has only married Arthur because he threatened to expose her supposedly scandalous Shanghai past, Michael plots to buy her out of the marriage. Fortuitously, Arthur's partner, George Grisby (Glenn Anders), offers Michael money to help him stage his own murder; Michael accepts, only to be arrested as the primary suspect when Grisby actually turns up dead. Things take a turn for the worse when Elsa convinces Michael to let Arthur defend him during the trial. As Arthur begins to deliberately sabotage the case, Michael creates a diversion by swallowing pills and escaping the courtroom. After finding refuge in a Chinatown theater, Michael, before passing out from the pills, realizes that Elsa killed Grisby. When he regains consciousness, Michael finds himself in a funhouse hall of mirrors where he witnesses a fatal duel between Elsa and Arthur. Michael survives and stumbles home (*AFI Catalog*, s.v. *The Lady from Shanghai*).

Because this film marks Hayworth's singular departure from the infamous red tresses that facilitated her racial mobility, the multiple levels of racial and ethnic codes operating in *The Lady from Shanghai* become all the more significant. By cropping and dying Rita's hair blond, Orson Welles—director and the purported mastermind behind this decision—effectively destroyed Hayworth's image and made her truly "unknowable and treacherous" and thus a more viable femme fatale in the process (Dyer 1978b, 96). With her hair cropped to a "cinema swirl" and tinted a "topaz blonde" color, Hayworth seemed to more fully embody the femme fatale as a blonde—so much so that her character, Elsa Bannister, kills her husband in a gunfight (Dyer 1978b; *The Lady from Shanghai* Press Book 1948a). In his reverse-gendering of the tale of Samson and Delilah, Orson Welles supervised while Helen Hunt once again cut and dyed Hayworth's hair and a "a score of cameramen click[ed] away" (*The Lady from Shanghai* Press Book 1948c).

As a blonde, Hayworth embodied the extreme end of idealized white representation at the same moment she traversed back across the United States–Mexico border—this time as a purportedly more American star.[38] When she was cast as a blond femme fatale who does not dance, the signifiers of Hayworth's racialized difference were least plainly in view and thus symbolically more dangerous because they were semiotically more American. Because part of *The Lady from Shanghai* takes place in Mexico, studio publicity went to great lengths to fabricate how out of place the blond Hollywood star Hayworth seemed south of the border. Articles such as "Even Glamour Has Its Problems When Hollywood Goes Mexican" (*The Lady from Shanghai* Press Book 1948b) framed Hayworth's glamorous image as impractical for the exoticized and primitivized spaces of

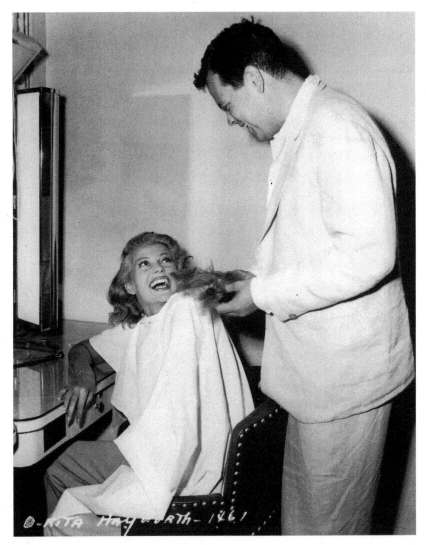

Figure 15. After Helen Hunt's initial cut of Rita's famous hair for her new "cinema swirl" coiffure, *The Lady from Shanghai* director and costar (and Hayworth's ex-husband) Orson Welles inspects the progress. Courtesy of the Margaret Herrick Library, Academy of Motion Picture Arts and Sciences.

Mexico; she purportedly required special makeup to withstand the "blazing tropical sun" and had a bodyguard to protect her from "crocodiles and snakes on land and cannibal fish in the water." Another article claimed that Hayworth was amazed to find that the peso ("approximately 20 cents") could purchase not one but "several hundred of the most gorgeous orchids [she had] ever seen." Beyond tropicalizing Mexico, such articles framed and represented Hayworth as an all-American woman by alienating her from the so-called foreign spaces of Mexico.

Rita Hayworth, Nation, and Iconic Womanhood

Unlike those of Dolores Del Rio before her or Rita Moreno after her, Hayworth's national and ethnic identities were framed as wholly American and of the United States despite the role her Spanishness and discovery in Mexico had played in the development of her sexual persona. As Hayworth gained landmark control of her career at the peak of her celebrity, she capitalized on the sexualization of her own body for personal profit.[39] In many ways, Hayworth's investment in herself as a business asset or property—something beyond national, political, or ethnic affiliation—was a precursor to Jennifer Lopez's multicultural business savvy. In fact, Lopez is one of the only Latinas to match the high-profile and leading roles that Hayworth played in her career. Unlike Del Rio, Miranda, or Moreno, both Hayworth and Lopez, it seems, knew the outermost sacrifices they were willing to make for their careers.

Although I have emphasized Hayworth's evolution within the U.S. national context, the matrix of race, gender, sexuality, and nation is not wholly removed from her international image. Rita Cansino's transition to Rita Hayworth was a long and public process, with the tension between these identities percolating differently across national and historical contexts. Both the Italian neorealist film *Bicycle Thieves* (1948) and the Manuel Puig novel *Betrayed by Rita Hayworth* (1968) represent the excesses of Hollywood (as an extension of the United States) through Hayworth's body. In *Bicycle Thieves*, Hayworth's image appears in advertising for *Gilda*; the image of Hayworth luxuriating and smoking in a strapless satin dress sardonically embodies the United States' opulence in the face of Italy's poverty in the aftermath of World War II. From an international perspective, Hayworth's racial mobility may equate to a kind of whiteface that makes her a more potent symbol of corruption, or as an accusation that she bought into the imperial system. The burden of the imperial critiques that have befallen Hayworth may not have been so prominent if her transformation had taken place outside this classical Hollywood period.

Domestically, Hayworth's image was no less fraught with the multiplicity of race, gender, and national identity. Racial mobility enabled Hayworth to occupy a kind of whiteness that afforded a mainstream career, yet the dangerous, sexual undertones of her appeal—strong star qualities, no matter how you cut or color them—depended on the routine mention of her history as a Spanish dancer, reifying an ever-present and underlying level of her exotic Otherness while evoking the myth of the Hollywood Latina. As Rita became a star, dance and exoticized dance performances remained a constant signifier of her (hyper)sexuality.

Rita Hayworth's racial mobility produced an all-Americanness under-pinned by a racialized sexuality, a simultaneity that served as the paradoxical foundation of her career as a Love Goddess and signaled a shift in the portrayal of white female sexuality within the United States. Like the other women in this project, Hayworth, through use of her body and its performance, signified sex-ual knowledge; unlike Del Rio, Miranda, or Lopez, however, Hayworth evinced an allure that was eventually and effectively rephrased as a general sex appeal as she increasingly whitened her look. Although a Hollywood Latina, Hayworth effectively settled her persona within the frame of whiteness, which perhaps explains her high-profile career and legendary status in Hollywood. Studio publicity, however, often worked to undermine or police the headstrong and sexually empowered dancing characters whom she portrayed. While Hayworth signaled the gestation and arrival of a newly sexual all-American girl, characters like Gilda or Elsa were symbolically punished or re-ethnicized by association. Although Hayworth's career evolved, her past was never very fully relinquished by the studios or the public.

Hayworth's popularity as the Love Goddess was so powerful that it antici-pated the girl-next-door sexuality lauded by *Playboy* magazine and other sex literature of the period. *Playboy*'s 1953 premier issue emerged at the end of Hayworth's box-office reign: *Salome* (1953) had just left first-run theaters, and *Miss Sadie Thompson* (1953) was completing postproduction. It is impossible to fully measure the impact of Rita Hayworth's image on the shaping of a 1940s mentality, but her musicals and pinup persona likely had a significant influence on the imagination of *Playboy* creator Hugh Hefner. While Hefner definitely preferred blondes, he produced a television biography about Hayworth titled *Rita* (2003) (Bennett 2004).[40] *Playboy* and the "singles culture" of the 1950s and 1960s were "premised on an ethic of success, prosperity and consumption" that motivated the postwar era (D'Emilio and Freedman 1997, 302–305). As the sexy siren preceding this sociocultural shift, Rita Hayworth was a prototypical liberated woman, the idealized female who could work in both public and private spheres, desire sex, and sustain a cosmetically desirable visage.[41] As an extremely successful product of cosmetic manipulation, Hayworth personified the consumption necessary to become a fully functioning member of a nation in transition. For women, whether factory workers or leading Hollywood stars,

World War II challenged, contested, and reified traditional gender roles.[42] Because race, gender, and class are and have been equally ensnared in the colonial or imperial project,[43] Hayworth's body and its racial mobility were entangled in and shaped by the war, by Hollywood, by the adoption of cosmetic markers of whiteness, and by the exoticized and sexualized Otherness she embodied.

CHAPTER 5

Rita Moreno, the Critically Acclaimed "All-Round Ethnic"

Following in the footsteps of previous Latinas in Hollywood, Rita Moreno has built a career shaped by national conceptions of race, gender, and their sexualization. Like Rita Hayworth, Moreno embodies the changing view of Latinas, and particularly the Puerto Rican Latina, in the U.S. imagination. Unlike her predecessors, however, Moreno has been able to gain professional recognition and remain employed while critiquing the conceptions of Latina-ness in Hollywood and beyond. A look at one of her early television appearances both accesses the historical base from which she emerged and suggests the agency she has exercised and continues to employ as a Latina.

A bass line thumps and Rita Moreno snaps her fingers. Two Muppet characters appear against a black background, seemingly providing the musical accompaniment for Moreno's cool snaps: humanoid Muppet Floyd plays bass guitar while monsterlike Animal drums in the background.[1] Moreno plays a lounge singer to perfection. Her wavy hair is coiffed about her bare shoulders, accentuating the cut of her red halter dress. As she sings "Fever," the song popularized by Peggy Lee, she is the epitome of coolness—until her performance is abruptly disturbed by Animal's improvised and overexcited drum solo. When she can stand it no longer, Moreno calmly walks upstage to Animal's drum kit and warns him—firmly and in Spanish—to stop interrupting her singing. Rita's warning, combined with a few stern glances, manages to delay Animal's outbursts until Animal's passion overwhelms him and he returns to wildly banging the drums. As a consummate professional, Rita finishes the song, but she punctuates it by smashing Animal's head between a pair of cymbals. Beaten, Animal responds: "That my kind of woman!"[2]

Rita Moreno's performance with Animal was the closing number of her guest appearance on the then-nascent primetime variety program *The Muppet Show* (1976). Still in its first season, *The Muppet Show* was establishing its tone and developing its characters. Moreno was an inspired choice as an early guest

Figure 16. In the first season of *The Muppet Show* (1976), Rita Moreno's guest appearance set the tone for Animal's "kind of woman." The pairings of Moreno and Animal largely bookend her appearance on the show.

performer because her range of talents—from comedic timing to dance—were fully utilized by the program's variety show format. She appears spontaneous despite the untold demands of rehearsal hours for the puppeteers, her animated gestures match the tone of the show, and she seems completely willing to lampoon herself. Watching the show, it is no surprise that the episode won Moreno an Emmy in 1977.

What can such a moment tell us about the trajectory of the Hollywood Latina and Moreno's role in this mythology? In other words, what kind of woman is Animal's kind of woman—and as a Hollywood Latina, why does Moreno fit the bill? By the time Rita Moreno debuted on the Hollywood screen, the racialized and sexualized myth of the Hollywood Latina was entrenched in the national imaginary and overtly informed the early roles available to her. As a result, Moreno played a string of temporary and often ill-fated lust interests for white leading men in the 1950s and 1960s, professional experiences that seemingly made her an outspoken critic of Hollywood representation. More explicitly than the other women in this project, Moreno's variegated career was distinctly marked by a political professional agency—a trajectory that correlates with larger U.S. social and cultural struggles of Latinos/as in terms of racial and gender equality. Moreno's vocal dissent about being a Latina performer was often aired in press interviews; her career can be read as a continual reworking of these expectations, even when she had little choice but to take roles within these racialized and sexualized traditions. Expanding on the efforts of the Hollywood Latinas before her, Moreno transformed temporary, sexualized roles into a formidable body of work.

Rita Moreno is a transitional figure in the myth and power of the Hollywood Latina. Despite the mainstream success of women like Dolores Del Rio, Carmen Miranda, and Rita Hayworth, none of them were able to change the range or representation of Latina performers. Nearly twenty-five years after Del Rio's debut, Moreno was met with the same, non-star-making roles of wench, native, and peasant (Beltrán 2004). Although Moreno never gained the leading lady status of Hayworth (or, in later years, Jennifer Lopez), she is the only Hollywood Latina nominated for any mainstream award of achievement and remains one of the most critically acclaimed performers in Hollywood: she has won an Academy Award, a Tony Award, two Emmys, and a Grammy.[3] Moreno's hard-won professional and political pursuits mark a progressive turn that enabled subsequent Hollywood Latinas like Jennifer Lopez to forge multimedia careers and mainstream stardom as Latinas. Without the cultural and political work of Rita Moreno, the apolitical tenor required of Lopez for a mainstream career would not have been possible. Moreno's supporting-role stardom—built from the longevity, diversity of roles, and continued critical acclaim of her career— makes her a pivotal figure in the myth of the Hollywood Latina.

While Moreno's honors have moved the Hollywood Latina into the critical spotlight, she has been unable to shake the importance of dance and racialized sexuality as key components of Latina embodiment. It is striking that three out of four of Moreno's award-winning screen roles have relied on dance as a signifier of her racialized or sexualized characterizations, while the fourth award-winning role omits dance but explicitly characterizes Moreno as a prostitute. Moreno's critical acclaim began in 1962 when she won an Academy Award for her role as Anita, the sassy, sexy Puerto Rican girlfriend of the Sharks' gang leader Bernardo (George Chakiris) in the film version of *West Side Story* (1961). Thirteen years later, she won a Tony for *The Ritz*, a 1975 stage production adapted for the screen one year later. In the play and the film, Moreno is cast as Googie Gomez, a "caricature of the Latin bombshell" who sings and dances in a gay bathhouse (Universal Studios Publicity Department 1981). In 1977 and 1978, Moreno was recognized with two Emmys for her guest appearances on *The Muppet Show* and *The Rockford Files*. In *The Muppet Show*, Moreno played a series of sassy and sensuous characters on a family-friendly prime-time variety program, while on *The Rockford Files* Moreno was cast as a plucky prostitute.

In this chapter I explore Moreno's award-winning roles within the context of the Hollywood Latina. I trace the role of dance and racialized sexuality in each of these roles to show how the mythological trajectory of the Hollywood Latina has ultimately reproduced itself as urban, multicultural, and multiplatform. In spite of this mythological reformation, Moreno's willingness to critique the media industry, coupled with the historical moment of her critical acclaim, powerfully distinguishes her from many other Hollywood Latinas.[4] Using television, Moreno highlighted her multifaceted talents and maximized her exposure beyond the limitations of Hollywood film, a process that set the multimedia stage for performers like Jennifer Lopez to follow. After a brief description of Moreno's early years in Hollywood, I provide an overview of the racial and cultural tensions surrounding Puerto Rican identity in New York to contextualize the national and cultural climate within which Moreno began her film career as well as the racialization of some of her early roles. I build on this theme to show how Moreno's body—and the Puerto Rican female bodies that mark the latter half of the twentieth-century Hollywood Latina—came to signify racialized sexuality through urban space, dance, and an affiliation with blackness. Using the film conventions of casting, characterization, costuming, publicity, and choreography, I analyze Moreno's early characters—especially Anita in *West Side Story*—to show how Moreno's in-betweenness was more closely aligned with blackness and urban space. I conclude with an analysis of the sonic and visual cues that illustrate the many ways Moreno negotiated the racialization and sexualization of her Tony-winning role in *The Ritz* and Emmy-winning roles in *The Rockford Files* and *The Muppet Show*.

Despite Moreno's outspokenness about her visual and aural representation, as well as her singularity as a recognizable Latina performer in cinema during the 1960s and 1970s, little academic attention has been paid to the whole of her career.[5] Confronting the limitations of Latina representation, Moreno chose to move her career laterally and opted for a wide array of roles across a spectrum of venues so as to carve out a living while challenging the status quo. As a result, Moreno's career has the most historical breadth of the women in this study; sixty years after she began her media career, Moreno remains a strong and visible performer. Yet for all of Moreno's maneuvering, her oeuvre follows the ordained trajectory of Latina representation, especially where critical recognition of her screen performances is concerned.

She was born Rosa Dolores Alverio in Puerto Rico and came to New York as a young child with her mother, a sweatshop seamstress. Eventually Rosa's mother married and took the last name Moreno (Miller 2000; Twentieth Century-Fox ca. 1956, 3–4).[6] Rosa's interest in dance was nurtured with formal training from the age of five, and she was soon a professional entertainer (Universal Studios Publicity Department 1981). Early studio biographies often focused on the formation of Moreno's career and especially favored the ways in which it followed a familiar Hollywood Latina legacy in the United States. Her early dance training was guided by the Spanish dancer Paco Cansino, a former member of the Dancing Cansinos and Rita Hayworth's uncle (Miller 2000; Twentieth Century-Fox ca. 1956, 3–4). By the age of ten, Rosa worked as a child actor for radio programming and as a dancer at parties, at large functions, and on early television. According to publicity biographies, one of her early routines included a Carmen Miranda impersonation (Twentieth Century-Fox ca. 1956, 3–4). The mention of Hayworth and Miranda in Moreno's studio biographies and general publicity highlights how her legacy was crafted in line with her predecessors, but it also attests to the intimate community from which Latino/a performers emerged.

The success of Dolores Del Rio, Carmen Miranda, and Rita Hayworth no doubt impacted the studios' desire for a performer like Moreno, but the early part of her career attests to the limitations of their expectations for a nonwhite female performer. After a childhood of performing on New York stages, on radio programs, and in television, Moreno signed a seven-year contract with MGM in 1949 when she was eighteen years old. At MGM, Rosa Dolores Alverio Moreno was encouraged to change her name to Rita Moreno; it is under this name that she was cast in a series of roles in the tradition of the spitfire and Other woman (Beltrán 2004, 149).[7]

"As We See Her": Mobilizing/Racializing the Puerto Rican Body

During the 1950s, after signing with MGM and later Twentieth Century-Fox, Moreno was cast in a long line of racialized and sexualized roles in which she played a hot-tempered Latina or a Native American—the generic brown temptress who served mainly as the temporary love interest to a white leading man. She quickly filled the hot-tempered Latina role in films such as *Pagan Love Song* (1950) and *The Toast of New Orleans* (1950). With films like *Fabulous Señorita* (1952) and *Latin Lovers* (1953), Moreno's stock-in-trade became losing the film's leading man to a white actress or serving as the film's jealousy-inducing figure (Twentieth Century-Fox ca. 1956, 3–4, 6–7).

Although Moreno admits that she was not always "conscious of casting stereotypes in those days," she quickly became an outspoken critic of Latino/a representation in Hollywood, and some of these critiques were surprisingly included in press coverage ("Rita Moreno" ca. 1955; Twentieth Century-Fox ca. 1956). Moreno's political consciousness seemingly emerged from a growing awareness of her early screen worth in terms of costuming. Commenting on one of what she called her "barefoot parts," Moreno remarks: "Once I was an Indian maiden in *Jivaro* [1954] with Rhonda Fleming. There she was, in frills, all pink and blonde and big-breasted. Right next to her, I had an ugly wig on, brown-shoe-polish make-up and wore a tattered leopard skin. I felt ugly and stupid, and every time I looked down at my bare feet, I grew more ashamed" (*TV Guide* 1983, 27). Another interview finds Moreno musing that "teeth mashing, hoop earrings and off-the-shoulder blouses were [her] trademark"—what she calls the "Rita Moreno Kit"—generic signifiers of tempestuous looseness that easily transferred from one brown female body type to another (Bell 1976). Hoop earrings, off-the-shoulder blouses, and bad attitudes bring to mind a variety of ambiguously ethnicized female bodies—from Gypsies to Spanish señoritas to Mexican or Italian peasants. For Moreno, these signifiers were accompanied by "teeth mashing," an action specific to the kind of performance required to denote an animalistic temperament such as excessive jealousy or fervid sexuality. As Mary C. Beltrán (2009) has noted, such roles also often required Moreno to speak in broken English, an aural cue that was seemingly intended to enhance the vulgarity of her costumed appearance.

Moreno's first big break from hoop earrings and animal skins came in the role of Zelda Zanders in the film *Singin' in the Rain* (1952), a nonethnicized role that notably was facilitated by a change in hair color. Crediting Gene Kelly with casting her in the role, Moreno stated: "[Kelly] put me in a red wig. It never occurred to him to say, 'No, she's too Latina, her name is Latina.' He just thought I'd be fine for it" (Miller 2000). Although Kelly showed great foresight by casting Moreno in a nonethnic role, her actual appearance was deemed too ethnic without the temporary modification of her hair—an adjustment akin to those that Hayworth had made before her and Lopez would after.[8] Unfortunately, Moreno was pushed "right back to the ethnic stuff" after her few scenes as Zanders, and MGM dropped her contract immediately after the film (Miller 2000). Moreno would go on to do a lot more "ethnic stuff" as a freelance actress and, soon after, as a signed Twentieth Century-Fox player.

As a brown-complexioned Puerto Rican woman emerging in the 1950s, Moreno often explicitly signified sexuality and blackness on the Hollywood screen, and her career trajectory embodies the social, cultural, and political climate of racial formation and Latino/a identity in New York and on the U.S. East Coast. With the exception of Carmen Miranda in the early part of her career, the Hollywood Latinas who came before Moreno were framed by the western United States and affiliated with whiteness. Mexican actress Dolores Del Rio was framed as Spanish and debuted in Los Angeles, while Rita Hayworth, although born in New York, began her racially mobile star trajectory in a nightclub along the western United States–Mexico border. Unlike Del Rio's, Moreno's surname and working-class background prevented an inflated cultural cachet or symbolic whitening through an affiliation with Spain; her look, including black curly hair and an "olive complexion," similarly limited her access to the mainstream, nonethnic roles that Hayworth eventually enjoyed (Beltrán 2004, 128).

The specific tonality of Moreno's in-betweenness was shaped by her cultural and regional origins as a Puerto Rican woman from New York, which placed her at the crux of nonwhiteness (specifically blackness) and the city in the

Figure 17. As Zelda Zanders in *Singin' in the Rain* (1952), Rita Moreno proves that hair and costuming make all the difference for the Hollywood Latina. Donning a red wig for this brief role, Moreno challenges the idea that the darkness of her skin was the sole constraint of her casting.

1950s. The decade marked the beginning of massive suburbanization through which the population was reorganized and redistributed as white residents moved from urban centers like Harlem to predominantly white (segregated) housing developments such as Levittown in New York. In 1954, hard-won civil rights initiatives such as the Supreme Court decision in *Brown v. Board of Education* shifted this social and political restructuring to a national level, as white communities fled to exclusive suburban developments so as to resist federal initiatives for racial integration of schools and housing. In the cultural climate of the late 1950s and 1960s, mainstream (white) media narratives shifted their focus from the city to the suburb: television was increasingly filled with suburban and nonethnic white characters, while the *New York Times* decreed urban spaces to be synonymous with overcrowding, nonwhite or ethnic bodies, and criminal behavior (Robinson 1955; Stoever-Ackerman 2010).

During this period, national discourses on labor, civil rights, and racial identification conflated black and Puerto Rican cultural identities within the U.S. national imagery. In New York, Puerto Rican identity was effectively "African Americanized" in the 1950s as a result of the shared oppression of these groups. As white workers (and other European immigrants) became upwardly mobile after World War II, African Americans and Puerto Ricans became and remained the cheapest sources of labor in the New York manufacturing industry. These jobs were increasingly identified as racialized positions, making already low-paying jobs even less lucrative for nonwhite workers while reinforcing a racialized hierarchy supported and reified by *New York Times* articles about Puerto Rican delinquency (Grosfoguel and Georas 2001, 106). Like African Americans, Puerto Ricans were often denied their full rights as citizens, a denial linked to long-standing racial and colonial oppression by the United States that stemmed from slavery or colonization and was exacerbated by the challenges of urban living (Grosfoguel and Georas 2001, 105–107).[9]

A second wave of migration from Puerto Rico further destabilized U.S. notions of race. As Puerto Rican families settled on the East Coast, the complex racial and cultural heritage of Puerto Rican families troubled the traditional lines of U.S. racial segregation by disturbing what U.S. imagery had defined as one racial category or the other (Stoever-Ackerman 2009). Because one family unit could easily include both light- and dark-complexioned members, the cultural and governmental inability to easily categorize Puerto Ricans as black or white eventually meant that they were racialized as a distinct group—first in New York and eventually throughout the United States (Grosfoguel and Georas 2001, 105–107). This racialization was directly related to the capitalist and imperialist goals of the United States. To fill post–World War II demands for labor, the U.S. government encouraged Puerto Ricans to migrate to New York through incentives like reduced airfares, even as it simultaneously used the island as a "symbolic showcase" for capitalism (Grosfoguel and Georas 2001, 107–108). To quickly and artificially promote the island as an economic haven, the U.S. government relocated the island's poorest populations by sending them to New York; many of the relocated people were mulatto, highlighting the socioeconomic racial hierarchy already operating on the island. In exchange for cheap labor, the United States purportedly refurbished Puerto Rico as an ideal "bootstrap" community. On the mainland, however, the government did little to assist the relocated population to settle in New York; because many Puerto Ricans ended up in high-poverty urban ghettos, the United States had effectively racialized and ghettoized a new low-wage labor force (Grosfoguel and Georas 2001, 107–108).

The resulting racial and spatial hysteria served as a backdrop and framed the first decade of Moreno's screen career, making the contours of her in-betweenness all the more significant in terms of whiteness and blackness. As Puerto Rican communities expanded in New York, commonly held assumptions about race and the traditions of the black/white binary were challenged anew. The conflation of urban space and the so-called Puerto Rican racial problem in popular culture took root in the 1950s with films like *Blackboard Jungle* (1955) and the stage production of *West Side Story* (1957), both of which emphasized and popularized the connection between juvenile delinquency and Puerto Ricans in New York (Stoever-Ackerman 2009).[10] As the nation reorganized its racialized hierarchy, Moreno's best-known production, the film adaptation of *West Side Story*, contributed to the classifying and racializing of "Puerto Ricans" as a discrete minority for a large percentage of the United States (Grosfoguel and Georas 2001).

When Moreno was signed with Twentieth Century-Fox in 1955, her roles increasingly signified the complexity of this racialization and its impact on her in-betweenness. In *Untamed* (1955), Moreno was cast as a "biracial African girl" who served as the temporary companion of one of the white male leads until the white female character became available (Beltrán 2009, 77). Even when Moreno was cast as a Latina or Native American, her characters shared the fate of the tragic mulatto by dying—in films such as *Seven Cities of Gold* (1955) and *The Vagabond King* (1956) (Bogle 2001).

Around the time of *Untamed*, the multiplicity of Moreno's image—whether racialized or sexualized—was underscored by the use of "cheesecake" publicity and its emphasis on her moving body. As Beltrán has observed, Moreno was a regular "excessive and inviting" subject of this kind of photography. One spread in particular highlights this multiplicity—even when race seemed to be deemphasized (Beltrán 2009, 85). In the publicity piece "What Does Hollywood See In Rita?" the monthly digest magazine *Pageant* uses a series of photographs to spotlight Moreno's role in the upcoming film *Untamed*. After crediting three men with "her belated [Hollywood] discovery," the short article assigns "photographer David Sutton to reconstruct the event" and show "Rita as they saw her" (Sutton ca. 1955). In the spread, each man credited with shaping Moreno's career is shown in a contemplative, authoritative stance: cameraman Frank Powolny points the camera at the audience in a fairly phallic way, director Henry King holds his hands in directorial gesture, and Fox's head costume designer Charles Le Maire stands with arms wrapped about his body, chin resting in his right hand. Moreno's corresponding poses seemingly respond to each gaze and are titled accordingly: "As the photographer sees her," "As the director sees her," and "As the designer sees her." The photographer's image of Moreno is presented as "bathed in warm light, with bare feet drawn up seductively and her face composed in the traditional glamour fashion: lips half-parted and moistened, eyes wide open and beckoning." The director's image shows Moreno "listening attentively and registering the emotions he calls for," while she becomes "the perfect vehicle for one of

[Le Maire's] creations, carrying furs and diamonds with the aplomb of a duchess, and considerably more sex appeal." The artificial nature of these poses is supposedly highlighted by an accompanying photo of Moreno "as she sees herself," brushing her teeth while "mug[ging] and mim[ing]" in the mirror.

It is the series of images that seemingly respond to the general public's gaze that is the most telling in terms of the myth of the Hollywood Latina. Following the heading "As you see her" is a series of seven images of Moreno dancing. The left panel features a full-page image of a barefoot Moreno completing a turn, legs crossed and skirt twirling about her as she smiles to the camera with her arms thrown playfully above her head. On the right page appears a series of six smaller images, each showing Moreno midturn. Although she wears a different dress in this series than in the full page image, the cut is the same: the fitted bodice features thin straps at shoulders and seems to highlight the fullness of the skirt below her waist. Moreno wears high heels in each of these pictures, and she interacts with her dress in different ways while highlighting her legs in each image. As we will see with *West Side Story*, the fullness of Moreno's skirt and the power of her turns reveal her legs and thighs in ways that underscore the sexual connotation of the dance movement. By the fourth of the six images in the series, Moreno has seemingly increased the speed of her turns; she is holding a fold of skirt in each hand, and the fabric has risen so high that it now reveals her fitted bloomers beneath. Because these images are black and white, the contrast of Moreno's light-colored dress and light tan skin makes the darkness of her hair and bloomers seem more revealing because they visually pop. The caption seemingly explains the emphasis on Moreno's poses, stating: "Puerto Rican born Rita lisped her way into show business by giving recitations at the age of four. By five, however, she had discovered her true medium: dancing. A prize student of the famous Paco Cansino, she began appearing in Greenwich Village night clubs. . . . When TV was just getting started, R donned purple lipstick and brown eye-shadow, then the standard make-up for the new medium, and made a number of appearances as a dancer." Although the write-up is built around Moreno's emerging film career at Twentieth Century-Fox, its emphasis on her dancing and her early work in television suggests that these are some of the many ways that "we" would continue to "see" her.

"A GIRL LIKE THAT": THE HOLLYWOOD LATINA MOVES TO THE CITY

A year after *Untamed*, Moreno was cast as Tuptim in *The King and I* (1956)—a professional turning point that enhanced the "all-round" nonwhiteness of her in-betweenness. Cast as a Burmese princess, Moreno was a studio replacement for the black actress Dorothy Dandridge (*AFI Catalog*, s.v. *The King and I*). In one of the first nonpeasant roles of her career, Moreno was aware that the role called for "another dark-skinned, dusky-skinned beauty"; as the one contract performer at Fox who fit the bill, she was cast (Twentieth Century-Fox ca. 1956, 2; Miller 2000). Operating as what she has called the "equal opportunity, all round ethnic person," Moreno, with her casting in *The King and I*, may have in fact helped mediate the film's Thailand setting and themes of slavery and freedom (Miller 2000).

In the play, set in nineteenth-century Siam (now Thailand), a young widowed English teacher named Anna (Deborah Kerr) is hired to teach English to the children of the king (Yul Brynner). Anna is displeased to find that she does not have her own residence (as agreed upon her hiring) and must live in the palace with her son and the king's many wives. When Anna attempts to address the king about her housing, she witnesses the presentation of a gift to the king from the prince of Burma—a new wife, the noble Tuptim (Moreno). Charmed by the royal children, Anna reluctantly agrees to "enlighten" them and the king's wives. While Anna and the king repeatedly butt heads, she remains outspoken: she continues to petition for a house and teaches the children that their custom of slavery is wrong. In time, Anna realizes that Tuptim pines for her lover, Lun Tha (Carlos Rivas), the man who delivered her to the palace. When Anna plans a lavish banquet on behalf of the king's efforts to impress the British ambassador and ward off British imperialism, Tuptim entertains the guests by narrating a performance of "The Small House of Uncle Thomas," an adaptation of *Uncle Tom's Cabin* by Harriet Beecher Stowe. After the banquet, Anna and the king share an intimate dance until they are interrupted with news that Tuptim has been caught attempting to escape with her lover. Anna's pleas weaken the king's resolve to punish Tuptim with a whipping; incapable of beating Tuptim, the king loses face in front of his men, while Anna decides to leave for England. When the king falls ill, Anna delays her departure and learns that the king respects her and is grateful for her help. At his death, the king leaves his kingdom to his eldest son—Anna's reluctant but apt pupil—who abolishes slavery in the kingdom (*AFI Catalog*, s.v. *The King and I*).

Given the close connection between African Americans and Puerto Ricans in New York at the time, the racialization of Moreno's body filled the same kind of ethnic/racial function as a black body would have—but in the midst of the civil rights era, she was crucially not black. Unlike *Singin' in the Rain*, in which Moreno was cast as a generic musical performer, in *The King and I* the racial connotations of her body are in full operation, despite the fact that she was not playing a Latina in the film. The replacement of Dandridge with Moreno in the role highlights the in-betweenness of Moreno's Latina body and suggests

Figures 18 and 19. In this publicity spread for *Untamed* (1955), Rita Moreno is shown dancing, the supposed way the general public knows and views her body. Courtesy of the Cinematic Arts Library, University of Southern California.

Figures 18 and 19. (*Continued*)

that her difference may have helped mediate the film's slavery themes without becoming too explicit for a country still adjusting to the Civil Rights Act. With Dandridge in the role, the racialized hierarchy of the film would have made such associations too evident during a sensitive historical moment. The film's allusion to *Uncle Tom's Cabin* and the threatened whipping of Tuptim's body as punishment for running away might have been ill received if Dandridge had depicted Tuptim. The casting of Moreno, an "equal opportunity, all round ethnic person," may have diffused the racial tensions seemingly considered inappropriate within such a lavish and expensive musical production. In this case, it seems the racist practices of Hollywood made the cross-racial casting of Tuptim an attempt at preemptive damage control.

Only a few years later, the musical film version of *West Side Story* put racial tensions center stage, and Moreno's brightest cinematic moment marked her as the female embodiment of Puerto Rican juvenile delinquency in Hollywood. The racial and class tensions that underpinned the United States' social/ spatial/racial reformation were the centerpiece of the Broadway production; debuting in 1957, *West Side Story* presented audiences with a negotiated idea of interethnic romance the same year that schools were being racially integrated in Little Rock, Arkansas. As an updated version of *Romeo and Juliet*, *West Side Story* was originally called *East Side Story* and focused on the more "ethnic" tale of star-crossed Christian and Jewish lovers (Briggs 2002, 173). The plot was quickly abandoned because it mimicked the well-known 1920s Broadway production *Abie's Irish Rose* and because the tension between Christians and Jews was no longer the crucial cultural concern that it once was (Negrón-Muntaner 2000, 89–90).

Reconceived as a story of intergang conflict, *West Side Story* was inspired by sensationalist press about Latino gang activity on the West Coast and immediately transposed onto the so-called Puerto Rican problem of New York (Briggs 2002, 167; Negrón-Muntaner 2000, 89; Stoever-Ackerman 2010, 79). The play focused on the racial tensions of an already polarized urban space, and its narrative was presented as a struggle between white immigrant "Americans" and Puerto Rican "foreigners" (Negrón-Muntaner 2000). The production's racial divide was embodied by the Jets and the Sharks, who sang and danced about race, delinquency, and urban space as though it were a violent, juvenile dilemma.

Although the Puerto Rican/Shark female character Anita had much to do with the production's popularity on stage and in film, an extensive exploration of Moreno's role in the film and its impact on her career has yet to be completed beyond scholarship on the film/production itself (Beltrán 2004; Negrón-Muntaner 2000; Sandoval-Sánchez 1999). Broadway legend Chita Rivera was originally cast in the role and crafted Anita into one of the most complex characters of the production. Sexy and self-assured, Rivera's Anita left an indelible mark on Broadway and Rivera's legacy; while Rivera's extensive and esteemed career is beyond the scope of this project, like Moreno's career it remains in need of greater scholarly attention (Negrón-Muntaner 2000, 93; Román 2002, 7).[11] Because most discussions of Moreno's career concentrate on *West Side Story*, I will not belabor the usual points about the film.[12] Instead I use the film to frame Moreno's characterization and tour-de-force performance as an important facet of her critical and popular appeal and as an anchor point in the myth of the Hollywood Latina.

West Side Story tells the tale of Maria (Natalie Wood) and Tony (Richard Beymer), young lovers from different sides of the color line and gang line, who live in the then working-class upper West Side of Manhattan. Tony and Maria fall in love after meeting at a dance, despite the fact that he is a former member of the Polish American gang the Jets and she is the younger sister of Bernardo (George Chakiris) from the rival Puerto Rican gang the Sharks. When Tony and Maria are caught embracing, their respective cliques use the opportunity to settle a neighborhood turf war through a rumble. Despite Tony's attempts to broker a fair fight, Bernardo and the Jets' leader Riff (Russ Tamblyn) prepare their men with additional artillery—just in case. The night of the fight, Maria asks Tony to stop the rumble because any battle will make her relationship with Tony impossible. While attempting to negotiate peace, Tony inadvertently escalates the fight, and Riff and Bernardo challenge each other with knives. Bernardo unexpectedly kills Riff, prompting a shocked and angered Tony to stab Bernardo and flee. Despite Tony's confession of murder to Maria, she loves him and they plan to escape the city. As Tony dodges the police and a vengeful Shark named Chino to prepare their departure, Anita (Moreno), Maria's fiery friend and Bernardo's mourning girlfriend, discovers Maria's plan. Although angry, Anita agrees to help the couple rendezvous by delivering information in Jets territory on Maria's behalf. As Anita approaches the rendezvous point, the Jets harass and implicitly rape Anita until the shop owner discovers them. Shaken and furious, Anita lies and says that Chino killed Maria. Upon hearing the news, Tony seeks out Chino. When Tony sees Maria near the playground, the two approach each other and Chino shoots and kills Tony. As the Jets and Sharks congregate around Tony's dead body to begin their battle anew, Maria grabs Chino's gun and accuses both gangs of murdering the three young men. Maria mourns for Tony as his body is carried away by both Jets and Sharks in a solemn, if temporary, moment of truce (*AFI Catalog*, s.v. *West Side Story*).

As one of the rare celluloid Latinas with gravitas, Moreno's Anita was also an embodiment of the racialized and gendered depiction of New York. While the Jets and Sharks embodied the ostensible American–Puerto Rican tensions at the center of the film, Rita Moreno's Anita anchored the Puerto Rican female image within Hollywood and Puerto Rican women within the U.S. imaginary. The mass distribution of the film and its popularity among audiences and critics pushed Moreno's Anita into the national consciousness. Legitimized and canonized by the production's successful box office, critical acclaim, and multiple Academy Awards, Anita's and the Sharks' images prospered despite Nuyorican and Latino/a ambivalence about their communities' depiction on the stage and in film.

Although not the lead female, Anita embodies the limits of the film's ethnic borders and serves as the film's primary agent for tolerance, and cross-cultural and cross-generational exchange. In one scene, her character cheekily critiques Puerto Rico while extolling the virtues of the United States in the rooftop number "America." By allowing Maria and Tony to secretly meet in the dressmaking shop where she and Maria work, Anita enables one of the young couple's first interactions. Unlike Bernardo or the Sharks, Anita is not as quick to judge the Jets, and later agrees to help Maria rendezvous with Tony even though he has murdered Bernardo. Anita, however, cannot and does not cross the racial line by falling in love with a white character, thus highlighting the limits of her transgressive potential. Casting plays a large role in these limitations: Rita Moreno is the only Puerto Rican in the cast, whereas Maria is played by mainstream star Natalie Wood (born Natasha Nikolaevna Zakharenko).

The limits of Anita's trangressive potential are most clearly demarcated by dance and the way her body is racialized and sexualized as a colonial subject in the film. While dance is a key component of the musical, the question of who dances and how illustrates the relationship between this bodily performance and the film's depiction of racialized sexuality. Like the other delinquent Jets' and Sharks' women, Anita clearly knows how to move; her bravado as a dancer signifies her sexual experience, while the kinds of movements she performs distinguish her from the white American bodies depicted in the film. We are introduced to Anita's prowess in the "Mambo" dance sequence, but she continues to mesmerize us with her movements in "America."

In addition to Anita's featured solos in "Mambo" and "America," her strength as a character, dancer, and sexual figure is highlighted by the ways in which her characterization contrasts with Maria's choreography. While most members of the Sharks and Jets dance during the "Mambo" scene at the gym, we do not see Maria dance until she meets Tony, and this inaugural union is chaste—a sweet duet of bodies that barely touch. As a symbolic sexual awakening, however, the impact of this dance is evident in the musical number that follows the next diegetic day. In "I Feel Pretty," a lovesick Maria is believed to be "in an advanced state of shock" because of how wildly she moves and sings. Yet Maria's dance moves in "I Feel Pretty" never match the vitality or brashness of Anita's dances. Despite their shared lineage and corroboration at the end of the film, neither woman fully inhabits the other's world: Maria is noticeably absent from the critique of "America," while Anita does not participate in "I Feel Pretty."

Wood's Maria and Moreno's Anita operate according to very different mythologies. As others have noted, the casting of Natalie Wood in the film role of Maria exacerbates the separation of the two women on an ideological and symbolic level (Negrón-Muntaner 2000; Sandoval-Sánchez 1999). While Anita and Maria are West Side Story's most sympathetic nonwhite characters, the fact that they are nonwhite women follows the colonial frame of the Hollywood Latina that posits nonwhite women as available and nonwhite men as threats. Fulfilling this legacy of in-betweenness, Anita and Maria offer a cultural and social median between the white characters and the Puerto Rican men in the film. But as Sandoval-Sánchez (1999) and Negrón-Muntaner (2000) have observed, casting an ethnically white actress like Wood in the role of Maria highlights the limits of representing nonwhite women as virtuous figures and emphatically suggests that Anita's sexuality is a seemingly inherent aspect of her Puerto Rican-ness.

As Anita, Rita Moreno is the film's authentic representational Latina; a sassy and sensual character, it is she who ultimately falls victim to the traditions of the hypersexualized mythology of the Hollywood Latina. The film's costuming and choreography reinforced popular expectations about Latina sexuality by signifying race, class, and gender through the performers' moving bodies as choreographed by Jerome Robbins and framed by Robert Wise (Negrón-Muntaner 2000, 94). The costuming of the "Mambo" sequence exemplifies this racialized and sexualized characterization. Negrón-Muntaner (2000) has observed that the film's production designer worked hard to artificially distinguish the racialized Sharks from the Jets through the use of makeup, hair color, and costuming. By mobilizing these details, the film effectively constructs and reiterates the racial difference between a "white" gang and a "Puerto Rican" gang, highlighting how tenuous such distinctions are and how many layers of filmic conventions were required to capture ideological assumptions about the Latino/a body (Negrón-Muntaner 2000, 94). This difference is most evident in the fact that Anita's sexual agency does not go unpunished: her final scene in the film is an implicit rape scene with the Jets, an extreme and violent example of the screen Latina's temporary status and inability to cross the racial line.[13] The intensity of this scene, with the experience of racism still too real, left Moreno in tears during the shooting of the scene (Gross 2001).

The stylized precision of West Side Story's production design is so thoroughly detailed that the colors of Anita's costumes take on additional symbolic weight in terms of sexuality and racialization when contrasted with the costume colors of Maria and the Jet girls. In the "Mambo" scene, Moreno is costumed in a purple dress with capped sleeves, a fitted bodice, and a billowing knee-length ruffled skirt; her compatriots wear dresses of reds and purples with similarly excessive amounts of fabric in the skirt, which swing and rise easily. In contrast, the Jet women wear orange or sky-blue dresses with skirts that appear more fitted; their spins and kicks still cause a swirl of skirt, but the dresses' range of movement is more contained and the twirling hemlines fall lower on the body, usually at thigh level. In contrast, the layers of Anita's skirt often rise to her hip or waist, enhancing her energetic movements: each leg kick or sweep becomes a grand and dramatic gesture, and her legs are unhindered by the restrictions of a straight skirt. The cut and color of her costumes—purples, blues, blacks, and reds in the "Mambo" scene and beyond—suggest a deeper sensuality than any of the other women in the film (Negrón-Muntaner 2004).

Figure 20. In *West Side Story* (1961), the cut of Moreno's dress (*left*) has more swing and shows more of her legs than does the costuming of the Jet women and echoes the style of dress featured in the publicity for *Untamed* (figs. 18 and 19).

This intersection of costuming, characterization, and movement becomes a key means of representing the characters' sexual identities. As the dance challenges become increasingly energetic and competitive, the movement of the women follows the cut of their dresses: straight lines and short gestures for the Jet women, supple, sweeping movements from Anita and the Shark women, discreet movements for Maria in her virginal white dress, and failed but imitative male choreography for Anybodys in androgynous pants and tank top. Such distinct movements were by design; part of Jerome Robbins's brilliance was his character-based choreography, akin to Jack Cole's individualized choreography for the personas of the women he worked with like Rita Hayworth and Marilyn Monroe (Miller 2000).

Just as the dance sequences in *West Side Story* tell us much about the racialization and sexualization of specific characters like chaste Maria and saucy Anita, the nondance musical number "A Boy Like That" illuminates how the Hollywood Latina has also been aurally imagined and reproduced. "A Boy Like That" follows Bernardo's murder in the film. When Anita seeks consolation from Maria, she discovers that Maria has just slept with Tony. "A Boy Like That" expresses Anita's anger and sense of betrayal, and eventually builds into a powerful duet ("I Have a Love") between the women. As a backdrop, the setting and bodies of the scene are visually coded as Latino/a: the apartment matches the purples, blues, and reds associated with the Sharks in the film (as in "Mambo"), while the two Latinas in the frame—one real and one diegetic—are colored Puerto Rican through the use of brown makeup. These stylized signifiers set the tone for Moreno's aural representation in the scene. As the only Puerto Rican in the film cast, Rita Moreno gave a performance that became a touchstone of aural authenticity for non–Puerto Rican actors such as George Chakiris (Bernardo). In one interview, Chakiris notes that he and the Shark actors used Moreno as their sonic "guide" (Gross 2001).[14]

Both Natalie Wood and Rita Moreno lip-synch to prerecorded tracks, but unlike Wood, Moreno performs her other songs herself; "A Boy Like That" is

Moreno's only song that does not feature her real singing voice. While the dubbed vocal performance compensates for Moreno's higher vocal range, it undercuts the ferocity of her physical performance. As Moreno's facial expressions and posturing exhibit an angry and forceful delivery, singer Betty Wand's vocal interpretation of the lyrics overly amplifies the supposed sound of a Latina body in lieu of the emotional urgency of the song. Moreno's assertive body language is thus mismatched with the generic quality of Wand's artificial accent, a kind of aural brown-face that flattens the scene's intensity.

In a 2001 interview, Moreno expressed her disapproval of the vocals in "A Boy Like That," claiming that Wand's lack of acting skills resulted in a restricted interpretation that did not match the physical intensity of the scene. She explains: "[Wand] just couldn't get it the way I wanted it . . . to sound. . . . It should have almost been a growl . . . you know, barely sung. And she ended up sounding . . . almost like a cliché Mexican" (Gross 2001). Despite Moreno's coaching, Wand could only articulate the song's Latina-ness, a sonic interpretation that solely relied on a stereotypical accent to tell its story. This racialized vocal performance is incompatible with the emotional depth Moreno produces onscreen because it was only—always, and already—aurally Other.[15]

"Easy on the Eyes, but Hard on the Ears": Moreno's Vocal Body of Work

While Moreno's visibility was greatly improved as a result of her role in the film version of *West Side Story*, she was dismayed to find that critical acclaim did not improve the roles she was offered. Ultimately, for Moreno, *West Side Story* led to a seven-year film hiatus because she refused the slew of stereotypical gang-girl roles that followed. Gradually, Moreno's unwillingness to submit to the cinematic status quo resulted in a series of award-winning roles on stage and in television. Because Moreno's attempts to diversify the kinds of roles she played ultimately remained marked by her role as Anita, I both watch and listen to Moreno's subsequent award-winning performances to understand how her role as Anita may have impacted her career trajectory more than a decade later. If, as Stoever-Ackerman argues, the color-line is as aural as it is visual and forms "an interpretive site where racial difference is coded, produced, and policed" (2010, 65), then the sonic layers of Moreno's Puerto Rican performances warrant deeper consideration—especially when paired with the bodily performance of dance as a racialized and sexualized signifier.

If we fast-forward a few years, we can imagine how such an experience may have impacted Moreno's perspective on her own physical and aural representation in Hollywood. One publicity piece suggests that the Tony Award–winning character Googie Gomez, featured in *The Ritz*, was actually conceived by Moreno during the production of *West Side Story*. As the story goes, Moreno reportedly created the outlandish Puerto Rican caricature/alter ego, eventually nicknamed Googie, to entertain herself and friends on set. Moreno's incarnation of an amateur entertainer with an overly enunciated Puerto Rican accent enabled her to laugh at the institutional representations of Hollywood Latinas by lampooning a passionate but talentless type of character (Universal Studios Publicity Department 1981). After Moreno performed a song as Googie at a party, playwright Terrence McNally used the character in his script *The Ritz*, and Moreno was eventually cast in the role she originated. The stage version of the role won her a Tony Award.

In *The Ritz*, the character Googie is a bad actress and a bad dresser, but she is passionate about her craft. Set in a New York bathhouse, the film focuses on Gaetano Proclo (Jack Weston). Just before Proclo's low-stakes mobster father-in-law dies, he orchestrates Proclo's assassination at the hands of his son Carmine Vespucci (Jerry Stiller). Fleeing the Vespuccis, Proclo asks a cabdriver to take him to the last place anybody would look for him. The cabdriver takes Proclo to a gay bathhouse called The Ritz, where he is followed by Vespucci. Hiding out, Proclo encounters a series of gay male "types," including the nice yet desperate Chris (F. Murray Abraham) and a so-called chubby-chaser named Claude (Paul B. Price), who is immediately enamored of Proclo's hefty frame. While Vespucci hires an assassin to kill Proclo, Proclo meets the resident entertainer, Googie Gomez (Moreno). Believing that Proclo is a Broadway producer, Gomez stalks Proclo and foils each assassination attempt. In a madcap finale, Proclo's wife (and daughter of the Vespucci mobster) finds Proclo at the Ritz and rectifies the situation by canceling the assassination and announcing that her family owns both the taxi service and the bathhouse.

While Googie Gomez originated as Moreno's caricature of the Hollywood Latina, *The Ritz*'s setting and her characterization produce a grotesque version of this mythology. The film's urban setting, coupled with the emphasis on gay bathhouse culture, reinforces the racialized sexuality of Gomez as a character. As the only woman (and one of the only visibly racialized figures) in the space, Gomez's body is doubly marginalized in the narrative. Several characters continually suspect that Gomez is a transvestite, and the film presents her exaggerated performance of "Puerto Rican-ness" as suspect and inadequately feminine. But her marginalized position—as bad performer (with little rhythm or voice), Puerto Rican, and "transvestite"—makes her affiliation with the city and queerness a compelling variation of the typical racialized and sexualized characterization depicted by the performing Puerto Rican/Latina female body in Hollywood film.

In 1976, the same year *The Ritz* debuted, Moreno made a guest appearance on the fifth episode of *The Muppet Show*'s first season. In the space of thirty minutes and four sketches, Moreno humorously used multiple facets of her persona to reassert control over her screen voice. Moreno's first sketch is a silent dance number in which she plays a hard drinking, sexy, violent woman who mistreats a human-sized Muppet in an apache-style tango. The remainder of her appearances highlight her vocal performance of English. As "Rita Moreno," we hear no discernible accent in her English; this vocal lack of national or regional affiliation is revealed to be Moreno's true speaking voice in the third sketch, where she appears as "herself" in a staged candid conversation with Kermit the Frog. Her final sketch, the lounge performance of "Fever" described in the opening of this chapter, also features Moreno's unaccented "American English."[16] Although this sketch underscores Moreno's sultriness and animal magnetism—she is, after all, Animal's "kind of woman"—Moreno is able to casually, coolly, and comically switch from her unaccented English to a smooth Spanish reprimand of Animal.

While these final scenes consciously employ Moreno's everyday accent, it is the way Moreno is introduced to the show through her first two sketches that reveals how audiences might be expected to continue seeing and hearing Moreno. After the apache number, which I explore in a moment, Moreno's first speaking part on the show is a sketch titled "Is Conversation a Dying Art?" This sketch sets up Moreno's sonic Puerto Rican-ness. Here, a panel of mock experts discusses the fate of interpersonal communication; as one of the guest panelists, Moreno couples an energetically exaggerated Puerto Rican accent with feisty posturing to develop the flamboyant character Tiffany Gonzalez—a seeming clear nod to Googie, since Moreno was likely plugging the film at the time. Gonzalez's rapid-fire and heavily accented English irritates another panelist, Miss Piggy, the Muppet version of the all-American blonde. When moderator Kermit loses control of the panel, an argument erupts between Piggy and Gonzales: Piggy claims to be unable to understand Gonzalez, while Gonzalez indirectly threatens Piggy in Spanish. The physicality of the quarrel between the two female characters delightfully animates both the Muppet and the Latina caricature as real beings. Because Moreno appears in a sparkly gold top and sports curly hair (the curliest it appears in the show), her accent and costuming yet again reinforce a particular impression of the outlandish Latina. Like Carmen Miranda before her, Moreno, speaking in accented English, has the potential to become an easy source of racialized humor. Although it seems that Moreno is intentionally mocking the visual-aural link of this traditional screen representation, the moment is hegemonically contained when the Muppet critics—curmudgeonly old white men who regularly mock the show from the audience—comment that Moreno "is easy on the eyes, but hard on the ears."[17]

After a brief but silent introduction by Kermit, in which Animal appears behind her and suggestively chews on her bare shoulder, Moreno performs her first number: a violent dance sequence in the tradition of an apache tango—a dance style featured in the Dolores Del Rio film *Wonder Bar* (1934). Cast as a hard-drinking woman, Moreno gives a facetiously sexy performance in which she operates as both a witty reversal of the usual gender dynamic of the apache dance's violence and an exaggerated version of the "dark temptress" role. Moreno enters a saloon and hits on a human-sized Muppet (called a Whatnot). Reprising her usual role as the Other woman to the production's female blonde, Moreno succeeds in pulling the Whatnot away from Miss Piggy, with whom he is flirting, several times throughout the dance. Wearing a sparkly red beret, matching shirt, and a tight black skirt with a slit to the hip, Moreno antagonizes her reluctant male partner throughout the dance. Pausing only to down shots of liquor, Moreno's character ultimately spins and knocks the Whatnot around the room until he finally retaliates by knocking her through a hole in the wall; he then collapses to the floor himself. As a dance sequence without dialogue, the number effectively characterizes Moreno for audiences—whether they are familiar with her work in *West Side Story* or *The Ritz* or seeing her as another generic, dancing Hollywood Latina.

The Muppet Show's multiple framings of Moreno in the course of five skits provide an insightful look at the way Latina mythology was shifting in the 1970s and how Moreno used biting humor to maintain control of her persona during that shift. Moreno's performances are either dance or performance oriented—such as the sexy apache and the sultry closing number "Fever"—or emphasize her feistiness, as in "Is Conversation a Dying Art?" By the time Moreno appears in "Fever," her fiery sultriness is fully evident, clarifying what kind of woman Animal desires.

Although Moreno's career continued beyond the 1970s and into the present, the underlying complications of the Hollywood Latina mythology draw a straight line between her last Emmy Award–winning performance on the program *Rockford Files* and her more recent work on the premium cable program *Oz* (1997–2003). While these examples illustrate how Moreno's vocal control has greatly impacted our reading of her career, other performances have aurally marked her racialized persona even when her character's voice, accent, and name have not. In her Emmy Award–winning guest performance on a 1978 episode of *The Rockford Files*, Moreno plays a plucky prostitute named Rita Capkovic. Although Moreno is sexualized by her character's profession,

Figure 21. In *The Muppet Show*, Rita Moreno's first two sketches mark the range of her popular depiction. In the first sketch (*top four images*), she is shown dancing an apache tango; she abuses her dance partner in between swigs of liquor and steals him from Miss Piggy. In the following sketch (*bottom two images*), Moreno uses an amplified Puerto Rican accent for comedic effect, once again irritating the Muppet version of an all-American blonde, Miss Piggy.

the show does little to mark Capkovic as an ethnic character beyond her vaguely Eastern European surname—that is, until the final scene in the show. After Capkovic inherits a large sum of money, she thanks the private detective Rockford for saving her life and gifts him with an antique roadster. As friends crowd around to admire the car, Capkovic proudly presses the car's horn; it blares the first few bars of "La Cucaracha," a song that Curtis Marez has shown long signifies Latino/a criminality and drug use (Marez 2004, 212). (The same bars from "La Cucaracha" are whistled by one of the Jets at the start of Anita's

symbolic rape scene at Doc's store—her last scene in the film.) Even when
Moreno's characters are not Latina, her sonic cues are.

As a prostitute on *The Rockford Files* and a prison nun on *Oz*, Moreno plays
roles that most clearly distinguish the function of hypersexuality and criminality in the persona of the Hollywood Latina. In *The Rockford Files*, Moreno is
explicitly cast in a sexualized role as a prostitute; in *Oz*, Moreno's hypersexuality functions on a much more subtle level. First, the casting of Moreno as a nun
works against type; given her oeuvre of sexual characters—from Anita to *The
Rockford Files*—the decision to cast Moreno as a character who is traditionally
considered celibate seems to cast against her type and persona. But Moreno's
screen introduction as Sister Peter Marie in her first scene of *Oz* illustrates her
modernity as a religious character. She is every bit as spunky as Moreno's characters tend to be, and her character's first lines of dialogue revolve around the sex
lives of the prison's inmates. The connotations of racialized sexuality, the inner
city, and criminality circulate through these two roles, regardless that the characters' professions seem to be polar opposites.

In the trajectory of the Hollywood Latina, Moreno is a transitional figure
because she proves that the promise of Hayworth's stardom could not be fulfilled without full physical and representational assimilation. Moreno has
struggled against the institutional constraints of Hollywood—from racism to
sexism to ageism—but her options never really widened or improved in terms
of leading roles. Instead, Moreno made a living while continuing to vocalize
her position within the industry; she opened crucial lines of dissent in the popular press while she was promoting whatever work she was in at the time.

Moreno regularly called for new and varied roles for Latinos/as, while
recognizing the progress and limitations of Latino/a self-representation. She
continued to critique the industry and racial/ethnic representation in general,
while occasionally remarking on how far black representation had developed in
terms of mainstream representation, in comparison with how little developed
were representations of groups such as Asians and Asian Americans (Welsh
1986). Over the course of her extensive career, Moreno has regularly rallied for
varied Latino/a roles in the industry. Wary of self-ghettoizing, however, she has
promoted the importance of mainstream Latino/a representation and encouraged Latino/a–produced content that aims beyond an exclusively Latino/a
audience (Tunison 1995). Thanks to the trials and tribulations of Rita, Anita,
Googie, Tiffany, and more, the Latina body may still be framed as little more
than visually desirable, but she is now, at least, less aurally undesirable.

Moreno's decisions and continued critiques have explicitly and implicitly
paved the way for Latinas, like Nuyorican Jennifer Lopez, to follow and to
refashion Latina-ness in subsequent media eras. Without Moreno, it is unlikely

that Lopez would be able to visually represent Latina-ness without also sounding like a stereotypical Latina. While Lopez's career has almost fulfilled Moreno's wish for mainstream representation, it has required its own share of negotiations, including multiple media channels, cosmetic modification, and racialized sexuality. Moreno's work and public critiques through performance and commentary established the foundation for the Hollywood Latina stardom of the late twentieth century.

CHAPTER 6

Jennifer Lopez, Racial Mobility, and the New Urban/Latina Commodity

To this day, Jennifer Lopez's career signals the peak of the Hollywood Latina. Building on nearly a century of the visual mythology developed from Dolores Del Rio to Rita Moreno, Lopez's stardom illustrates how the end of the twentieth century proved ripe for the commodification of in-betweenness and racial mobility. The multiplicity of media outlets and mainstreaming of black popular culture facilitated Lopez's rise to fame and have successfully reproduced a hierarchy of light female nonwhiteness that is marketable as both urban and multicultural. Lopez has crafted her multimedia and multidemographic career to exploit all facets of the Hollywood Latina myth and claim both financial and cultural agency of her image as a brand. Framed against the ostensibly multicultural 1990s and 2000s, Lopez's image exemplifies the malleability of the iconographic Latina body, while her career highlights how self-commodification necessarily negotiated her representation across Hollywood film, music television, and beyond.

In this chapter, to show the culmination of the Hollywood Latina's evolution, I focus on Jennifer Lopez as dancer-actor-singer-magnate within the visualized realm of popular music and the Hollywood film frame. Lopez built her career by compartmentalizing the traditions of the Hollywood Latina: she was able to shed the general limitations of Latina nonwhiteness in Hollywood film because she (and her team) largely compartmentalized her Puerto-Rican-from-the-Bronx roots on MTV. As cultural tastes shifted toward a commodified form of blackness in the late 1990s and early 2000s, Lopez maximized her commercial potential by visually emphasizing the codified sensuality of her nonwhite female body in accordance with an alleged urban style (that is, a black/nonwhite/ethnic aesthetic) as signaled by Rita Moreno's career during the 1960s and 1970s.[1] Because Lopez is the first Latina performer to star in mainstream leading roles since Rita Cansino became Rita Hayworth, her negotiation of these media spheres is a crucial detail in the current myth of the Hollywood Latina.

Unlike previous chapters, which focused on the film frame, this chapter emphasizes the compartmentalization of Lopez's nonwhiteness on MTV as a means for enabling a progression toward whiteness on the Hollywood screen. To address the ambiguity that Latina bodies have been presented with in Hollywood, I have theorized that representational Latina bodies oscillate between the normalcy of whiteness and the exoticism of blackness in visual culture. This in-betweenness demarcates the ambiguously racialized space that Latinas have been assigned in the hierarchy of visual representation, a representational space that Latinas have maneuvered within and around to maximize their careers in Hollywood. To show how Lopez has negotiated in-betweenness and racial mobility across the realms of Hollywood film and music television, I begin with a brief history of MTV and its emphasis on marketing and racialized representation to question the relationship between the hyperproduction of Lopez's body as nonwhite and MTV's increased representation of and reliance on nonwhite performers and performance. After detailing the role that in-betweenness and dance played in the film *Flashdance* (1983) and Lopez's video remake of the film in "I'm Glad" (2003), I turn to her origins as a dancer on the television program *In Living Color* to contextualize the historical period of racialization that facilitated her mainstream roles in Hollywood film. The centrality of Lopez's body in each business venture that followed—from film to music video to fragrance and retail fashion—illustrates how Lopez's sensuality was transformed from a largely visible pleasure to one both tangible and wearable. As a racially mobile performer, Jennifer Lopez has made in-betweenness an urban commodity available to a new wave of nonwhite female performers.

As a result of the Latina mythology that preceded her, Jennifer Lopez embodies the most commodifiable representation of urban U.S. nonwhiteness. By combining the media processes of Hollywood film and television—a newer medium that has made hip-hop and urban styles accessible for all ranges of the racialized spectrum—Jennifer Lopez has created a unified fan base of white, black, Latina, and everything in between and outside of these parameters. Lopez's career is the full fruition of the Hollywood Latina because she has wielded her in-betweenness with the greatest deftness by turning its inherent visuality into tangible commodities. With a catalogue of brands, Lopez has packaged herself into a product for each of the five senses: sight (film/video), sound (music), smell (perfume), touch (clothing), and taste (style or, including her now defunct restaurant, food) (Fox 2008; Madre's 2004; Madre's Out to Lunch 2008; Shuster 2002).

Lopez's rise to mainstream Hollywood fame necessitated representational manipulations that echoed whiteness, but her mainstream film success was only attainable because her nonwhiteness was simultaneously accentuated and regulated in the realm of music video performances (Ovalle 2007, 2008). While becoming more than "just a Latina actress" required that Lopez straighten and lighten her hair and assume roles with Anglicized names, her Hollywood crossover—from supporting Latina roles to ethnically nondescript leads in romantic comedies—was ultimately possible because she was simultaneously featured as a dancing singer on MTV (Handelman 1998; Ovalle 2008).[2] As the trajectory of the Hollywood Latina has made plain, Latinas are in-between bodies in the hierarchy of visual representation and have functioned as ambiguously racialized performers working within the scope of whiteness and blackness. Like Dolores Del Rio, Rita Hayworth, Carmen Miranda, and Rita Moreno before her, Lopez found that fame is not divorced from her representational ability to oscillate between the normalcy of whiteness and the exoticism of blackness in visual culture.

MTV: The Advertising Stage and Its Representational Bodies

While the industry of Jennifer Lopez—built around her body and movement—has been made most visible and viable by MTV, the cable network's and media brand's role in this production (including the legacy of music videos) has been largely overlooked. Over the years, MTV and Jennifer Lopez have seemingly collaborated for mutual benefit: the network has magnified Jennifer Lopez's rise to multimedia fame and chronicled the expansion of her enterprise, while she has mediated the network's increasing visual commodification of nonwhiteness for the U.S. market.[3] The Lopez-MTV symbiosis—symbolic or financial—was most evident when Jennifer Lopez premiered the video for her single "I'm Glad" on MTV in 2003. In the music video, Lopez embodies the character Alex from the 1980s cultural and box office hit *Flashdance* (1983). The video, conceived and directed by David LaChapelle, showcases Lopez's technical skill as a dancer while using costumes, scenarios, and movement from the film to promote Lopez's then recently released music single.

Although it is tempting to attribute Lopez's revival of *Flashdance* to a sort of postmodern nostalgia for the 1980s, the myth of the Hollywood Latina suggests that this seamless reincarnation was instead indebted to the combined visual spectacle of racialized sexuality, the female body, and dance performance—now set in an urban context. With Lopez appearing in *Flashdance* fashion and movement, her body performed anew the codification and commodification of an ambiguously nonwhite female sensuality within the MTV frame. As a visual adaptation organized around a dancing brown female body, the video "I'm

Glad" makes explicit what *Flashdance* made implicit in terms of racialized sexuality and in-betweenness.

Because MTV was built on the principles and formal conventions of advertising, its eventual diversification of on-screen racial representation was only a matter of market and marketability. The channel's ingenuity was to sell advertisers airtime for programming that was in itself a string of commercials for record label products—and then to get its "unique" target demographic (twelve- to thirty-four-year-olds) to tune in (Banks 1996, 173; Ebenkamp 2003, 32; Hartman 1987, 19). The network has since nurtured an uncanny ability to naturalize product placement by effectively synergizing adolescence, music, and commercial products—including everything from soda to the musical performers themselves (Ebenkamp 2003, 30).[4] When MTV debuted in 1981, the cable channel was aimed at white male adolescents and primarily focused on mainstream rock and roll; this began to change with the debut of Michael Jackson's spectacular "Billie Jean" in 1983 (Hartman 1987, 17).[5] While it took many more years for MTV to incorporate black performers into its regular video rotation, it took nearly no time at all for advertisers to realize the salability of music performers, particularly black performers. As early as 1984, Jackson appeared in high-profile and long-format music video–styled advertisements for Pepsi-Cola, and soon after, Whitney Houston was peddling Diet Coke (Hartman 1987, 21).[6]

Around the time of "Billie Jean," Hollywood began to recognize MTV as a cultural force.[7] In 1983, a pre-Viacom Paramount Pictures released a low-budget feature film, with an unknown lead actress, titled *Flashdance*, the first film to be marketed on the cable channel and the source of Lopez's "I'm Glad" homage (Abramowitz 2000, 248).[8] *Flashdance* tells the tale of an ambiguously racialized young woman with the upwardly mobile dream of becoming a ballerina. With a formal style inspired by music videos—including rapid-fire editing, dance performances created in the editing room, an overreliance on soundtrack, and the seductive haze of fog machines—*Flashdance* went on to gross $90 million, nearly eleven times its production budget. In addition, the film inspired a raggedy-ballet fashion trend that was embraced by young women and likely worn while they danced to the best-selling soundtrack in nightclubs and living rooms across the nation.

While the film's marketing excess is worthy of scrutiny, it is not divorced from the racial politics operating below the film's surface: when embodied by an in-between female body, the intersection of dance and racialized sexuality continues to prove popular. At the core of *Flashdance* is the commodification of nonwhiteness, most evident in the film's reliance on black/Latino urban dance styles like break dancing and the strategic racial ambiguity of its lead

actress. Jennifer Beals, a biracial actress, brought a sort of tomboy innocence
and charm to the role of Alex. While the film never explicitly addresses Alex's
identity, it seems to intentionally operate on the underlying double meaning of
Beals as a performer.[9] Her name is gender neutral. By day, she is the only
female welder in an otherwise male company; by night, she is an exotic dancer.
She is independent and sexually aggressive yet sweetly concerned about her
friends.[10] As a character, Alex is illegitimate.[11] She has no biological relatives
written into the film and is instead surrounded by a surrogate family composed
of one white and naive best friend, a semidiverse social network of strippers
(including a token black female friend), and an older perceivably Russian mentor named Hanna.[12]

Whether intentional or not, Beals's lurking nonwhiteness legitimized the
incorporation of marginalized and sexualized dance styles into Alex's narrative;[13] her ambiguously raced body was crucial because it produced a female
protagonist—rare in Hollywood regardless of race—imbued with the tough
sexual knowing and self-assurance often attributed to nonwhite women
(McRobbie 1997, 219). As a biracial woman, Beals, with her light-skinned physical features—not quite white and not quite black[14]—better sold the fusion of
(what one review called break dancing) an "acrobatic style of ghetto street
dancing" with the sanctioned performance of ballet, a traditionally white dance
form (Langway and Reed 1983, 55). Beals's significance as a mediating body
with the "right look" was further highlighted by the fact that she did not, in
fact, dance in *Flashdance*. Instead, the illusion of Beals as a dancer was created
through clever editing and uncredited double dance work provided by professional dancer Marine Jahan and Puerto Rican breaker Crazy Legs (né Richie
Colon).[15]

Like Alex/Beals, Jennifer Lopez is culturally hybrid, and her body is similarly affiliated with urban space and dance performance. While Alex's body
was read against the backdrop of Pittsburgh, Lopez's body (like Moreno's)
has been framed by and continually read through the multicultural lens of
New York—specifically the Bronx. This representation of Lopez's body as
urban and Bronx-based has been particularly central to her music career as
depicted on MTV. As an in-between body, Beals lacked the ability to dance and
did not fulfill the promise of her casting, which may have resulted in her otherwise lukewarm career; as a contemporary Hollywood Latina, however, Lopez
has bona fide technical skill as a dancer, and it has played a significant role
in her success.[16] A decade after Michael Jackson peddled Pepsi and Jennifer
Beals pretended to dance, Lopez became the Latina face for Coke in the
English-language market. Shortly after this major advertising debut, Lopez
emerged as a music performer on MTV—at the precise time that hip-hop and

"black cultural tastes" became "extremely efficient devices for extracting profit from the consumption habits of America's youth" (Smith 2003, 75).

"I'M GLAD": AUTHENTICATING FLASHDANCE

According to Lopez, the decision to remake *Flashdance* in the form of the music video "I'm Glad" came from director LaChapelle. Lopez's only goal for the track was to dance solo, without the traditional aid of backup dancers. In the video, LaChapelle re-creates the sets, iconography, and costuming of *Flashdance* as a backdrop for Lopez. Although her dancing body moves with updated choreography and to her own soundtrack, Lopez's performance and the overall effect are uncannily satisfying. The adaptation works because Lopez, like Alex in *Flashdance*, is a girl with a dream to move beyond her station in life through dance and hard work. As Angela McRobbie reminds us, tales of upward mobility are—for women—presented as most attainable when depicted through the body and especially through dance. At that moment in time, Lopez fully embodied this particular "fantasy of achievement" (McRobbie 1997, 223–229).

As an adaptation of the original film, Lopez's hypervisible body in the music video "I'm Glad" makes explicit the racialized sexuality implicit with Beals's body in *Flashdance*. Comparing the two media helps further our understanding of how gendered and racialized representations have shifted in popular culture over the past twenty-five years through the lens or promotion of MTV. While black popular culture has been mainstreamed since *Flashdance*, this has largely functioned around the black male body—as evinced in Christopher Holmes Smith's discussion (2003) of the hip-hop mogul. The black female body has largely been embraced through multiracial or light-skinned female performers like Halle Berry, Mariah Carey, and Beyoncé. While Lopez has arguably brought "the butt" into the commodified space of mainstream beauty standards,[17] she has simultaneously—if only symbolically—replaced or "stood in" for the black/biracial female in mainstream media. Because Lopez has only collaborated with black or brown men in the realm of music, she performs as a lighter, safer stand-in for a black woman or a darker, sexual stand-in for a white woman. The hyperpresence of Lopez as a nonwhite figure seemingly affirms black masculinity while denying black femininity in this visual representation of music. By omission, black female sexuality remains as yet untamed, too dangerous or too black for mainstream consumption.[18]

Because black female sexuality has been continually denigrated and made taboo, *Flashdance* takes great pains to show that Alex does not quite fit into the white world of ballet without actually identifying her as black. Instead, the film displaces her blackness from her actual body to how it is framed, juxtaposed, and fragmented. Alex's out-of-place body highlights her unique ability to navigate the traditionally masculine realms of steelwork and men's club audiences while simultaneously casting her as too dark and unfeminine for the traditional ballet world. Scenes that place Alex in the all-white ballet academy frame her racialized and sexualized ambiguity through casting, costuming, and hair. In one tracking shot, Alex's difference is starkly on display: her wild hair, baggy jeans, boots, and army jacket stand out against a marbled hallway of white ballet dancers with slicked-back hair and pale pink, skintight leotards. Her unwanted difference is most pointed when a close-up of Alex's dirty work boots is juxtaposed with the clean yet worn shoes of the ballet dancers as they whisper about her.

While upward mobility is clearly a central theme of *Flashdance*, the dance binary utilized by the film to illustrate this ascension (ballet and hip-hop) frames the economic tension along racial lines. If Alex's difference is apparent in the ballet school, the fetishistic framing of her dancing body and encounters with b-boys (break-dancers) on the street more firmly affiliate her with blackness. In the scene cut to the soundtrack single "Maniac,"[19] the dance double Marine Jahan's hips and torso are shot in close-up. In this tight frame, Jahan's taut legs pump up and down as she frantically touches her glisteningly wet thighs in an excessive and masturbatory dance sequence. Because the images of Jahan's hips and legs are intercut with shots of Beals's face, we are led to believe the two are of the same body. As Daphne Brooks (2006, 5) posits, the black body has historically been fragmented; when this compartmentalization is visualized and combined with dance as in the "Maniac" sequence, the reading of Beals's body as nonwhite—however implicit—is reinforced. Soon after this sequence, blackness becomes more visible and explicit when Alex encounters a trio of b-boys performing in an alley. As the sequence progresses, a crowd accumulates around the black and brown break-dancing bodies. The crowd is primarily composed of black people—old, young, short, tall, lean, and fat— and marks the most significant representation of black bodies in the film. The only other explicitly black body in *Flashdance* is Alex's one black friend, the only dark-skinned dancer at the club. Oddly, Alex's black friend never actually dances; according to the racialized logic of the film, it seems she doesn't need to dance to authenticate her race or sexuality.

While black popular culture has transitioned from the margins to the center, one of the most successful female bodies in this process has been a woman who can signify nonwhiteness without actually being black. Jennifer Lopez has made a career by explicitly carrying the weight of nonwhiteness on her actual body—specifically her butt—because of her dance background and its continued role in her fame.[20] For example, in the shots that faithfully re-create the "Maniac" sequence in "I'm Glad," Lopez's gyrating pelvis is authenticated as her own: an establishing shot tilts to connect—face to fanny—what *Flashdance* associated by way of juxtaposed frames. This authenticity is furthered by the "wiggle and jiggle" of Lopez's body in the frame, the result of vigorous choreography combined with skimpy costuming. Yet the obvious athleticism of Lopez's body was overruled as excessively fleshy movement and modified in editing.[21] Lopez states:

> I really worked out and did the diet thing . . . and then after the video . . . there's always that one guy who's like, "We should retouch this." I was like, "You're going to leave everything the way it is. That's how it wiggles and jiggles in real life, that's how they're going to see it in the video." And I noticed—[the editors] sent [the video] to me and they had shaved off a little bit of my hips and—I was like, "That ain't me—those are not my hips. Just leave them the way they are. Do me a favor—don't touch my hips. Don't try to make me look skinnier. It's fine, it's fine the way it is." And that's what they did. (Gable 2003)

Despite the training and physical intensity of the dance, Lopez's body did not represent the ideal performance of femininity. The desire to police Lopez's flesh illustrates the ingrained equation of unfirm flesh with a lack of physical or moral discipline (Banet-Weiser 1999, 68). Lopez's will to "keep it real" illustrates her significant creative control and representational agency. The authority that Lopez seems to have over her music video image is dependent on the fact that she—body and all—remains a high-demand commodity.

Angela McRobbie's reading of Alex in *Flashdance* offers another opportunity to evaluate Lopez's response to the modification of her hips in the context of her own impact on the representation of female agency and body. McRobbie asserts that Alex's body is her only means of expression—"her only 'commodity'" (1997, 229). In the 1980s, this commodity was the hyperaerobic body, a white female body so slender and athletic that the female dance double captured in "Maniac" could easily be swapped out with a break-dancing male body in the finale performance of "What a Feeling!" Although *Flashdance*'s narrative and signified sexuality relied on Beals's ambiguous racialization, it was the "small, muscular and round" buttocks featured in "Maniac" that exemplified Alex's discipline and drive (a discipline ironically matched only by her ravenous sexual appetite) (Kael 1983; Bordo 1993, 110).

In 2003, that idealized hard body was softened—though no less disciplined—with the rise of Lopez. Where Beals (et al.) was framed by an urban space, Lopez's body is an urban space. With a self-proclaimed and visualized urbanness in songs and videos like "Jenny from the Block" or "I'm Real" (with Ja Rule) on

Figure 22. From *Flashdance* (1983) to "I'm Glad" (2003), the in-between female body dances her butt off. *Top:* Jennifer Beals's face was a separate shot from the buttocks of her dance double. *Bottom:* "I'm Glad" authenticated Jennifer Lopez as a bona fide Hollywood Latina by showing her dancing in shots that tilt from face to fanny.

MTV, Lopez's body also came to signify the city and its symbolic nonwhiteness.[22] For example, the shots that re-create the break-dancers-in-the-alley moment of *Flashdance* replace the film's crowd of black faces with the lone figure of Lopez. While this replacement is primarily because "I'm Glad" is Lopez's music video and therefore prioritizes her body, it also establishes that as a culture we no longer need to authenticate representations of break dancing as urban or street—or, at the very least, that Lopez can do all of this on her own. Lopez's biography—as a Bronx-born Puerto Rican descendent who went from "*In Living Color* to movie scripts" (Lopez et al. 2001)—expands *Flashdance*'s narrative of upward mobility to explicitly include nonwhite (as well as white) audiences.

While Beals and Lopez both promoted the image of nonwhiteness through their respective media forms, both women's bodies were at the center of a music, dance, and fashion explosion propelled by MTV. As a brown woman, Lopez has translated nonwhiteness into an accessible and therefore commodifiable style. Lopez has utilized her particular version of in-betweenness to reinforce her brand through music singles and videos—effectively using MTV as much as it has used her. However, none of this would have been possible without the legitimization of Hollywood and the whiteness required for its most

Figure 23. In *Flashdance*, black bodies authenticate the urban space of break dancing (*left*); in "I'm Glad," the singularity of Jennifer Lopez's body against an urban backdrop provides the same signification (*right*).

hallowed space—the close-up. By looking at Lopez's emergence as a dancing body, we can better understand the reverse progression—from fanny to face—that facilitated Lopez's Hollywood stardom.

THE HOLLYWOOD LATINA AND THE LOPEZ FACTOR

The genius of Lopez's branding is her local-global packaging of Latinidad. By popularizing an ethnic/Latina-ness defined and contained by the decidedly U.S. urban center of New York, Lopez maximized her representational potential while retaining an "Americanness" in the media's eye (Dávila 2001, 158). While there should be no doubt that this delicate balance is proof of Lopez's creative business savvy, it would be careless to overlook the late 1990s/early 2000s context of racialized sexuality, gender, and cultural production within which her career trajectory developed—or the history of Puerto Rican racialization in New York that framed the emergence of Lopez's immediate Latina predecessor, Rita Moreno. The inflection of Lopez's nonwhite female image as interpreted across multiple media frames (television, film, music videos) helps illustrate the complex and contradictory locations of her success and the limits of contemporary in-betweenness.

Beginning in the 1980s and accelerating during the late 1990s and early 2000s, the term "urban" became a thinly veiled synonym for nonwhiteness, particularly in terms of black representation or black popular culture as affiliated with the urban center.[23] As a physical place, the city has long framed contemporary discussions of blackness; in New York, this blackness was often conflated with Puerto Rican-ness. The urban/blackness conflation is particularly true in the construction of blackness as a racialized signifier of authenticity in mainstream U.S. popular culture. John Jeffries's work on the relationship

between the social construction of race, the city, and black popular culture suggests that the "repertoires of black popular culture" must be understood within
the context of urban space. These "repertoires," as identified by Stuart Hall,
encompass three elements: style as subject, emphasis on music over the written word, and "deliberate use of the body as a canvas" (Hall 1998, 27; Jeffries
1998, 158). Jeffries builds on Hall's repertoires by asserting that the U.S. urban
space—a potentially dehumanizing space filled with low-paying jobs, harsh living conditions, and continued racism—serves as a lived space where these elements are continually "transformed and remixed" (1998, 154). In the face of
continual degradation and oppression, urban black popular culture provided
an arena where black subjects could "reaffirm" their humanity (Jeffries 1998,
162). Jeffries warns, however, that as cultures are hybridized for better commodification, these reaffirming maneuvers are in danger of being displaced.
Given this history it is possible to see how black and nonwhite representation
has been a fraught enterprise despite the popularization and incorporation of
black and hip-hop culture into mainstream media since the Reagan era (Gray
1995, 18).

It is against this backdrop, around 1990, that Lopez achieved her mainstream media break. Lopez "won a dance contest to become a Fly Girl" on the
popular television series *In Living Color*, Fox network's "attempt to capitalize
on the commercial success of black youth culture" (Gray 1995, 134; Larkin
2006, 318).[24] *In Living Color*'s comedy sketches were punctuated by hip-hop
music breaks performed live by up-and-coming artists or spun by the show's
resident DJ, a format that simultaneously mainstreamed black sketch comedy
while fixing it within an urban milieu. The Fly Girls, a house company of lithe
female dancers, accompanied these music breaks with creative dances choreographed by Rosie Pérez; the women were occasionally accompanied by (black)
male dancers but invariably clothed in wildly colorful fashions. Thus, each Fly
Girl embodied the repertoire of black popular culture through fashion (style)
and movement (body), while fiercely moving to hip-hop (music). The performances were initially framed against the urban mise-en-scène (city) of a
darkly lit rooftop framed by fire escapes,[25] a set that thematically tied the Fly
Girls to the show's black-centered humor and seemingly imbued their strong
yet seductive movements with an urban flavor.

The Fly Girls primarily functioned as racialized and spatialized signifiers,
cueing the audience to tune in or tune out from the program as needed. The
spectacle of these moving female bodies was intended to recapture the audience's attention between programming and advertising; the kinetic and colorful appeal of their costumed and choreographed bodies primed us for the next

televisual message. The carefully constructed multicultural crew of (mostly nonwhite) female dancers epitomized the commodifiable function of the nonwhite female form and its movement. Because Fly Girl performances were not the show's main event, their creative contributions were transitional and (unlike the rest of the cast) located wholly on the body. It is possible that the Fly Girls, like the show itself, suffered from the television industry's push for (white) mainstream audiences. Like Herman Gray, I find *In Living Color* an "ambivalent" and "contingent" representation of blackness (and nonwhite femaleness) in spite of executive producer Keenen Ivory Wayans's initial creative control and the choreography of Pérez (Gray 1995, 138–146).

Perhaps because of its kinetic American Dreaminess, the Fly Girl origin-story has remained an often-repeated and deeply entrenched part of Lopez's sexy, sassy, and upwardly mobile persona. After her tenure as a Fly Girl ended, she worked as a backup dancer for Janet Jackson and was featured in the Jackson video "That's the Way Love Goes" (1993).[26] In 1995, Lopez's acting career accelerated with appearances in *Mi Familia* (1995) and *Money Train* (1995). Two years later—the same year Lopez appeared in her breakthrough role in *Selena* (1997)—Lopez was a featured performer and dancer in the Sean "Puffy/P.Diddy" Combs long-format music video for "Been around the World" (1997). The combined effect of Lopez's high-profile role as the slain Tejana singer/fashion designer Selena and her appearance with Sean Combs marked a turning point in her career.[27] While Lopez lip-synched Selena's original songs, her strengths as a performer and the visibility of *Selena* encouraged Sony to sign Lopez as a recording artist (Handelman 1998, 82).

In many ways, Lopez's music career picked up where Selena's left off; two years after *Selena* and the Combs video, Lopez debuted her first album, titled *On the 6* (1999). This freshman musical effort furthered Lopez's emerging "Jenny from the Block" persona. As a recording artist, her nonwhiteness was an acknowledged asset to be celebrated and exploited as a result of its multimarket appeal. Thanks to MTV, Lopez's burgeoning music career and Bronx-rooted heritage were made immediately visible with videos for *On the 6*, an album named for the Bronx-Manhattan train Lopez used to commute (Larkin 2006, 319; Ovalle 2008).[28] The album featured two early collaborations that signaled her later musical trajectories and highlighted the multidemographic potential of Lopez as a recording artist. The first, "Feelin' So Good," was produced by Sean Combs and featured fellow Bronx-Latino rappers Big Pun(isher) and Fat Joe. The second song, "No Me Ames," was a Spanish-language duet with Marc Anthony. These collaborations foreshadowed her later work with black rappers like Nas, Ja Rule, and LL Cool J, as well as her more recent turn toward Spanish-language albums such as the Marc Anthony–produced *Como ama una mujer* (2007).

Although the end of the 1990s signaled the rise of the "hip-hop mogul," Lopez emerged as one of the few women operating within this new business world; through music, Lopez was able to stretch beyond the mainstream to engage both black and Latino/Spanish-language markets. Christopher Holmes Smith identifies the hip-hop mogul as a hybrid of American traditions—male, entrepreneurial, and prestigiously wealthy—with the flair of a new class of blacks and Latinos/as emerging from the entertainment industry (Smith 2003, 69). Smith finds hip-hop moguls like Russell Simmons and "bad boy for life" Sean Combs to be typically young, black, and "tethered either literally or symbolically to America's disenfranchised inner cities" (Smith 2003, 69). As a Diddy protegée, Lopez is the only woman whom Smith identifies as a mogul, a detail that underscores her persona as a strong-willed businesswoman as well as her affiliation with the city.[29]

As a musical performer favored by the camera and vetted by both Emilio Estefan and Sean Combs—heavy music muscle from the realms of Latino/a crossover and hip-hop, respectively—Lopez was the perfect multifaceted and multicultural celebrity poised at the cusp of the new century.[30] Her singles and videos became transatlantic hits, even before she heavily ventured into Spanish-language recordings with *Como ama una mujer* (Larkin 2006, 319). But the force of Lopez's musical success may in fact be due to her technical position as a pop performer signed to Sony Records' then-nascent label Work Group (Sandler 1998). With Lopez, Sony gained a highly visible personality, while Lopez benefited from a lucrative "multi-album, multimillion-dollar recording contract" that outbid a "multifaceted deal by Capitol Records and sister label EMI Latina" (Sandler 1998). Lopez's business savvy is evident not only in the millions of dollars she has earned but in her decision not to sign with EMI, a deal that would have placed her on the Latin-specific label that previously signed Selena.

A telling write-up by *Variety* hints at other reasons for Lopez's being particularly attractive to Sony. "Insiders note the inking [contract signing] evokes *shades of Mariah Carey*, as Mottola is also dating Lopez and the pair's appearance together at the conglom's recent post-Grammy party has become tabloid fodder" (Sandler 1998, emphasis mine). While the writer is clearly alluding to Mottola's then-recent divorce from Carey, it is interesting that the word "shades" is used to compare the two women. Both of these nonwhite female artists (Carey is biracial) fit comfortably within the zone of brownness or in-betweenness visually preferred by mainstream media—a significant coincidence, whether or not Lopez and Mottola were romantically involved (she has publicly denied it).

The Seductive Safety of Lopez's In-Betweenness

As we have seen, a significant component of Lopez's mainstream representation is its simultaneity as authentically urban and appealingly safe, expanding the limits of female representation while diversifying (but not disrupting or destabilizing) mainstream media's emphasis on whiteness. The sexualization of Lopez's nonwhite body figures largely into this marketability.[31] As a woman whose nonwhiteness is continually coded by the media as "not black," Lopez conveys a sexualization that is tempered as sensual—seductive yet safe. As Lopez transitioned from backup dancer to actress, her roles increasingly relied on her ability to function as a mediating body: as a Latina in film, she was the ideal in-between woman. Lopez's role in *Money Train* exemplifies this aspect of her career. In the film, Lopez is cast as the Latina love interest, a role meant to mediate the sexual and racial tensions between an unlikely pair of brothers played by Wesley Snipes and Woody Harrelson. In one interview, Lopez remarked: "They wanted a Latina. . . . They wanted somebody who could be with Wesley and with Woody" (Murray 1997, 72).[32] In a film that challenges the racial taboos of mixed-race families, Lopez's in-betweenness served as a convenient bridge, a detail utilized by the film's publicity: one *Money Train* advertisement literally places the body of Lopez between and against close-ups of Snipes and Harrelson (Ovalle 2007, 228). Because this role was early in Lopez's career, her racialized position was beyond her control; it seems, however, that this convenient position was consciously exploited by both Lopez and MTV.

The variety of Lopez's media venues—including film, print, interactive media, music videos, and television appearances—has provided multiple visual spaces through which her racial mobility has been displayed. Because each medium encodes its message differently, these multiple planes have enabled Lopez's image to utilize multiple bodily codes and narratives. Like Moreno, Lopez understood the traditional limits of her career as a Latina. A 1998 interview illustrates Lopez's consciousness of her Hollywood identity and the need to aim beyond her limited type. She says, "My managers and agents and I realized that I'm not white . . . so I've always wanted to show that I could play any kind of character. Not only a range of emotions, but also race-wise" (Handelman 1998, 82).

Like Moreno, Lopez saw the value of moving beyond traditional Latina roles and the compromises that would be required to exceed these limitations—especially in terms of hair and cosmetic style. Although Lopez would never change her name as Rita Hayworth did, her film representations would echo the medium's conventions of lightness and whiteness even when she was cast in roles that reiterated her difference through characterization and character name.

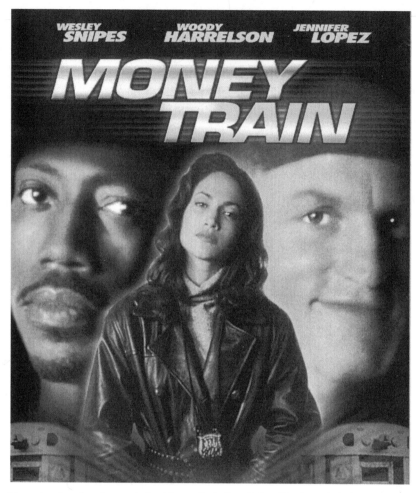

Figure 24. In advertisements for *Money Train* (1995), Jennifer Lopez's in-between body literally borders the whiteness and blackness of unlikely brothers played by Woody Harrelson and Wesley Snipes.

THE LIGHTENING WHITENING OF THE HOLLYWOOD CLOSE-UP

The Hollywood film's close-up directs the audience's full attention to the subject of the frame's composition and presents the audience with the most valuable or informative detail within a scene. Important gestures, objects, or other visual cues are indicated through full magnification within the frame. The shot's cultural value, however, resides primarily in its use to capture the film star's face: within this frame, the star may use this space to emote, react, glow, or simply be. Traditionally, cinematographic technology has been organized around the proper exposure of the face; because the face has historically been white, the medium has long been ideologically and technologically ill prepared for the nonwhite star. Richard Dyer has identified how traditional cinematic lighting and framing techniques have, technically and culturally, reinstated whiteness by operating according to mechanical requirements standardized for white complexions—even when recording black bodies. More symbolically, back-lighting (creating a specific glow or halo around the star to signal importance) has reinforced the mythical representation of white virtuousness—a technique most commonly used with white female stars. Brightness cues the framed subject's "idealized representation" by cultivating the illusion of a "glow" (Dyer 1997, 127, 132).[33] This artificial glow effectively and economically collapses lightness, beauty, and subject/narrative positioning in a single shot.

The fiery Hollywood Latina has not typically received the full cultural weight of the close-up and has most often been relegated to character actor or sup-porting roles. The spatial value of the close-up is exemplified on the April 1997 cover of *Vanity Fair*. While the outer magazine cover features blondes Cameron Diaz, Kate Winslet, and Claire Danes, the inside cover highlights emerging actresses Jennifer Lopez, Charlize Theron, and Fairuza Balk. Captioned "Not Quite Ready for Their Close-Ups," these three actresses complete a ten-person spread, following other performers such as Renée Zellweger, Minnie Driver, Alison Elliott, and Jada Pinkett (pre-Smith) (*Vanity Fair* 1997, 88).

Lopez's position in this Hollywood lineup indicates the newness of her celebrity and the unmet potential of her nonconforming image as a brunette.[34] Like the front cover, the image of Lopez, Theron, and Balk seems to privilege blondeness. Lopez and Balk, both brunettes, are seated and flank Theron, who stands at the center of the picture; Theron's nude-colored dress, blond hair, and central placement in the light make her the image's focal point. Although such composition may be a coincidence, Theron is afforded another image on the same page, whereas Lopez and Balk are not. While Theron may not have her close-up, her blondeness clearly deserved more screen and page time.

Like those of Rita Hayworth, Lopez's early Hollywood film roles were identi-fied by Spanish surnames until her look became more malleable. As Lopez's hair color and hairstyle began to change, overtly Latina characters and names—like Grace Santiago in *Money Train* (1995), Terri Flores in *Anaconda* (1997), and Selena Quintanilla in *Selena* (1997)—disappeared from her films. As Lopez's nonwhite difference was increasingly marked through and compartmentalized in her music videos on MTV, her Hollywood image was increasingly lightened to help mobilize her climb toward less ethnically defined roles—initially tran-sitioning to whiteness through Italian American characters as Hayworth did through Irish American characters (Roediger 2005). Since the beginning of her

Figure 25. From *Money Train* to *Angel Eyes* (2001): In the first decade of Jennifer Lopez's career, her close-ups (or lack thereof) highlight the importance of lightened and straightened hair in the process of racial mobility.

career, Lopez's hair has shifted from a dark and curly mane (as featured in *Money Train*) toward lightened and straightened hair in films like *Angel Eyes* (2001) and *Monster-in-Law* (2005).[35] Although Lopez has rarely gone completely blond for a film role (with the near exceptions of *Angel Eyes* and *Monster-in-Law*), she routinely employs dramatic hair highlights or her image is adjusted to effectively lighten and brighten her face, as the publicity stills for *Angel Eyes* and *The Wedding Planner* illustrate. In *The Wedding Planner* posters and other art work, Lopez's hair and complexion nearly match those of Matthew McConaughey; in *Angel Eyes*, her face becomes a blown-out ghost of whiteness.

Evidence of this transition toward the close-up exists in the casting of Lopez's romantic interests: each leading man in Lopez's Hollywood films (and real life in the case of Sean Combs, Ben Affleck, and Marc Anthony) has helped usher her racial mobility. Since *Anaconda*, Lopez's romantic leads have consistently been white (or white ethnic) males: George Clooney (*Out of Sight*, 1998), an animated Woody Allen (*Antz*, 1998), Matthew McConaughey (*The Wedding Planner*, 2001), Ralph Fiennes (*Maid in Manhattan*, 2002), Richard Gere (*Shall We Dance*, 2004), and Alex O'Loughlin (*The Back-up Plan*, 2010).[36] As Mary C. Beltrán has noted in her work on Lopez as a crossover star, it was Lopez's pairing with white leading man Clooney in *Out of Sight* that announced her status as a "rising global star property," particularly because she followed the film with her music career (Beltrán 2002, 76). Clooney's pairing with Lopez, in turn, marked him as a bona fide Hollywood sex symbol.

As an in-between and racially mobile body, Lopez, as an incarnation of the Hollywood Latina, functions as a safe—that is, marketable—racial middle ground, not too far removed from the center or from either polarized/racialized margin. While her career appears to be in decline, she remains the median of the racial representational scale through which U.S. culture still operates

Figure 26. Advertisements for *The Wedding Planner* (2001) and *Angel Eyes* illustrate how dramatic hair highlights or image adjustments effectively lighten and brighten Jennifer Lopez.

(Schwartz 2010). In the case of Lopez, heterosexual men of any racial identity—as suggested by her role in *Money Train* and her video debut "If You Had My Love" (1999)—can access her as an object of sexual desire. Yet women and gay men (as well as white or nonwhite audiences in general) can also desire her—sexually or at the very least as a figure of emulation due to her upward mobility, nonwhiteness, and/or fabulousness. While these assertions are obviously oversimplified, they speak to the centrality of Lopez's body in her allure. Her body—racialized, gendered, and/or sexualized—links each commodity. At first we could experience how her body looked, how it performed. But now we can be like her: we can buy her fragrance, dance to her music, learn her moves, and wear her clothes.

The simultaneity of Lopez's commodified and racialized representations—moving toward whiteness in Hollywood and blackness via MTV—has maximized her commercial appeal. She is so massively marketable because she has tapped into the corps of pop with an accessible image that flaunts a hip-hop aesthetic through origin story, media trajectory, and supposed nonwhite/atypical Hollywood physique.[37] Lopez holds our gaze with her movement and makes us want to follow along. We may objectify her, but we may also move with her, be moved by her. We are voyeurs—in a multiplicity of ways and multi-oriented perspectives—but she wills us to remain. We buy Lopez as a singer precisely because we first understood her as a dancer. And we stick around because we "wanna" buy what she's selling: a dream, a neighborhood, some Latin-fusion food, a picture that kind of looks like us on the screen, and so forth.

The myth of the Hollywood Latina has persevered because of its ubiquity; her image is so easy to dismiss or overlook because it is so hypervisible that it becomes invisible. In a post-Lopez period, a whole wave of brown women—from Shakira to Beyoncé to even Hilary Duff in Middle Eastern brownface ("Stranger," 2007)—are utilizing the codes of in-betweenness in hopes of tapping the fashion or cosmetics industries. For example, in 2007 Beyoncé announced her first Spanish-language single. The song's release followed her successful video collaboration with Shakira, titled "Beautiful Liar"; a significant draw of this video is the viewer's inability to discern the brown body of Shakira from the brown body of Beyoncé in terms of hair style, movement, and complexion. As pop performers, the ability of nonwhite female performers to look and sound alike speaks volumes to the marketable in-betweenness that Lopez has opened up and popularized in recent years. The entrepreneurial push provided by Lopez suggests that the next Hollywood Latina may not be Latina at all so long as she remains (racially) mobile in the frame.

Notes

CHAPTER 1 — MOBILIZING THE LATINA MYTH

1. As I later explain, the distinction "Spanish" is wholly entangled in the myth of the Hollywood Latina, despite key distinctions between Spain–Spanish and Latin America or the United States–Latina.

2. In 2005, the U.S. Postal Service unveiled its Hispanic heritage commemorative stamp series titled "Let's Dance/Bailemos!" All four featured illustrations of dancing couples, with the dancing Latina prominently featured in three of the four designs.

3. Like the white/black racial binary, representations of gender (and hetero-sexuality) work according to dominant power structures by supporting and reifying one another.

4. Judith Ortiz Cofer (2007) briefly began to explore this myth in her short, personal essay "The Myth of the Latin Woman." The article was originally published in 1992.

5. Cinema studies' emphasis on representation has enabled me to rethink identity politics and the term "Latina," an identification I use to unify the women and goals of this project.

6. While Rick Altman provides this coupling dynamic to better frame the musical, Adrienne McLean develops this point by highlighting how musicals have largely been validated through male-centered analyses around authorship—either in terms of the performer (Astaire, Kelly, etc.) or auteur (Minnelli, Freed Unit, etc.) (Altman 1987; McLean 2004).

7. This hierarchization functions like the colonial model of race and gender, as outlined by Maria Lugones (2007).

8. These claims of in-betweenness and racial mobility are not meant to prioritize one racial representation or identity over another. Rather, I aim to nuance the representational hierarchy that continues to favor poles rather than spectra in a continued hegemonic effort to recenter whiteness. I use these terms to further theorize the phenomenon through which black is read differently from brown, brown differently from white, and everything else—yellow, red, interracial—is diffuse or further marginalized beyond an "American" or Hollywood body. My goal is to further this discussion of look and performance across various racialized and sexualized representations on screen.

9. Duna was chosen to test whether dark hair and an "olive complexion" would photo-graph "attractively" in Technicolor (Berry 2000; Higgins 2000, 361).

10. Although Lucy and Ricky Ricardo (Lucille Ball and Desi Arnaz) are seemingly the exception that proves the rule, Arnaz's Cuban identity is often affiliated with Caucasianness (Sandoval-Sánchez 1999, 55).

11. As Frances Negrón-Muntaner notes, "The interracial exchange [of *West Side Story*] becomes a safe spectacle for white audiences. . . . The fact that the two principal 'Puerto Rican' characters are 'white' actors makes *West Side Story* a drag ball of sorts, where white (male) America can inhabit the dark and dangerous skins of Puerto Ricans and desire Natalie Wood safely (protected by her whiteness) while indulging in Rita Moreno from Bernardo's masquerade [as a "Euro-American" or Greek actor playing Puerto Rican]" (Negrón-Muntaner 2000, 92). Examples like these reinforce Judith Butler's assertion that bodies that matter are discursively constructed and reified by hierarchies of race and gender (Butler 1993, 10).

12. On-screen depictions of interracial romance have been a component of Hollywood since the silent era, but it was expected that the coupling would not suggest procreation (Courtney 2005; Hershfield 1998).

13. While James Mandrell's use of the phrase "between and betwixt" and Alicia Arrizón's work on Latina performance have greatly contributed to my understanding of in-betweenness, I have found the work of Asian American scholars like Gary J. Okihiro and Celine Parreñas Shimizu to be particularly insightful on the racial ambiguity of bodies that are not quite white, not quite black, in terms of social and racial/identity formation as well as performance (Arrizón 1999; Gúzman and Valdivia 2004; Mandrell 2001; Okihiro 1994; Shimizu 2007).

14. I thank Sangita Gopal for her insight on this point. I am also indebted to scholars such as Melissa Blanco Borelli and Cindy García, whose work at the intersection of Latina representation and dance studies illustrates the complexity and intimacy of the brown female body's dance mobility, racialized identity, and agency (Blanco Borelli 2008; García 2008).

15. Pioneer Pictures was cofounded by a Technicolor stockholder, millionaire John Hay (Jack) Whitney; *La Cucaracha* was its first live action film, a test of the production process as a "prototype" Technicolor film (Higgins 2000, 360–361).

16. The actual airdates for "Mural" are unknown, but the commercial was available on the Jell-O Channel Web page (http://brands.kraftfoods.com/jello/explore/channel/) as late as December 2008. I thank Michael Aronson and Jennifer Stoever-Ackerman for drawing my attention to these examples.

17. The excitement and enticement of these colorized bodies were so tempting that by the end of the Technicolor era, three of Hollywood's top ten new star performers were identifiably Latina: Carmen Miranda, Rita Hayworth, and Maria Montez (Basten 1980, 102–126). The early Technicolor palette of blues, greens, and reds was also believed to favor "dark" rather than "white" skin—a hilarious association given the fair complexions of Miranda, Hayworth, and Montez (Higgins 2000, 361; Marez 2004, 215).

18. As quoted by Sarah Berry, Technicolor's production adviser stated that Steffi Duna was qualified for the role because of her exotic look and "natural rhythm," which came from being "weaned on gypsy music" while growing up in Budapest (2000, 119).

19. The English lyrics of Chatita's song compare a woman to a rose, which prompts her to declare that Pancho will now "feel [her] thorns" before sabotaging Pancho's performance.

20. As Curtis Marez observes, the song "La Cucaracha" was firmly linked with marijuana; this association underscores a reading of Pancho and Chatita's coupling as part of a "violently erotic dance number" (Marez 2004, 212).

21. In "Mural," as in "Spa" and "Wiggle Room," the Latina and her female companions become the edible embodiment of the very diet desserts they crave; such associations are common in food advertising campaigns aimed at female consumers, and Susan Bordo's chapter on diet advertising in *Unbearable Weight* features several Jell-O product campaigns (Bordo 1993; Brook 2008). "Mural," however, takes this association to a new level in terms of racialized sexuality.

22. Neither "Wiggle Room" nor "Spa"—the other two commercials available on the Jell-O Web site during the "Mural" campaign—features men. In "Wiggle Room," an all-female and predominantly white cast dance independent of each other to a girl-power jingle by the Go-Gos. While the lyrics in "Mural" seem to address the male dancer as "Baby" on behalf of our Latina, "Wiggle Room" declares independence: "It's a tight squeeze, so c'mon please / Give me some wiggle room / That's what I want" (http://brands.kraftfoods.com/jello/explore/channel/).

23. Although born in New York, the U.S. film industry matured in Southern California beginning around 1910. In this locale, the industry was deeply subject to the racial and national tensions fostered by Prohibition (1919–1933) and the Depression (1929–1939). Built on land that had only recently been incorporated into the United States after the Mexican American War, Hollywood had as its backyard the United States–Mexico border at a time when Prohibition-era nightclubs were increasingly erected along the southern edge of the border. These spaces became notorious for liquor, women, and dance. The combined historical period and location set the stage for the Hollywood Latina's entrance.

24. Rita was dubbed "The Love Goddess" by Winthrop Sargeant (1947) in his *Life* magazine article "The Cult of the Love Goddess."

CHAPTER 2 — DOLORES DEL RIO DANCES
ACROSS THE IMPERIAL COLOR LINE

1. As Jolson sings about being "in the arms of a lovely Latin daughter," his parting-legs gesture actually occurs offscreen since the frame line ends at his hips. The moment, however, is no less racialized or sexualized because of its brevity or lack of visibility, since Jolson's own bodily presence and performance are marked by contradictions of racialized and sexualized representation (Hischak 2008, 380; Rogin 1996, 34).

2. Mary C. Beltrán has argued that the variety and quantity of Del Rio's roles enabled her to exceed Latin typecasting, but I suggest that the casting and movement of Del Rio's body always betrayed her racialized persona (Beltrán 2005, 65).

3. Because most of these films—with the exception of *What Price Glory?*—are unavailable for viewing, my assertions rely on the *American Film Institute [AFI] Catalog* (2003–2010) for information.

4. This argument builds on the works of Mary C. Beltrán and Joanne Hershfield and their positioning of Del Rio's star text within the conventions of Hollywood film (Beltrán 2004, 2005, 2009; Hershfield 1998, 2000).

5. As the Depression soon took its toll on the economy, many Mexican Americans were erroneously blamed for the economic crisis and deported regardless of their citizenship status, which highlighted the secondary status of Mexican Americans in the United States, especially California.

6. In the early colonial period, Spanish notions of whiteness and blackness were tied to racialized notions of religious beliefs that identified whites with Christianity and blacks or Others with non-Christianity. For a more nuanced approach to this topic, see Triana (2010).

7. Of course, this general tendency does not account for the variegated circumstances that impact racialization, such as class, demography, local conditions or circumstances, and so forth. Many thanks to Tania Triana for her insight on this complex issue.

8. Del Rio "often complained of the peasant-style clothes she had to wear in her films" and strove to move beyond the limitations of her early roles (Hershfield 2000, 22–23).

9. In California, the Great Depression exacerbated the social, labor, and racial tensions already mounting between Anglos and Mexican Americans (Sandoval 2005).

10. Ultimately, the division and marginalization of Del Rio's career encouraged her to return to Mexico; there she embarked on a high-profile career that was no less marred by

racialized, sexualized, and nationalized perceptions of class as a result of her time in Hollywood.

11. In fact, while still Rita Cansino, Rita Hayworth was slated by Fox Studios to star in the Technicolor remake of *Ramona*, a move they hoped would "establish Rita as the next Dolores Del Rio" (García 2005).

12. This slippage—between Spain/Mexico and fact/fiction—remains so entrenched that even Joanne Hershfield's otherwise comprehensive research on Del Rio overlooks the complex racial-cultural relationship among Spain, Mexico, and the United States. For example, she dismisses a *Motion Picture Herald* description of the "Spanish" dancing described by *In Caliente* publicity (the film is set in Mexico) by asserting that the studio was simply "confusing Mexico with Spain" (Hershfield 2000, 48–49). In fact, the *Herald* article Hershfield references directly quotes several "catchlines" from the Warner Bros. press book for *In Caliente*, illustrating how such so-called confusions were either deliberate or heavily informed by a regional and national preference for Spanish (not Mexican) diversions (*In Caliente* Press Book 1935).

13. Joanne Hershfield and Mary C. Beltrán identify this period of Del Rio's Hollywood career as both its apex and point of decline (Hershfield 2000, 34; Beltrán 2005, 67).

14. Del Rio's *Girl of the Rio* (1932) illustrates how Latinas visually reinforced the hypersexual image and mediated the racialized gender hierarchy of Hollywood narratives. In the film, Del Rio plays a cantina girl harassed by the film's primary Mexican male character and longing for the heroic white male character. Because films like *Girl of the Rio* often characterized the Mexican male character as vulgar and criminal, the narrative could safely conclude the film with Del Rio and other "cantina girls" like her falling in love with the white male. In his analysis of the film, Marez posits that such representations fall just short of actual "looseness or prostitution," but I suggest that the act of dance and the continued racial ambiguity of Del Rio's early representations meant that these qualities were always just below the surface (Marez 2004, 167, 172).

15. As the Code became an established part of the production process, photos of actresses in costume were submitted to the Production Code Administration for clearance before principal photography began.

16. Joanne Hershfield (1998) does not mention the complexities of Luana's characterization as a Pacific Islander in her otherwise astute article "Race and Romance in *Bird of Paradise*." However brief, Jane Desmond's mention of *Bird of Paradise* is perhaps the best context of Del Rio's role in the film as it pertains to Pacific Islander female bodies; Desmond's book *Staging Tourism: Bodies on Display from Waikiki to Sea World* (1999) was a significant help as I was thinking through the concept of in-betweenness.

17. Although some men do join the dance, the majority of dancing bodies on screen are female.

18. As Del Rio became more selective of the types of characters she would play, her Warner Bros. contract was nearly rewritten from scratch to meet her standards. M. Lewis, presumably Del Rio's lawyer, advised Warner Bros. to carefully examine the contract, "as there [was] almost nothing standard about it" (Lewis 1934).

19. The presence of Etta Moten "emphasiz[es] the presence of the African heritage in Brazilian culture and introduc[es] an image later immortalized by Carmen Miranda" (Freire-Medeiros 2002, 54). By comparison, the Latin group is serenaded by two dark-haired, presumably Latina singers dressed in evening gowns.

20. For additional information on the training of dancers from the 1920s until the present, see Billman (1997) and Keller (1997, 91).

21. The article credits playwright Harry Lee (*Wonder Bar* Press Book 1934c) as its writer, one of the few mentions of writers in the *Wonder Bar* press books.

22. *The Fugitive* opens with a spoken prologue, acknowledging that "this picture was entirely made in our neighboring republic Mexico, at the kind invitation of the Mexican government and of the Mexican motion picture industry" (*AFI Catalog*, s.v. *The Fugitive*).

CHAPTER 3 — CARMEN MIRANDA SHAKES IT FOR THE NATION

1. This book, with its focus on Hollywood film, does not address the multiple meanings Miranda may have exhibited as a popular stage performer in the United States, although the two are closely related.

2. For a compelling analysis of Miranda's movement in terms of samba and rumba rhythms, see Coelho (1998, 155–158).

3. This period of Latin American musicals is largely concentrated in the early 1940s. The desired escapism that these films provided began to evaporate as World War II came to an end.

4. *The Streets of Paris* even legitimized two burlesque performers, introducing a duo named Abbott and Costello to Broadway audiences (*Encyclopaedia Britannica* on line premium service, s.v. "Abbott, Bud; and Costello, Lou").

5. Oddly, the Production Code office, charged with regulating the decency of film content in the United States, had "strongly urged" the studio to "consult [their] Foreign Department to make certain that the finished picture contain[ed] nothing that might cause [them] difficulty with [their] release in Latin America" (Breen 1940).

6. This biography was included in Paramount studio's promotional materials for *Scared Stiff* (1953) (Paramount Studios 1953). However, variations of this text have circulated in multiple forms since 1941. Alberto Sandoval-Sánchez cites a similar quote, which Shari Roberts also uses in her essay on Miranda (Roberts 1993, 11, 21n38; Sandoval-Sánchez 1999, 209).

7. The two categories of the Production Code that specifically impacted Miranda's career were "Costume" (category VI) and "Dances" (category VII).

8. *The Gang's All Here* (1943) required significant correspondence regarding the costuming—most of it concerning Miranda.

9. I have been unable to discover whether the Shuberts were entitled to a percentage of her film work or only her stage appearances.

10. In a telegram from Carmen Miranda to Hedda Hopper, dated February 14, 1946, Miranda states: "Darling Hedda. Notice your item about me being offered four thousand dollars in London. This figure is incorrect as I am now getting ten thousand dollars a week at the Roxy and have also been offered engagements at Palm Island Miami ten thousand dollars per week and Detroit Chicago theatres also offered ten thousand dollars a week. I cannot accept these engagements as I am returning to Hollywood immediately after finishing here at Roxy. I am having wonderful time here and business is terrific see you soon love Carmen Miranda." The text is modified from the uppercase, unpunctuated telegram. Hedda Hopper Collection, file 1821, Margaret Herrick Research Archive, Academy of Motion Picture Arts and Sciences.

11. The sixth shot in the opening sequence is a dissolve from cardboard cutouts of the band in a travel agency window to the actual band performing on a soundstage version of a stage on a beach. The band "comes alive" from the cutouts and begins to play, underscoring the commodified bodies of the Good Neighbor policy that seemingly perform on cue or command.

12. Studio publicity and Miranda herself described her singing as "with movement." Also see Gil-Montero (1989, 80) and Roberts (1993, 17).

13. This integrated musical structure—in which musical numbers are integral to the plot's development—often conflicted with the practice of including nonwhite performers

in musical numbers, since use of the structure meant that these racially integrated numbers could not be easily removed if the picture was to be distributed in Jim Crow states (Griffin 2002).

14. Davis complicates the role of Miranda's whiteness and its imperial function within a multiracial Brazil, stating: "the administration required an image, a face, that could be applauded by the upper, middle and popular classes. . . . Less than fifty years after the abolition of slavery . . . that face would naturally be one of a white person: Carmen Miranda, born in Portugal but raised in Brazil" (Davis 2000, 184).

15. The only other English-language writing on Miranda currently exists in the form of articles, dissertations, and theses (Coelho 1998; Ellis 2008; Stam 2004; Walters 1978).

16. Interestingly, the school was Maria's introduction to radio; the school supported itself by occasionally producing radio programs featuring the talents of its students.

17. Also see *Bananas Is My Business* (1995) by Helena Solberg. Solberg's intervention in Miranda's career is largely organized around gender and class; the filmmaker does not fully engage or critique race—especially whiteness and privilege—in Brazil or the United States.

18. The denial of this hierarchy was linked to the fact that Brazil had a multiethnic demographic (Jensen 1999, 278).

19. "Race was omitted from the 1920 census, while the 1964 constitution forbade any mention of racism" (Bollig 2002, 161).

20. *Banana da terra* was Miranda's last film produced in Brazil and was not affiliated with Hollywood.

21. This transformation occurred as Miranda began the transition toward visual media. The timing may be coincidental, but the ornate image that Miranda embodied would become ideal as she became a Broadway and Hollywood star in the United States. Or, as Davis states, "Her journey north occurred precisely at the moment when she had made the appropriation of a black musical icon complete" (Davis 2000, 197).

22. *Banana da terrra* was Miranda's biggest and last film in Rio. Miranda's Brazilian film career was brief, consisting of short sequences that captured her singing on a stage. These films include *Carnival Songs in Rio* (1932), *Voz do carnival* (1933), and *Alô, alô Brasil!* (1935). Both *Carnival Songs in Rio* and *Voz do carnival* were minor "documentary takes of artists"; copies of these films no longer exist (Gil-Montero 1989, 49).

23. The only English-language account that is wholly attentive to the racial implications of Miranda's Afro-Brazilian performance is Coelho's "Carmen Miranda: An Afro-Brazilian Paradox" (1998). The dissertation is an impressive study of Miranda's embodiment of Afro-Brazilian culture, especially in terms of performance and movement, as well as her shift in performance style in the early part of her Hollywood career.

24. As a whole, the documentary seems problematically uncritical of the racial tensions of representation in both the United States and Brazil.

25. These gestures, however, were not a spontaneous or natural occurrence, as was often reported through Miranda's famous quote in which she claimed that dance came naturally—the dance just needed to come out of her belly.

26. Coelho (1998, 192) is one of the few scholars to note the dilution of Miranda's black Brazilianness as her Hollywood presence accelerated. See also Stam (2004).

27. According to Gil-Montero and the lore of Miranda's discovery, much of Shubert's enthusiasm for Miranda may have been inspired by Henie's interest in Miranda—and Miranda's style. One variation of the story has Henie exclaiming, "Oh, Shubert, what a beautiful dress!" An accompanying version of the tale has Miranda giving a baiana dress to Henie, who then wears it at a Carnival party held aboard the ship upon its return to New York. Miranda's ability to make black style marketable showed her potential—beyond performance (Gil-Montero 1989, 55–56). By contrast, Coelho has determined that the discovery was an orchestrated event organized by a married American couple living in Rio.

Claiborn Foster and Maxwell Jay Rice, an actress and the "regional director of Pan American Airlines in Brazil," respectively, invited Shubert to see Miranda and even hosted an event to introduce the producer and performer. While this account removes some of the sensationalism of the Shubert discovery, Rice's inclusion in this narrative points to some of the larger transnational aspects of Miranda's commodification (Coelho 1998, 108–109).

28. This quotation comes from a draft of the actual article, which may or may not have made it into *Modern Screen* (Hall 1940). This article relies on quotes from Miranda, written in parenthetical transliterations of her "bad" English.

29. This information is gleaned from a caption that accompanies a Corbis image of Carmen Miranda dated December 19, 1941. The caption reads: "Carmen Miranda (left, believe it or not!) hands a life-size manikin [sic] twin of herself a ticket to Rio de Janeiro, which she had just purchased at the Pan American Airways ticket office, at New York's Airline terminal. The manikin replica of the glamorous Brazilian singing star of *Sons o' Fun*, will fly first to Havana and then to Rio, dressed in the latest Bonwit Teller fashions. In cooperation with the Nelson Rockefeller Committee on Inter-American Affairs, the 'twin' will be exhibited as a 'silent Good Neighbor,' displaying North American fashions to South American women" (Bettmann Archive 1941).

30. Because Miranda's hair was rarely visible—or rarely visible without significant ornamentation—this lack of hair prevented her from manipulating one of the most ready signifiers of female whiteness: hair color and style. As we will see with the careers of Rita Hayworth and Jennifer Lopez, the modification of hair contributes greatly toward the standardized codes of whiteness.

31. Miranda's hair was so rarely exposed in film roles that her present-day incarnation as a paper doll shows her undressed likeness wearing a hair cap (Tierney 1982).

32. A group of apparently Latin performers—a chorus line composed of light-complexioned, dark-haired men and women—follows Rogers and Astaire. The dancers wear costumes that seemingly amalgamate various Latin American styles: fringed mantillas, hair combs, beads, and sheer folk skirts. The choreography is listless and primarily involves choreographed formations across the floor. The Latin dancers wear sheer skirts that reveal their legs, which contrasts with the long black and opaque gown worn by Ginger Rogers, and can be read as more explicitly sexual, and therefore nonwhite.

33. Although the presence of Etta Moten "emphasiz[es] the presence of the African heritage in Brazilian culture," it also indicates a sort of essentialized "blackness" in Hollywood film, where black Americans can stand in for black Latin Americans, thus flattening race across national borders (Freire-Medeiros 2002, 54).

34. Latinness mediates racialized performances; in this case, it is a series of dances—from white to black—that become progressively more sensual (Kinder 1978, 40).

35. Early in the film, Melvin denigrates the rumba as "vulgar," even though the bodies in motion within the frame are tame in every way.

36. In fact, DirecTV's synopsis (2009) summarized the film *A Date with Judy* as "a Santa Barbara, Calif. teen thinks her father is having an affair with a Latin dancer."

37. A Google search for Carmen Miranda images shows how many different people, and animals, have invoked the spirit and image of Miranda in the years since her death.

CHAPTER 4 — RITA HAYWORTH AND THE COSMETIC BORDERS OF RACE

1. In fact, McLean argues that significant intimate components of Hayworth's past were public knowledge. For example, Barbara Leaming's biography of Hayworth, *If This Was Happiness*, gained popularity by alleging that Rita was sexually abused by her father. McLean points out that fan magazines and other popular publications had discretely made similar allegations nearly forty years earlier. Other traditional biographies, including the

Hugh Hefner–coproduced documentary *Rita* (2003), have largely overlooked the importance of Hayworth's Spanish lineage in the trajectory of her Hollywood career (Leaming 1989, 17–18; McLean 2004, 66–67).

2. Although *Being Rita Hayworth* concentrates on Hayworth's stardom and emphasizes the role that dance played in determining Hayworth's agency, McLean (1992) previously explored Rita's early career as an ethnic performer.

3. Such tendencies continue. The early half of the novel *The People of Paper* by Salvador Plascencia provides a fantastical account of Rita Hayworth's Mexican origins.

4. Rita is also rumored to have appeared as an uncredited dancer in various short films (Parish 1972, 219).

5. The Dancing Cansinos were originally a brother-sister team composed of Eduardo and his sister (Parish 1972, 220). Both Leaming and Parish mention Eduardo's epiphanic moment ("All of a sudden, I wake up! Wow! She has a figure! She ain't no baby anymore!"), but Leaming alleges that this statement hinted at Eduardo's sexual abuse of Rita in her youth.

6. According to Leaming, Rita's hair color change was orchestrated by Eduardo and counts as one of the many ways in which he manipulated Rita. Leaming points out that in 1913 Eduardo and Elisa "had wasted no time in Americanizing their costumes" once in the United States, "but [along the border] Eduardo dressed Margarita as a *Spanish* girl so that the audience would perceive them to be a *local* couple" (Leaming 1989, 16, emphasis added).

7. Joe Schenck was an instrumental figure in the 1935 Twentieth Century and Fox merger.

8. Historian George Sánchez has demonstrated how ambiguous and complex the identity panic was for both whites and Mexicans. The 1930s pushed many bodies south of the border, from repatriated Mexicans and Mexican Americans to Anglo-Americans seeking liquor and gambling during Prohibition and all others seeking employment along the border (Beltrán 2005; Kobal 1978, 45; Sánchez 1993, 209–226).

9. McLean (2004) does an excellent job of illustrating how this origin myth—considered to be a revelation in some more contemporary biographical accounts—was actually a standard representation of Hayworth as her career became more mainstream. McLean, however, does not fully explore the cultural impact on Hayworth's representational evolution in terms of race, gender, and sexuality.

10. The *American Film Institute Catalog* suggests that Rita Cansino was actually in the cast of *In Caliente*, although her appearance is hard to determine (*AFI Catalog*, s.v. *In Caliente*).

11. One can easily add Native American to the list of interchangeable brown women viewed as comparables in Hollywood, a point made by Beltrán, Hershfield, and others (Beltrán 2005, 68; Hershfield 2000, 15).

12. Representational Irishness in the United States, as I use it here, operates like Spanishness as a kind of racialized whiteness, irrespective of its European connections. As Matthew Frye Jacobson and Mark Quigley have noted, the racialization of Irishness as a white identity challenges an easy equation of Irishness = whiteness (Jacobson 1998; Quigley 2009).

13. This term is frequently used in biographies to describe the process of dying Hayworth's hair from brunette to auburn.

14. See information about Crawford in O'Neill (2002).

15. Of course, Hayworth is blond in *The Lady from Shanghai* (1948), the exception that proves the rule. The film is discussed at length later in the chapter.

16. Noticing that two men are following her, Arthur's character puts a sword to their throats. When she recognizes their U.S. dialect, however, she is excited to see them;

the scene implies that she expected them to be South American and therefore an immediate threat, whereas two scraggly and stalking men from the United States were immediately safe company.

17. The exceptions are Doña Sol in *Blood and Sand* (1941), Maria Acuña in *You Were Never Lovelier* (1942), and Carmen in *The Loves of Carmen* (1948). Of these, both Doña Sol and Carmen are Spanish, while Maria is Argentinean.

18. From the September 1940 issue of *Motion Picture*, as quoted by McLean (2004, 37).

19. The original film version of this novel featured Rudolph Valentino, another star presented as an "exotic-erotic spectacle," speaking to both the versatility of ethnicity and the sensuality attributed to the Spanish subjects in these films (Hansen 1991, 260).

20. *Blood and Sand* was Rita's first film with Fox after her contract was cancelled; she then returned, commanding a significantly higher price.

21. *You'll Never Get Rich* was one of the first Hollywood films to incorporate war into its mise-en-scène (Mueller 1985, 187).

22. By the finale, Astaire's character has regained the lead in the narrative, rigging the diegetic finale performance so that he and Sheila (Hayworth) marry without her consent. By ending in marriage, Hayworth's partnership with Astaire in *You'll Never Get Rich* lent her the legitimacy of Astaire's "gentlemanly" persona.

23. McLean also stresses that musicals have largely been validated through analyses that emphasize male authorship—either in terms of the performer (Astaire, Kelly, etc.) or auteur (Minnelli, Freed Unit, etc.) (McLean 2004).

24. For example, John Mueller continually compares Astaire's partners to Rogers in his book *Astaire Dancing* (1985). For an interesting revision of the Rogers-Astaire dynamic, see Edward Gallafent's *Astaire and Rogers* (2004), which chronicles the pair's films as a serial.

25. This domestication was further developed in Hayworth and Astaire's second film together, *You Were Never Lovelier* (1942), in which Hayworth plays the daughter in a wealthy Argentine family; here, Argentina operates primarily as an exotic locale (it does not figure much into the narrative of the film) but also subtly invokes Hayworth's difference.

26. With the exception of brunette Cyd Charisse in *The Band Wagon* (1953) and *Silk Stockings* (1957), Hayworth is perhaps the most sexual or sexualized of Astaire's star partners.

27. Like the importance of women in the general genre, this female power is often disregarded or subjugated in favor of the male performer. See McLean's discussion of the musical female and "women's musicals" (McLean 2004, 112–117).

28. The Cole Porter song in itself exemplifies the function of in-betweenness. "So Near and Yet So Far" was not actually an Afro-Cuban rumba but a U.S. consumer-friendly approximation called a "latune"—a "tune with a Latin beat and an English-language lyric" that was popular in the United States from the 1930s (as evident in *Flying Down to Rio*) until the 1960s (Firmat 2008, 180–181, 184).

29. Second only to that of Betty Grable, Hayworth's pinup status made her a lasting iconic figure; in 1982 Stephen King referenced her image in his novella *Rita Hayworth and the Shawshank Redemption*.

30. After the release of *Cover Girl*, *You'll Never Get Rich* and *Cover Girl* were then released as a double feature. Audiences were asked to judge "the dance battle of the century" among Hayworth, Astaire, and Kelly.

31. Fred Astaire is considered the more "gentlemanly" dance performer of the musical era, contrasted with the more contemporary, working-class persona of Gene Kelly (Billman 1997, 66). It was not until Kelly starred with Hayworth in *Cover Girl* that he was recognized as a star—just as Hayworth had not achieved such acclaim until her partnership with Astaire. This process was echoed when George Clooney became an identifiable sex symbol after his pairing with Jennifer Lopez in *Out of Sight* (1998).

32. For an excellent example of Cole's style, see The *"I Don't Care" Girl* (1953).

33. While Cole was called in for Hayworth during *Cover Girl*, he fully crafted her choreography in the films *Tonight and Every Night, Gilda*, and *Down to Earth*—the very films that earmark her "Love Goddess" period (Billman 1997, 79).

34. The magazine *Life* is incorporated into the narrative. In one scene, a *Life* photographer tries to take Rosalind's picture. As she poses, she slyly covers her/Hayworth's famous legs with a copy of *Life* magazine; at the insistence of the photographer ("For the boys!"), Rosalind/Hayworth reveals her gams.

35. Beyond its history across racialized communities within the United States, the jitterbug was also popularized in Europe during World War II. The remaining Hayworth performances include the comedic pantomime of female soldiers in "The Boy I Left Behind," a drama-tragedy inspired modernesque performance in "Cry and You Cry Alone," and a tame vaudevillian striptease in "Anywhere."

36. Instead of marrying Paul, Rosalind chooses to remain with the theater company and pay homage to friends who died as the result of a bomb.

37. According to one source, this association with an atom bomb upset Hayworth and was a publicity stunt orchestrated by Harry Cohn (Morella and Epstein 1983, 99–100).

38. While one *Lady from Shanghai* press book article mentions Hayworth's origins and her discovery in Agua Caliente, its connection between Hayworth and Mexico is much more ambiguous than had been the case for previous publicity campaigns.

39. McLean argues that Hayworth was one of the first actors to receive a percentage of studio profits when she formed her own production company, Beckworth (McLean 2004, 12, 211n28).

40. The film is frequently sold as *Playboy Presents Rita*. In an odd serendipity, the image of Marilyn Monroe (shot in 1949) that graced *Playboy*'s debut centerfold bears an uncanny, if coincidental, resemblance to Hayworth's publicity shot, especially the pose and hairstyle, for *Cover Girl* (1944) ("Hugh Hefner on a Life Less Ordinary" 2007).

41. One press book encouraged exhibitors to aim publicity at women because they were "the nation's shoppers." Like women's work during the postwar era, Hayworth's domestic labor was necessary to the economic life of the postwar period, particularly as white, nonworking-class women were increasingly rushed back into the home.

42. Page Dougherty Delano's article (2000) on the use of makeup by women during the war offers a fascinating example of the complexity of these gendered structures during and after the war.

43. For more about the matrix of gender, race, and class as an imperial project, see Anne McClintock's *Imperial Leather* (1995). Although McClintock focuses primarily on British imperialism, there is much overlap with nation building in and by the United States.

CHAPTER 5 — RITA MORENO, THE CRITICALLY ACCLAIMED
"ALL-ROUND ETHNIC"

1. Animal is described as the Muppet Band's "savage, frenzied drummer" (*Wikipedia*, s.v. *Muppet Show*).

2. The Muppet named Sweetums was originally given the line "That's my kind of woman" in the first season's fourth episode (the same episode in which Animal's role is expanded), but the phrase became more frequently associated with Animal, especially as he became more of a crazed womanizer. The phrase "My kind of woman" was occasionally simplified to the shrieked "Woo-man!" as Animal chased women.

3. One exception is Jennifer Lopez's Golden Globe nomination for her performance in *Selena*. Although Rosie Pérez is not included in this project, she received an Academy Award nomination for Best Supporting Actress for her work in *Fearless* (1993).

4. As I mentioned in chapter 2, Dolores Del Rio's open objection to depictions of Mexicans and Mexico was a precursor to her abandonment of Hollywood film.

5. A recent exception is Mary C. Beltrán's chapter on Rita Moreno in *Latino/a Stars in U.S. Eyes* (2009).

6. Rita's mother's profession was typical for Puerto Rican women during the period, but studio biographies often mentioned that her specialty was lingerie. In publicity materials, studios used this detail to reinforce and enhance Rita's representation as a sexpot. In *Popi* (1969), Moreno's character works as a seamstress in a sweatshop that produces intimate apparel.

7. Moreno's first role was in the independent film *So Young, So Bad* (1950), in which she played Dolores Guerrero, a suicidal ward of the Elmview Corrective School for Girls.

8. Moreno praised Gene Kelly's "theater sensibility, or New York sensibility" as the reason he was able to see beyond her ethnic type—a capacity that, she says, few people had, which limited the kinds of roles she received for the length of her career. Moreno also notes that she might have been able to remain at MGM if Gene Kelly had remained at the studio and continued to cast young roles (Miller 2000).

9. As a commonwealth of the United States, Puerto Rico exemplifies in-betweenness on a state and national level. For example, although Puerto Ricans are citizens of the United States, they do not have full access to rights as voters while living on the island itself.

10. Although the film version of *West Side Story* iconized the "Puerto Rican problem" for the nation at large, Stoever-Ackerman has shown how films like *Blackboard Jungle* (1955) had already begun to sonically depict Puerto Rican bodies as a kind of racialized noise in New York (Negrón-Muntaner 2000; Stoever-Ackerman 2009).

11. Such oversights have often resulted in fans and interviewers confusing Moreno with Rivera, despite the fact that they only shared the one role from *West Side Story* (Miller 2000).

12. Aside from the chapters on Moreno in Beltrán's work (2004, 2009) and Negrón-Muntaner's (2000, 2004), Moreno's career has been given little scholarly attention.

13. When Anita ventures into the soda shop to give Tony Maria's message, the Jets attack her with words and gestures—"pierced ear," "gold tooth," and the whistled tune of "La Cucaracha"—that signify the many ways that Latinas have been racialized, sexualized, and mobilized since the early part of the cinematic century as evinced in the careers of Dolores Del Rio, Carmen Miranda, and Rita Hayworth.

14. Interestingly, the *West Side Story* shooting script available in the Bob Wise Collection at the University of Southern California Cinematic Arts Library includes written dialect for the Jets but not the Sharks, suggesting that the sonic expectations of the Latino/a characters were self-evident.

15. This shift is most noticeable at the moment in "A Boy Like That" when Rita Moreno's dialogue as Anita suddenly shifts to the lyrics of the song.

16. While this use of the term "unaccented" is problematic, it speaks to the regionally/ethnically unmarked code used to signify "American English."

17. It is interesting that in this sketch, the "white male" Muppets either ignore or insult Gonzalez and that her Spanish dialog uses a Caribbean term, which contrasts the English reference she makes to (Mexican) enchiladas. This contrast suggests a tension between Moreno's improvised "play" and how that play is framed by script.

CHAPTER 6 — JENNIFER LOPEZ, RACIAL MOBILITY, AND THE NEW URBAN/LATINA COMMODITY

1. This chapter's usage of the term "blackness" should not suggest that there is one form—authentic or otherwise—of blackness. Like whiteness or brownness, blackness is malleable, highly constructed, and in many ways has been shaped and repackaged by MTV.

2. I suggest that this crossover process continued beyond the early period that Beltrán discusses in her insightful article "The Hollywood Latina Body as Site of Social Struggle" (2002).

3. Beyond the usual appearance on "Making the Video" (an MTV series that goes behind the scenes with performers on their video shoots), Lopez also collaborated with MTV to executive produce "Jennifer Lopez: Beyond the Runway" in 2005 and the short-run series *DanceLife* in 2007. Lopez's celebrity standing with MTV made her the perfect person to announce the channel's latest Latino venture at the 2006 MTV Video Music Awards: MTV Tr3s. Aimed at the U.S. Latino/a market, MTV Tr3s applied a specific cultural filter to the MTV brand. Says Lucia Ballas-Traynor, general manager of MTV TR3S: "You take a global brand like MTV and what it stands for: everything music, youth, cool, hip. Regardless of the ethnic origin you have to start with that. Then you apply the cultural filter, which in the case of MTV TR3S is Latino" (as quoted in Nemer 2006).

4. In effect, music videos function like commercial jingles by programming us to recall specific images (performers, movement, fashion, and other inanimate products) when cued by a particular song (Kinder 1984, 3).

5. MTV's consistent reinvention is a necessity of its business model in that it must continually remain relevant to an ever-pubescent audience.

6. I believe this rock focus catered to the U.S. cultural (hegemonic) backlash after the disco period of the late 1970s. The visible whiteness of rock on MTV countered the black, gay, and urban origins of disco. For more on the roots of disco, see Richard Dyer's "In Defence of Disco" (1979). Michael Jackson experienced his own challenges entering the hallowed airwaves of MTV. Similarly, Prince struggled to cross over through MTV representation. While both were eventually successful, their early exposure was limited.

7. It was only a matter of time before Hollywood recognized the impact of MTV. After all, MTV was a joint venture funded by Warner Bros. and American Express.

8. The film, heavily influenced by and promoted on MTV, effectively "ingrain[ed] the music into the minds of the American public" to create a "95% awareness in the 'youth market'" (Salamon 1983).

9. I do not mean to suggest that race or ethnicity need be explained or excused by a film; in fact, the freedom for a nonwhite performer to simply be a character in a film can be seen as a triumph. However, the levels of ambiguity at work in *Flashdance* do not work to mainstream Beals/Alex's body so much as they function to suggest/reinforce the symbolic qualities of her nonwhiteness, namely, her sexual knowing and ability to dance.

10. Alex's concern for her friends can be framed as both maternal and paternal. In one scene, Alex rescues her naive white female friend from performing in a full-nudity bar. Alex storms the all-male-patron club, wearing baggy army-surplus work clothes and shoving men out of her way. After dragging her naked friend from the stage, she delivers a tough-love lecture outside the club. The scene accentuates Alex's androgyny while legitimizing her own strip performances as somehow more artistic (and thereby more classy).

11. The film was similarly illegitimate; it was all but abandoned by Paramount. Upon its success, everyone clamored to claim responsibility (Pollock 1983).

12. Alex's ritual visits to a Catholic priest emulate the white-ethnic Italian appeal of Tony Manero in the disco hit *Saturday Night Fever* (1978), a film similarly built on an urban dance trend and ubiquitous soundtrack.

13. Interestingly enough, even McRobbie misreads the character, suggesting that "Hispanic-born Alex is pleased to be able to leave her disco-dancing days behind her" (McRobbie 1997, 217).

14. Indeed, Beals's complexion was so fair that, Bogle notes, the studio forbade darker-complexioned black actor Denzel Washington from kissing Beals in *Devil in a Blue Dress* (1995) (Bogle 2001, 369).

15. It is rumored that several other b-boys (break-dancers) danced in Beals's stead, in addition to Jahan and Crazy Legs.

16. With the exception of *Devil in a Blue Dress*, Beals all but disappeared until the 2004 television series *The L Word*.

17. For more on the multiple framings of Lopez, see Beltrán (2002) and Ovalle (2007).

18. I thank Jennifer Stoever-Ackerman for her insight on this section, especially her attention to the racialized and gendered trends of Lopez's music collaborations and the inherent implications on the representations of black women.

19. The "Maniac" sequence begins when Alex's character catches a ballet performance on television. After attempting a pirouette in her living room and spilling her (product placement) Pepsi, she begins this iconic and hyperkinetically memorable dance montage.

20. For an excellent analysis of Lopez's butt, its authenticity, and all it can mean, see Negrón-Muntaner (1997).

21. Lopez's labor (physical exertion) on the set of "I'm Glad" was so intense that shooting was suspended for a day while she recovered from a dance-related injury ("Making the Video" 2003).

22. There are, of course, limits to Lopez's nonwhiteness. She was readily critiqued for her personal use of the term "niggaz" on "I'm Real," even though Ja Rule used the same term on the same track.

23. The thrust of this urban = black equation is so strong that even Sean Combs has expressed his dislike for the term "urban" because it is a limiting category—"just another way of saying 'black'" (Rozhon 2005, 1).

24. Fox was effectively the fourth network and challenged the traditional three-network structure of ABC, CBS, and NBC in both style and revenue.

25. This set piece is most reminiscent of the rooftop iconized by Rita Moreno's key film, *West Side Story* (1961).

26. The video was heavily played in MTV's rotation and marks one of the few and last times Lopez would work with another female recording artist.

27. In the video, Lopez salsas with Combs during a pyrotechnic-filled dance break, a segment wholly out of character with the spy-in-the-desert themed video. For more on how Lopez's music video career relates to her film career, see Ovalle (2007).

28. For more on the relationship between Lopez and MTV, see Ovalle (2008, 253–268).

29. Lopez seems to oversee many of the daily decisions of her business ventures and is a co-investor in Los Angeles' Conga Room (Fox 2008; Shuster 2002; Wilson and Feitelberg 2004). By 2008 Beyoncé Knowles and a few other women may have come close, but Lopez still led the pack.

30. Many thanks are extended to Irmary Reyes-Santos for her feedback on Emilio Estefan's role in Lopez's career.

31. For example, the infamous green dress Lopez wore to the 2000 Grammys (while escorted by Sean Combs) looms large in her mystique as a fashionably sexy body.

32. Lopez's comment prompted the article writer to (quite rightly) note, "Apparently, in Hollywood, brown is some kind of mediating color between black and white" (Murray 1997).

33. It is fitting that Lopez's first fragrance was titled "Glow" in 2007.

34. This conformity is supported by the fact that—as yet—Fairuza Balk has not achieved the same level of media representation as have Lopez and Theron. Of the three, Theron's persona is the only full "blonde." Although Lopez's media exposure is arguably far greater than that of the other two, Theron is the only star of the trio to be recognized by the Academy of Motion Picture Arts and Sciences.

35. In the commentary for her video "I'm Glad," Lopez remarks that her hair is naturally curly like the style featured in the video (Gable 2003).

36. Although Lopez and Harrelson exhibit romantic tension in *Money Train*, their relationship is tempered and mediated by her dance and eventual sex scene with Wesley Snipes.

37. As of 2006, Lopez's brand cleared $400 million in sales (DeCarlo 2006; Lockwood 2006).

Works Cited

Abramowitz, Rachel. 2000. *Is That a Gun in Your Pocket? Women's Experience of Power in Hollywood*. New York: Random House.

Albright, Ann Cooper. 1997. *Choreographing Difference: The Body and Identity in Contemporary Dance*. Hanover, NH: Wesleyan University Press; University Press of New England.

Aldama, Arturo J. 2005. "Native Americans/Mexicanos." In *The Oxford Encyclopedia of Latinos and Latinas in the United States* (e-reference edition), edited by S. Oboler and D. J. González. New York: Oxford University Press.

Almaguer, Tomás. 1994. *Racial Fault Lines: The Historical Origins of White Supremacy in California*. Berkeley: University of California Press.

Altman, Rick. 1987. *American Film Musical*. Bloomington: Indiana University Press.

American Film Institute [AFI] Catalog. 2003–2010. Online database: http://afi.chadwyck.com.

Aparicio, Frances R. 1998. *Listening to Salsa: Gender, Latin Popular Music, and Puerto Rican Cultures*. Hanover, NH: University Press of New England.

Appelbaum, Nancy P., Anne S. Macpherson, and Karin Alejandra Rosemblatt. 2003. *Race and Nation in Modern Latin America*. Chapel Hill: University of North Carolina Press.

Arrizón, Alicia. 1999. *Traversing the Stage: Latina Performance*. Bloomington: Indiana University Press.

Aufderheide, Pat. 1986. "Music Videos: The Look of the Sound." *Journal of Communication* 36:57–77.

Balzano, Michael P. 1983. "*Flashdance*: A *Rocky* in Toe Shoes." *Los Angeles Times*, July 31.

Banet-Weiser, Sarah. 1999. *The Most Beautiful Girl in the World: Beauty Pageants and National Identity*. Berkeley: University of California Press.

Banks, J. 1996. "Music Video Cartel: A Survey of Anti-Competitive Practices by MTV and Major Record Companies." *Popular Music and Society* 20(2): 173–196.

Barthes, Roland. 1972. *Mythologies*. New York: Hill and Wang.

Barzel, Ann. 1997. "The Moving Image: Dance and Television—70th Anniversary Issue." *Dance Magazine*, June, 120–124.

Basten, Fred E. 1980. *Glorious Technicolor: The Movies' Magic Rainbow*. Cranbury, NJ: A. S. Barnes.

Bell, Arthur. 1976. "Rita Moreno Outclasses Her Old Act." *Village Voice*, August 23.

Beltrán, Mary C. 2002. "The Hollywood Latina Body as Site of Social Struggle: Media Constructions of Stardom and Jennifer Lopez's 'Cross-over Butt.'" *Quarterly Review of Film and Video* 19(1): 71–86.

———. 2004. "Bronze Seduction: The Shaping of Latina Stardom in Hollywood Film and Star Publicity." Ph.D. dissertation, University of Texas, Austin.

———. 2005. "Dolores Del Rio, the First 'Latino Invasion,' and Hollywood's Transition to Sound." *Aztlán: The Journal of Chicano Studies* 30 (Winter): 55–86.

———. 2009. *Latina/o Stars in U.S. Eyes: The Making and Meanings of Film and TV Stardom.* Urbana: University of Illinois Press.

Bennett, Dan. 2004. "Hefner Releases DVD Homage to '40s Screen Siren Rita Hayworth." *Video Store* 26(24): 27.

Berg, Charles Ramírez. 2002. *Latino Images in Film: Stereotypes, Subversion, and Resistance.* Austin: University of Texas Press.

Bernardi, Daniel. 2007. *The Persistence of Whiteness: Race and Contemporary Hollywood Cinema.* New York: Routledge.

Bernstein, Matthew H., and Dana F. White. 2007. "*Imitation of Life* in a Segregated Atlanta: Its Promotion, Distribution, and Reception." *Film History* 19(2): 152–178.

Berry, Sarah. 2000. *Screen Style: Fashion and Femininity in 1930s Hollywood.* Minneapolis: University of Minnesota Press.

Bettmann Archive. 1941. "Carmen Miranda." Photograph.

Billman, Larry. 1997. *Film Choreographers and Dance Directors: An Illustrated Biographical Encyclopedia.* Jefferson, NC: McFarland and Co.

Blanco Borelli, Melissa. 2008. "'¿Y Ahora Qué vas a Hacer, Mulata?': Hip Choreographies in the Mexican *Cabaretera* Film *Mulata* (1954)." *Women and Performance: A Journal of Feminist Theory* 18(3): 215–233.

Blood and Sand Press Book. 1941a. "Bright Colors Fascinate Men Says Mamoulian." P. 26. Fox Studios Press Book Collection, Cinematic Arts Library, University of Southern California, Los Angeles.

———. 1941b. "Rita Hayworth Cast as Siren in New Hit Film." P. 24. Fox Studios Press Book Collection, Cinematic Arts Library, University of Southern California, Los Angeles.

Bodeen, DeWitt. 1976. *From Hollywood: The Careers of 15 Great American Stars.* South Brunswick, NJ: A. S. Barnes.

Bogle, Donald. 2001. *Toms, Coons, Mulattoes, Mammies, and Bucks; An Interpretive History of Blacks in American Films.* 4th ed. New York: Continuum.

Bollig, Ben. 2002. "White Rapper/Black Beats: Discovering a Race Problem in the Music of Gabriel o Pensador." *Latin American Music Review* 23(2): 159–178.

Bordo, Susan. 1993. *Unbearable Weight: Feminism, Western Culture, and the Body.* Berkeley: University of California Press.

Breen, Joseph I. 1940. *Down Argentine Way.* Production Code Administration Collection Files, Margaret Herrick Library, Academy of Motion Picture Arts and Sciences, Los Angeles.

Briggs, Laura. 2002. *Reproducing Empire: Race, Sex, Science, and U.S. Imperialism in Puerto Rico.* Berkeley: University of California Press.

Brook, Heather. 2008. "Feed Your Face." *Continuum: Journal of Media and Cultural Studies* 22(1): 141–157.

Brooks, Daphne. 2006. *Bodies in Dissent: Spectacular Performances of Race and Freedom (1850–1910)*. Durham, NC: Duke University Press.

Brown, Jayna. 2008. *Babylon Girls: Black Women Performers and the Shaping of the Modern*. Durham, NC: Duke University Press.

Butler, Judith. 1993. *Bodies That Matter: On the Discursive Limits of "Sex."* New York: Routledge.

Candelaria, Cordelia. 2005. "La Malinche." In *The Oxford Encyclopedia of Latinos and Latinas in the United States* (e-reference edition), edited by S. Oboler and D. J. González. New York: Oxford University Press.

Carmencita. 1894. Filmed by Thomas A. Edison, Inc. Produced by W.K.L. Dickson. Library of Congress.

Carr, Larry. 1979. *More Fabulous Faces: The Evolution and Metamorphosis of Dolores Del Rio, Myrna Loy, Carole Lombard, Bette Davis and Katharine Hepburn*. New York: Doubleday.

Coelho, José Ligiéro. 1998. "Carmen Miranda: An Afro-Brazilian Paradox." Ph.D. dissertation, New York University.

Cofer, Judith Ortiz. 2007. "The Myth of the Latin Woman: I Just Met a Girl Named Maria." In *Race, Class, and Gender in the United States: An Integrated Study*, edited by Paula S. Rothenberg. New York: Worth Publishing.

Coffman, Elizabeth. 2002. "Women in Motion: Loie Fuller and the 'Interpenetration' of Art and Science." *Camera Obscura* 17 (1): 72–105.

Corliss, Richard. 1983. "Manufacturing a Multimedia Hit." *Time*, May 9.

Courtney, Susan. 2005. *Hollywood Fantasies of Miscegenation: Spectacular Narratives of Gender and Race, 1903–1967*. Princeton, NJ: Princeton University Press.

Dávila, Arlene. 2001. *Latinos Inc.: The Marketing and Making of a People*. Berkeley: University of California Press.

Davis, Darién J. 2000. "Racial Purity and National Humor: Exploring Brazilian Samba from Noel Rosa to Carmen Miranda, 1930–1939." In *Latin American Popular Culture: An Introduction*, edited by William H. Beezley and Linda A. Curcio-Nagy. Wilmington, DE: SR Books.

DeCarlo, Lauren. 2006. "Sweetface Names President." *WWD: Women's Wear Daily*, May 17.

Delano, Page Dougherty. 2000. "Making Up for War: Sexuality and Citizenship in Wartime Culture." *Feminist Studies* 26(1): 33–68.

Delgado, Celeste Fraser, and José Esteban Muñoz. 1997. *Everynight Life: Culture and Dance in Latin/o America*. Durham, NC: Duke University Press.

Del Rio–Warner Bros. Studios contract. 1934. Dolores Del Rio production files. Warner Bros. Archives, School of Cinematic Arts, University of Southern California, Los Angeles.

DeLyser, Dydia. 2003. "Ramona Memories: Fiction, Tourist Practices, and Placing the Past in Southern California." *Annals of the Association of American Geographers* 93(4): 886–908.

D'Emilio, John, and Estelle B. Freedman. 1997. *Intimate Matters: A History of Sexuality in America*. Chicago: University of Chicago Press.

Desmond, Jane, ed. 1997. *Meaning in Motion: New Cultural Studies of Dance*. Durham, NC: Duke University Press.

———. 1999. *Staging Tourism: Bodies on Display from Waikiki to Sea World*. Chicago: University of Chicago Press.

Desmond, Jane. 2001. *Dancing Desires: Choreographing Sexualities On and Off the Stage.* Madison: University of Wisconsin Press.

Dyer, Richard. 1978a. "Postscript: Queers and Women in Film Noir." In *Women in Film Noir,* edited by E. Ann Kaplan. London: British Film Institute.

———. 1978b. "Resistance through Charisma: Rita Hayworth and Gilda." In *Women in Film Noir,* edited by E. Ann Kaplan. London: British Film Institute.

———. 1979. "In Defence of Disco." *Gay Left: A Gay Socialist Journal* 8 (Summer): 20–23.

———. 1986. *Heavenly Bodies: Film Stars and Society.* New York: St. Martin's Press.

———. 1997. *White.* New York: Routledge.

———. 2002. *Only Entertainment.* New York: Routledge.

———. 2004. *Heavenly Bodies: Film Stars and Society.* 2nd ed. New York: Routledge.

Ebenkamp, Becky. 2003. "They Guard Their MTV." *MediaWeek,* October 20, p. 28.

Ellis, Amanda J. 2008. "Captivating a Country with Her Curves: Examining the Importance of Carmen Miranda's Iconography in Creating National Identities." M.A. thesis, State University of New York at Buffalo.

Enloe, Cynthia. 1990. *Bananas, Beaches and Bases: Making Feminist Sense of International Politics.* Berkeley: University of California Press.

Feuer, Jane. 1993. *The Hollywood Musical.* 2nd ed. Bloomington: Indiana University Press.

Firmat, Gustavo Pérez. 2008. "Latunes." *Latin American Research Review* 43:180–203.

Fox, Killian. 2008. "I Liked It So Much I Bought the Restaurant." *Observer,* August 17.

Fregoso, Rosa Linda. 1993. *The Bronze Screen: Chicana and Chicano Film Culture.* Minneapolis: University of Minnesota Press.

———. 1999. "Re-imagining Chicana Urban Identities in the Public Sphere, *Cool Chuca Style.*" In *Between Woman and Nation: Nationalisms, Transnational Feminisms, and the State,* edited by C. Kaplan, Norma Alarcón, and Minoo Moallem. Durham, NC: Duke University Press.

Freire-Medeiros, Bianca. 2002. "Hollywood Musicals and the Invention of Rio de Janeiro, 1933–1953." *Cinema Journal* 41(4): 52–67.

Fuentes, Carlos. 1992. *The Buried Mirror: Reflections on Spain and the New World.* New York: Houghton Mifflin.

Gable, Jim. 2003. "Jennifer Lopez: The Reel Me." New York: Epic Music Video.

Gallafent, Edward. 2004. *Astaire and Rogers.* New York: Columbia University Press.

García, Cindy. 2008. "'Don't leave me, Celia!': Salsera Homosociality and Pan-Latina Corporealities." *Women and Performance: A Journal of Feminist Theory* 18(3): 199–213.

García, Emma. 2005. "Rita Hayworth." In *The Oxford Encyclopedia of Latinos and Latinas in the United States* (e-reference edition), edited by S. Oboler and D. J. González. New York: Oxford University Press.

"Gene Kelly, Anatomy of a Dancer." 2006. PBS American Masters series essay, http://www.pbs.org/wnet/americanmasters/database/kelly_g.html (accessed September 2006).

Gilda Press Book. 1946a. "Film Backgrounds in Latin America Becoming Popular (Feature)." In "Prepared Reviews/Theater Notices/Feature," 17. Columbia Studios Press Book Collection, Cinematic Arts Library, University of Southern California, Los Angeles.

———. 1946b. "Gal GI's Picked!" In "Theater and Lobby Suggestions," 10. Columbia Studios Press Book Collection, Cinematic Arts Library, University of Southern California, Los Angeles.

———. 1946c. "Hayworth, Ford Bring New Drama to State Screen (General Advance)." In "*Gilda* Publicity," 16. Columbia Studios Press Book Collection, Cinematic Arts Library, University of Southern California, Los Angeles.

———. 1946d. "Hayworth Scores as Spicy 'Gilda' in Dramatic Film (Review)." In "Prepared Reviews/Theater Notices/Feature," 17. Columbia Studios Press Book Collection, Cinematic Arts Library, University of Southern California, Los Angeles.

———. 1946e. "Hollywood Photographer Discusses His Subjects (Feature)." In "Glamour Girls vs. Tanks/5% Redheads/Rita Takes Punishment," 24. Columbia Studios Press Book Collection, Cinematic Arts Library, University of Southern California, Los Angeles.

———. 1946f. "Rita Hayworth Turns Dramatic at Height of Glorious Career (Biographical Feature)." In "Hayworth, Ford, MacReady, Calleia Biographies," 22. Columbia Studios Press Book Collection, Cinematic Arts Library, University of Southern California, Los Angeles.

———. 1946g. "Romantic Drama Stars Hayworth in New Type Role (General Advance)." In "*Gilda* Publicity," 16. Columbia Studios Press Book Collection, Cinematic Arts Library, University of Southern California, Los Angeles.

Gil-Montero, Martha. 1989. *Brazilian Bombshell: The Biography of Carmen Miranda.* New York: D. I. Fine.

Gonzalez, Juan. 2000. *Harvest of Empire: A History of Latinos in America.* New York: Viking.

Gray, Herman. 1995. *Watching Race: Television and the Struggle for "Blackness."* Minneapolis: University of Minnesota Press.

Griffin, Sean. 2002. "The Gang's All Here: Generic versus Racial Integration in the 1940s Musical." *Cinema Journal* 42(1): 21–45.

Grosfoguel, Ramón, and Chloé S. Georas. 2001. "Latino Caribbean Diasporas in New York." In *Mambo Montage: The Latinization of New York*, edited by A. Laó-Montes and A. M. Dávila. New York: Columbia University Press.

Gross, Terry. 2001. Interview with George Chakiris, Rita Moreno, and Marni Nixon. *Fresh Air*, National Public Radio.

Gúzman, Isabel Molina, and Angharad N. Valdivia. 2004. "Brain, Brow, and Booty: Latina Iconicity in U.S. Popular Culture." *Communication Review* 7(2): 205–221.

Hall, Gladys. 1940. "South America Looks at Hollywood through the Flashing Eyes of Carmen Miranda." Draft of article for *Modern Screen.* Gladys Hall Collection, Margaret Herrick Library, Academy of Motion Picture Arts and Sciences, Los Angeles. December 20.

Hall, Stuart. 1998. "What Is This 'Black' in Black Popular Culture?" In *Black Popular Culture*, edited by G. Dent and M. Wallace. New York: New Press.

———. 2000. "Encoding/Decoding." In *Media Studies: A Reader*, edited by P. Marris and S. Thornham. New York: New York University Press.

Handelman, David. 1998. "A Diva Is Born." *Mirabella*, July/August, 82–84.

Hansen, Miriam. 1991. *Babel and Babylon: Spectatorship in American Silent Film.* Cambridge: Harvard University Press.

Hartman, John K. 1987. "I Want My A.D.-TV." *Popular Music and Society* 11(2): 17–24.

Hershfield, Joanne. 1998. "Race and Romance in Bird of Paradise." *Cinema Journal* 37(3): 3–15.

———. 2000. *The Invention of Dolores Del Rio*. Minneapolis: University of Minnesota Press.

Higgins, Scott. 2000. "Demonstrating Three-Colour Technicolor: Early Three-Colour Aesthetics and Design." *Film History* 12(4): 358–383.

Hischak, Thomas S. 2008. *Oxford Companion to the American Musical*. New York: Oxford University Press.

"Hugh Hefner on a Life Less Ordinary." 2007. National Public Radio. April 23. http://www.npr.org/templates/transcript.

In Caliente Press Book. 1935. Warner Bros. Archives, School of Cinematic Arts, University of Southern California, Los Angeles.

Jacobson, Matthew Frye. 1998. *Whiteness of a Different Color: European Immigrants and the Alchemy of Race*. Cambridge, MA: Harvard University Press.

Jeffries, John. 1998. "Toward a Redefinition of the Urban: The Collision of Culture." In *Black Popular Culture*, edited by G. Dent and M. Wallace. New York: New Press.

Jensen, Tina Gudrun. 1999. "Discourses on Afro-Brazilian Religion: From De-Africanization to Re-Africanization." In *Latin American Religion in Motion*, edited by Christian Smith and Joshua Prokopy, 265–285. New York: Routledge.

Kael, Pauline. 1983. "Movie Review: *Flashdance*." *New Yorker*, June 27.

Katzew, Ilona, and Los Angeles County Museum of Art. 2004. *Inventing Race: Casta Painting and Eighteenth-Century Mexico/La invención del mestizaje: La pintura de castas y el siglo XVIII en México*. Los Angeles: Los Angeles County Museum of Art.

Keller, Gary D. 1997. *A Biographical Handbook of Hispanics and United States Film*. Tempe, AZ: Bilingual Press/Editorial Bilingue.

Kinder, Marsha. 1978. "Review of *Saturday Night Fever*." *Film Quarterly* 31(3): 40–42.

———. 1984. "Music Video and the Spectator: Television, Ideology and Dream." *Film Quarterly* 38(1): 2–15.

Klein, Herbert S. 1988 *African Slavery in Latin America and the Caribbean*. New York: Oxford University Press.

Knight, Arthur. 2002. *Disintegrating the Musical: Black Performance and American Musical Film*. Durham, NC: Duke University Press.

Kobal, John. 1978. *Rita Hayworth: The Time, the Place, and the Woman*. New York: Norton.

Kropp, Phoebe S. 2001. "Citizens of the Past?: Olvera Street and the Construction of Race and Memory in 1930s Los Angeles." *Radical History Review* 81:35–60.

The Lady from Shanghai Press Book. 1948a. "Beauty Shops (News Promotions/Campaign Ideas)." Columbia Studios Press Book Collection, Cinematic Arts Library, University of Southern California, Los Angeles.

———. 1948b. "Even Glamour Has Its Problems When Hollywood Goes Mexican (Feature)." P. 4. Columbia Studios Press Book Collection, Cinematic Arts Library, University of Southern California, Los Angeles.

———. 1948c. "Nations News Tickers Vibrate When Hayworth Bobs Hair (Women's Page Feature)." P. 5. Columbia Studios Press Book Collection, Cinematic Arts Library, University of Southern California, Los Angeles.

———. 1948d. "Rita Hayworth Goes to Mexico and All Mexico Goes for Rita (Feature)." P. 6. Columbia Studios Press Book Collection, Cinematic Arts Library, University of Southern California, Los Angeles.

Langway, Lynn, and Julia Reed. 1983. "Flashdance, Flashfashions." *Newsweek*, July 4, 55.

Larkin, Colin, ed. 2006. "Jennifer Lopez." In *The Encyclopedia of Popular Music*. New York: Oxford University Press.

Leaming, Barbara. 1989. *If This Was Happiness: A Biography of Rita Hayworth*. New York: Viking.

Lewis, M. 1934. Letter to Mr. R. J. Obringer regarding Dolores Del Rio's Warner Bros. Studio contract. March 20. Warner Bros. Archives, School of Cinematic Arts, University of Southern California, Los Angeles.

Lockwood, Lisa. 2006. "Andy Hilfiger to Rejoin Tommy's Team." *Women's Wear Daily*, June 7.

Loney, Glenn. 1984. *Unsung Genius: The Passion of Dancer-Choreographer Jack Cole*. New York: Franklin Watts.

López, Ana M. 1991. "Are All Latins from Manhattan? Hollywood, Ethnography, and Cultural Colonialism." In *Unspeakable Images: Ethnicity and the American Cinema*, edited by L. Friedman. Urbana: University of Illinois Press.

———. 1994. "Tears and Desire: Women and Melodrama in the 'Old' Mexican Cinema." In *Multiple Voices in Feminist Film Criticism*, edited by D. Carson, L. Dittmar, and J. R. Welsch. Minneapolis: University of Minnesota Press.

López, Ian F. Haney. 1996. *White by Law: The Legal Construction of Race*. New York: New York University Press.

Lopez, Jennifer, Troy Oliver, Cory Rooney, Leshan Lewis, Jeffrey Atkins, Irving Lorenzo, and Rick James. 2001. "I'm Real (Murder Remix)." Hollywood: Nuyorican Publishing (BMI), Sony/ATV Songs LLC (BMI), Cori Tiffani Publishing (BMI), Sony/ATV Tunes LLC (ASCAP), and Chocolate Factory Music (ASCAP).

Lorey, David E. 1999. *The U.S.-Mexican Border in the Twentieth Century: A History of Economic and Social Transformation*. Wilmington, DE: Scholarly Resources.

Lugones, María. 2007. "Heterosexualism and the Colonial/Modern Gender System." *Hypatia* 22(1): 186–209.

Macias, Anthony F. 2008. *Mexican American Mojo: Popular Music, Dance, and Urban Culture in Los Angeles, 1935–1968*. Durham, NC: Duke University Press.

Madre's. 2004. *LA Weekly*, July 16.

Madre's Out to Lunch. 2008. *Pasadena Star-News*, July 9.

"Making the Video: Jennifer Lopez, 'I'm Glad.'" 2003. *Making the Video*, season 10. MTV.

Maltby, Richard. 2003. *Hollywood Cinema*. Malden, MA: Blackwell Publishing.

Mandrell, James. 2001. "Carmen Miranda Betwixt and Between, or, Neither Here nor There." *Latin American Literary Review* 29 (January–June): 26–39.

Marez, Curtis. 2004. *Drug Wars: The Political Economy of Narcotics*. Minneapolis: University of Minnesota Press.

Maurice, Alice. 2002. "'Cinema at Its Source': Synchronizing Race and Sound in the Early Talkies." *Camera Obscura* 17 (49): 30–71.

McClintock, Anne. 1995. *Imperial Leather: Race, Gender and Sexuality in the Colonial Contest*. New York: Routledge.

McLean, Adrienne L. 1992. "'I'm a Cansino': Transformation, Ethnicity and Authenticity in the Construction of Rita Hayworth, American Love Goddess." *Journal of Film and Video* 44 (3–4): 8–26.

————. 2004. *Being Rita Hayworth: Labor, Identity, and Hollywood Stardom*. New Brunswick, NJ: Rutgers University Press.

McRobbie, Angela. 1997. "Dance Narratives and Fantasies of Achievement." In *Meaning in Motion: New Cultural Studies of Dance*, edited by J. Desmond. Durham. NC: Duke University Press.

McWilliams, Carey. 1946. *Southern California: An Island on the Land*. Salt Lake City, UT: Peregrine Smith Books.

Mendible, Myra, ed. 2007. *From Bananas to Buttocks: The Latina Body in Popular Film and Culture*. Austin: University of Texas Press.

Miller, Marla. 2000. Interview with Rita Moreno. *Archive of American Television* (on line). Academy of Television Arts and Sciences Foundation, Los Angeles.

Monroy, Douglas. 2001. "Making Mexico in Los Angeles." In *Metropolis in the Making: Los Angeles in the 1920s*, edited by Tom Sitton and William Deverell. Berkeley: University of California Press.

Morella, Joe, and Edward J. Epstein. 1983. *Rita: The Life of Rita Hayworth*. New York: Delacorte Press.

Mueller, John. 1985. *Astaire Dancing: The Musical Films*. New York: Knopf.

Mulvey, Laura. 1989. *Visual and Other Pleasures*. Basingstoke, UK: Macmillan.

Murray, Yxta Maya. 1997. "Jennifer Lopez." *Buzz*, April.

Nancy Goes to Rio Press Book. 1950. Special Collections, Cinematic Arts Library, University of Southern California, Los Angeles.

Negra, Diane. 2001. *Off-White Hollywood: American Culture and Ethnic Female Stardom*. London: Routledge.

Negrón-Muntaner, Frances. 1997. "Jennifer's Butt." *Aztlan* 22(2): 181.

————. 2000. "Feeling Pretty: *West Side Story* and Puerto Rican Identity Discourses." *Social Text* 18(2): 83–106.

————. 2004. *Boricua Pop: Puerto Ricans and the Latinization of American Culture*. New York: New York University Press.

Nemer, Brad. 2006. "How MTV Channels Innovation." *Business Week* (online), November 6.

Nericcio, William Anthony. 2007. *Tex[t]-Mex: Seductive Hallucinations of the "Mexican" in America*. Austin: University of Texas Press.

New York Times. 1945. "About Tanks and Rita Hayworth." October 21.

————. 1946. "Test Bomb Named 'Gilda,' Honoring Rita Hayworth." June 30, 3.

Noriega, Chon A. 2000. *Shot in America: Television, the State, and the Rise of Chicano Cinema*. Minneapolis: University of Minnesota Press.

Okihiro, Gary Y. 1994. *Margins and Mainstreams: Asians in American History and Culture*. Seattle: University of Washington Press.

O'Neill, Pat, Rosemary Comella, and Kristy H. A. Kang. 2002. *Tracing the Decay of Fiction: Encounters with a Film by Pat O'Neill*. DVD-ROM project. Los Angeles: Annenberg Center for Communication, University of Southern California, Los Angeles.

Ovalle, Priscilla Peña. 2006. "Shake Your Assets: Dance and the Performance of Latina Sexuality in Hollywood Film." Ph.D. dissertation, University of Southern California, Los Angeles.

————. 2007. "Framing Jennifer Lopez: Mobilizing Race from the Wide Shot to the Close-Up." In *The Persistence of Whiteness: Race and Contemporary Hollywood Cinema*, edited by D. Bernardi. New York: Routledge.

———. 2008. "Urban *Sensualidad*: Jennifer Lopez, *Flashdance*, and the MTV Hip-Hop Re-Generation." *Woman and Performance: A Journal of Feminist Theory* 18(3): 253–268.

Paramount Studios. 1953. Publicity material on *Scared Stiff*. Carmen Miranda clipping file. Cinematic Arts Library, University of Southern California, Los Angeles.

Parédez, Deborah. 2009. *Selenidad: Selena, Latinos, and the Performance of Memory*. Durham, NC: Duke University Press.

Parish, James Robert. 1972. *The Fox Girls*. Secaucus, NJ: Castle Books.

Peiss, Kathy Lee. 1999. *Hope in a Jar: The Making of America's Beauty Culture*. New York: Henry Holt.

Pike, Fredrick B. 1995. *FDR's Good Neighbor Policy: Sixty Years of Generally Gentle Chaos*. Austin: University of Texas Press.

Pollock, Dale. 1983. "Flashfight." *Los Angeles Times*, July 10, Calendar sec.

Proffitt, T. D. 1994. *Tijuana: The History of a Mexican Metropolis*. San Diego: San Diego State University Press.

Quigley, Mark. 2009. "White Skin, Green Face: House of Pain and the Modern Minstrel Show." In *The Black and Green Atlantic: Cross-Currents of the African and Irish Diasporas*, edited by P. O'Neill and D. Lloyd. London: Palgrave Macmillan.

Rainer, Peter. 1983. "This Film's a Flash in the Pan: *Flashdance* Essentially a Feature-Length Trailer." *Los Angeles Herald-Examiner*, April 15.

Richardson, Zella. 1944. Letter from the City of Atlanta Board of Review. Atlanta, GA, dated January 8, 1944. Production Code Administration Collection files, Margaret Herrick Library, Academy of Motion Picture Arts and Sciences, Los Angeles.

Ringgold, Gene. 1974. *Rita Hayworth: The Legend and Career of a Love Goddess*. Secaucus, NJ: Citadel Press.

"Rita Moreno: A Pint-Sized Spanish Spitfire Has Been Garnering King-Sized Compliments from Dancing Debut to Film Career." Ca. 1955. Unknown source. Rita Moreno clipping file. Cinematic Arts Library, University of Southern California, Los Angeles.

Roberts, Shari. 1993. "'The Lady in the Tutti-Frutti Hat': Carmen Miranda, a Spectacle of Ethnicity." *Cinema Journal* 32(3): 3–23.

Robinson, Layhmond, Jr. 1955. "Our Changing City: Harlem Now on the Upswing." *New York Times*, July 8.

Rodriguez, Clara E. 2004. *Heroes, Lovers, and Others: The Story of Latinos in Hollywood*. Washington, DC: Smithsonian Books.

Roediger, David R. 2005. *Working toward Whiteness: How America's Immigrants Became White: The Strange Journey from Ellis Island to the Suburbs*. New York: Basic Books.

Rogin, Michael. 1996. *Blackface, White Noise: Jewish Immigrants in the Hollywood Melting Pot*. Berkeley: University of California Press.

Román, David. 2002. "Comment—Theatre Journals." *Theatre Journal* 54(3): vii–xix.

———. 2005. *Performance in America: Contemporary U.S. Culture and the Performing Arts*. Durham, NC: Duke University Press.

Roman, Robert C. 1996. "Gene Kelly: 1912–96 (dancer), Obituary." *Dance Magazine*, April, 94–95.

Rozhon, Tracie. 2005. "The Rap on Puffy's Empire." *New York Times*, July 14, 1–6.

Said, Edward W. 1979. *Orientalism: Western Concepts of the Orient*. New York: Vintage Books.

Saito, Leland. 1998. *Race and Politics: Asian Americans, Latinos, and Whites in a Los Angeles Suburb*. Urbana: University of Illinois Press.

Salamon, Julie. 1983. "*Flashdance*: Good Legs, Big Mouth." *Wall Street Journal*, June 10.

Sánchez, George J. 1993. *Becoming Mexican American: Ethnicity, Culture and Identity in Chicano Los Angeles, 1900–1945*. New York: Oxford University Press.

Sandler, Adam. 1998. "Sony Puts Lopez to Work on Multi-Album Contract." *Variety*, March 11.

Sandoval, Gabriela. 2005. "California." In *The Oxford Encyclopedia of Latinos and Latinas in the United States* (e-reference edition), edited by S. Oboler and D. J. González. New York: Oxford University Press.

Sandoval-Sánchez, Alberto. 1999. *José, Can You See? Latinos On and Off Broadway*. Madison: University of Wisconsin Press.

Sargeant, Winthrop. 1947. "The Cult of the Love Goddess." *Life*, November 10.

Savigliano, Marta E. 1995. *Tango and the Political Economy of Passion*. Boulder, CO: Westview Press.

Schatz, Thomas. 1988. *The Genius of the System: Hollywood Filmmaking in the Studio Era*. New York: Pantheon Books.

Schwartz, Missy. 2010. "Jennifer Lopez: 5 Ways She Can Get Back on Top." *Entertainment Weekly*, March 26.

"She Saved Broadway from the World's Fair." N.d. Constance McCormick Collection, Cinematic Arts Library, University of Southern California, Los Angeles.

Shimizu, Celine Parreñas. 2007. *The Hypersexuality of Race: Performing Asian/American Women on Screen and Scene*. Durham, NC: Duke University Press.

Shohat, Ella. 1991. "Ethnicities in Relation: Toward a Multicultural Reading of American Cinema." In *Unspeakable Images: Ethnicity and the American Cinema*, edited by L. D. Friedman. Urbana: University of Illinois Press.

Shohat, Ella, and Robert Stam. 1994. *Unthinking Eurocentrism: Multiculturalism and the Media*. London: Routledge.

Shuster, Fred. 2002. "J-Lo Hopes Madre's Tops Charts; Performer Celebrates Opening Cuban-Style Eatery in Valley with Gala." *Pasadena Star-News*, April 13.

Smith, Christopher Holmes. 2003. "'I Don't Like to Dream about Getting Paid': Representations of Social Mobility and the Emergence of the Hip-Hop Mogul." *Social Text* 21(4): 69–97.

Smith, Stephanie A. 2006. *Household Words: Bloomers, Sucker, Bombshell, Scab, Nigger, Cyber*. Minneapolis: University of Minnesota Press.

Solberg, Helena. 1995. *Bananas Is My Business*. International Cinema Inc. production, in association with the Corporation for Public Broadcasting, Channel 4 Television, the National Latino Communications Center, and Riofilmes, S.A.

Stam, Robert. 2004. *Tropical Multiculturalism: A Comparative History of Race in Brazilian Cinema and Culture*. Durham, NC: Duke University Press.

Stanley, Fred. 1945. "Hollywood's Veterans." *New York Times*, September 16.

Stoever, Jennifer. 2007. "The Contours of the Sonic Color-Line: Slavery, Segregation, and the Cultural Politics of Listening." Ph.D. dissertation, University of Southern California, Los Angeles.

Stoever-Ackerman, Jennifer. 2009. "'Who Calls the Teacher Daddy-O?': *Blackboard Jungle*, the Sonic Color-Line, and Cold War Nationalism." Paper presented at the annual meeting of the American Studies Association, Washington, DC, November 5–8.

————. 2010. "Splicing the Sonic Color-Line: Tony Schwartz Remixes Postwar *Nueva York*." *Social Text* 28(1): 59–86.

Strawberry Blonde Press Book. 1941. Press Book Collection, Warner Bros. Archives, School of Cinematic Arts, University of Southern California, Los Angeles.

Sutton, David. Ca. 1955. "What Does Hollywood See in Rita?" *Pageant*, n.d., 134–141. Rita Moreno clipping file. Cinematic Arts Library, University of Southern California, Los Angeles.

Tenenbaum, B. A., ed. 1996. *Latin American History and Culture*. New York: Charles Scribner's.

Thompson, Kristin, and David Bordwell. 1994. *Film History: An Introduction*. New York: McGraw-Hill.

Tierney, Tom. 1982. *Carmen Miranda Paper Dolls in Full Color*. New York: Dover.

Triana, Tania. 2010. "Blackness Unmoored: Challenging White Supremacy in Cuba." Manuscript. University of Oregon.

Tunison, Michael. 1995. "Finally, a Hollywood Star for the Multi-Talented Moreno." *Entertainment Today*, July 14, 8.

TV Guide. 1983. "The Cutthroats Almost Got Her." January 15, 26–29.

Twentieth Century-Fox. Ca. 1956. "Rita Moreno Tintype." Sidney Skolsky Collection, Margaret Herrick Library, Academy of Motion Picture Arts and Sciences, Los Angeles.

Universal Studios. 1981. Press release on Rita Moreno, in *The Four Seasons*. Rita Moreno clipping file. Cinematic Arts Library, University of Southern California, Los Angeles.

Vanity Fair. 1997. "Not Quite Ready for Their Close-Ups." April, 88.

Variety. 1940. "Preview of *Down Argentine Way*." October 2.

————. 1987. Obituary of Rita Hayworth. May 20.

"Ventriloquism, Carmen Miranda and Experience Brazil 3–16–41." 1941. In "Bergen and McCarthy," Bergen files. Cinematic Arts Library, University of Southern California, Los Angeles.

Walters, Debra Nan. 1978. "Hollywood, World War II, and Latin America: The Hollywood Good Neighbor Policy as Personified by Carmen Miranda." Ph.D. dissertation, University of Southern California, Los Angeles.

Welsh, Michael. 1986. "There's Nothing 'Odd' about Rita: An Interview with Rita Moreno." *Faces International*, Rita Moreno clipping file. Cinematic Arts Library, University of Southern California, Los Angeles.

Williams, Linda. 1989. *Hard Core: Power, Pleasure and the Frenzy of the Visible*. Berkeley: University of California Press.

Wilson, Eric, and Rosemary Feitelberg. 2004. "J. Lo Gets Hands-On at Sweetface." *WWD: Women's Wear Daily* 188 (40): 6.

Wonder Bar Press Book. 1934a. "Dolores Del Rio in Dizzy Dance with Ricardo Cortez." In "*Wonder Bar* Exploitation Ideas." Warner Bros. Archives, School of Cinematic Arts, University of Southern California, Los Angeles.

————. 1934b. "Gaucho, Exotic New Dance Invented for *Wonder Bar*." Warner Bros. Archives, School of Cinematic Arts, University of Southern California, Los Angeles.

————. 1934c. "On with the Dance (Special Sunday Feature)." In "*Wonder Bar* Exploitation Ideas." Warner Bros. Archives, School of Cinematic Arts, University of Southern California, Los Angeles.

Index

About the Author

Priscilla Peña Ovalle is an assistant professor in the English Department at the University of Oregon, where she teaches film and television studies. After studying film and interactive media production at Emerson College, she received her Ph.D. from the University of Southern California School of Cinematic Arts while collaborating with the Labyrinth Project at the Annenberg Center for Communication.